Places of
Folklore and Legend

EXPLORE AMERICA

Places of
Folklore and Legend

THE READER'S DIGEST ASSOCIATION, INC.
Pleasantville, New York / Montreal

PLACES OF FOLKLORE AND LEGEND was created and produced by ST. REMY MULTIMEDIA INC.

STAFF FOR PLACES OF FOLKLORE AND LEGEND
Series Editor: Elizabeth Cameron
Art Director: Solange Laberge
Editor: Elizabeth Warrington Lewis
Assistant Editor: Neale McDevitt
Photo Researchers: Geneviève Monette, Linda Castle
Cartography: Hélène Dion, David Widgington
Designer: Anne-Marie Lemay
Research Editor: Robert B. Ronald
Contributing Researcher: Olga Dzatko
Researcher: Jennifer Meltzer
Copy Editors: Joan Page McKenna, Judy Yelon
Index: Linda Cordella Cournoyer
System Coordinator: Éric Beaulieu
Technical Support: Mathieu Raymond-Beaubien, Jean Sirois
Scanner Operators: Martin Francoeur, Sara Grynspan

ST. REMY STAFF
PRESIDENT, CHIEF EXECUTIVE OFFICER: Fernand Lecoq
PRESIDENT, CHIEF OPERATING OFFICER: Pierre Léveillé
VICE PRESIDENT, FINANCE: Natalie Watanabe
MANAGING EDITOR: Carolyn Jackson
MANAGING ART DIRECTOR: Diane Denoncourt
PRODUCTION MANAGER: Michelle Turbide

Writers: Rita Ariyoshi—Land of Fire
Rod Gragg—Daniel Boone's Kentucky; The Wild West
Eric Hause—The Lost Colony
Kim Heacox—Klondike Gold Rush
Jim Henderson—Texas Revolution
Bruce Hopkins—John Brown's Raid
Rose Houk—The Golden Spike
Robert Kiener—Paul Revere's Journey
Nathaniel Philbrick—The Faraway Land

Contributing Writers: Adriana Barton, Maxine Cuttler, Brian Polan

Address any comments about *Places of Folklore and Legend* to U.S. Editor, General Books, c/o Customer Service, Reader's Digest, Pleasantville, NY 10570

READER'S DIGEST STAFF
Editor: Kathryn Bonomi
Art Editor: Eleanor Kostyk
Production Supervisor: Mike Gallo
Editorial Assistant: Mary Jo McLean

READER'S DIGEST GENERAL BOOKS
Editor-in-Chief, Books and Home
Entertainment: Barbara J. Morgan
Editor, U.S. General Books: David Palmer
Executive Editor: Gayla Visalli
Art Director: Joel Musler

Opening photographs
Cover: The Alamo, Texas
Back Cover: Golden Spike National Historic Site, Utah
Page 2: Old Trail Town, Cody, Wyoming
Page 5: Hawaii Volcanoes National Park, Hawaii

Library of Congress Cataloging in Publication Data

Places of folklore and legend.
       p.   cm.—(Explore America)
    Includes index.
    ISBN 0-89577-905-6
    1. Tales—United States. 2. Legends—United States. 3. United States—Folklore. 4. United States—History. 5. United States—Description and travel.   I. Reader's Digest Association.
II. Series.
GR105.P55 1997
398'.0973—dc21   96-40045

CONTENTS

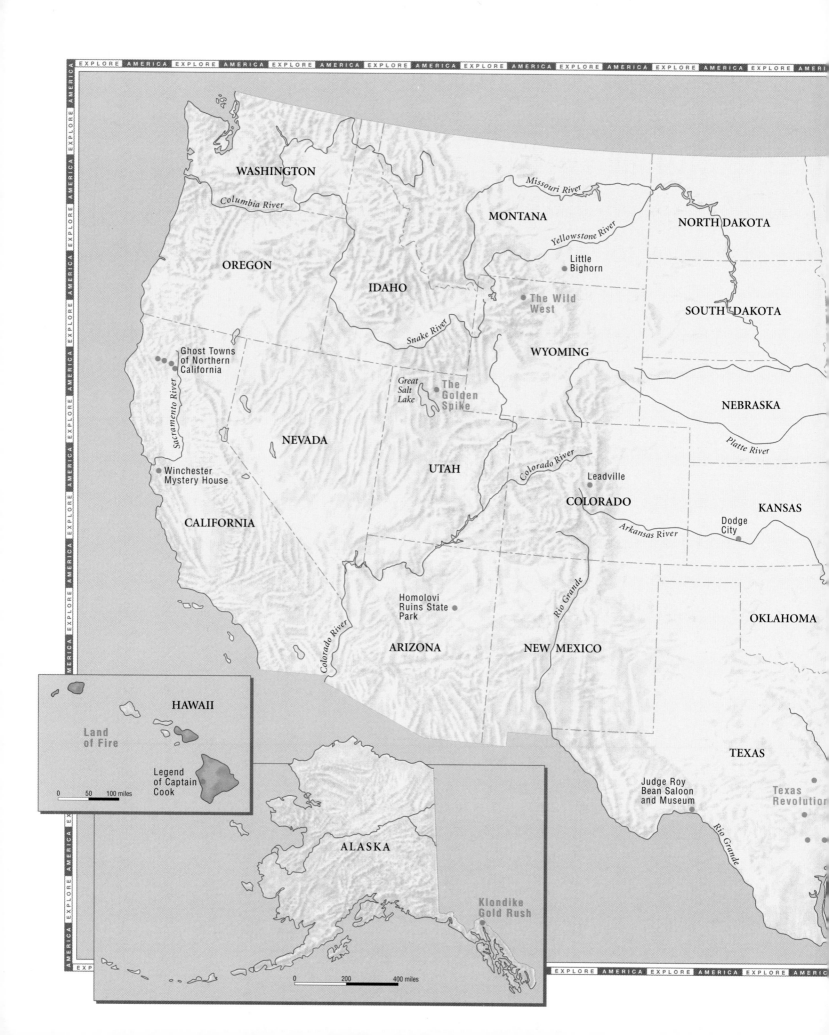

WASHINGTON

Columbia River

OREGON

IDAHO

MONTANA

Missouri River

Yellowstone River

Little
Bighorn

The Wild
West

WYOMING

NORTH DAKOTA

SOUTH DAKOTA

NEBRASKA

Platte River

Ghost Towns
of Northern
California

Snake River

Great
Salt
Lake

The
Golden
Spike

Sacramento River

NEVADA

UTAH

Colorado River

Leadville

COLORADO

KANSAS

Dodge
City

Arkansas River

Winchester
Mystery House

CALIFORNIA

Homolovi
Ruins State
Park

Colorado River

Rio Grande

ARIZONA

NEW MEXICO

OKLAHOMA

HAWAII

Land
of Fire

Legend
of Captain
Cook

0   50   100 miles

ALASKA

TEXAS

Judge Roy
Bean Saloon
and Museum

Texas
Revolution

Rio Grande

Klondike
Gold Rush

0   200   400 miles

PLACES OF FOLKLORE AND LEGEND

MAINE

Lake Superior

VERMONT
NEW HAMPSHIRE

Ancient and Modern Stargazers

Green Mountain Boys

Paul Revere's Journey

MASSACHUSETTS

Lake Huron

Lake Michigan

Lake Ontario

NEW YORK

The Faraway Land

RHODE ISLAND

Sleepy Hollow Country

CONNECTICUT

WISCONSIN

MICHIGAN

Lake Erie

MINNESOTA

Mississippi River

PENNSYLVANIA

NEW JERSEY

Fort McHenry

John Brown's Raid

Cradle of Liberty

IOWA

Johnny Appleseed

OHIO

D.C.

DELAWARE

MARYLAND

Stonewall Jackson

Nauvoo

INDIANA

Ohio River

WEST VIRGINIA

Ford's Theatre

The Underground Railroad

Riders and Outlaws

ILLINOIS

Pocahontas and John Smith

Missouri River

Daniel Boone's Kentucky

VIRGINIA

The Lost Colony

MISSOURI

KENTUCKY

NORTH CAROLINA

TENNESSEE

Mississippi River

SOUTH CAROLINA

ARKANSAS

GEORGIA

MISSISSIPPI

ALABAMA

LOUISIANA

Cane River Country

Fountain of Youth

FLORIDA

0   100   200   300 miles

READER'S GUIDE

"Listen, my children, and you shall hear,/ Of the midnight ride of Paul Revere," began Henry Wadsworth Longfellow as he transformed history into legend in his famous poem, Paul Revere's Ride. From the lost colony on North Carolina's Roanoke Island to the Alamo, in San Antonio, Texas, travelers uncover the stories that tell of America's past. Part I presents 10 handpicked sites (in orange on this map). Part II, the Gazetteer, provides photographs, maps, and capsule descriptions of 23 others. A legend explaining the symbols for facilities and map features can be found on the front inside cover.

VIRGIN ISLANDS

Land of Pirates

PUERTO RICO

0   50   100 miles

PAUL REVERE'S JOURNEY

On April 18, 1775, Paul Revere sped from Boston to Lexington on a history-making journey.

It was a cool, moonlit night during an unseasonably warm spring. A dark-haired, stocky man hurried from his house on North Square and headed through the warrenlike streets of Boston's North End. At age 40, Paul Revere was by build and inclination a man of action and by trade an artisan. When Revere swung into the saddle and clattered down the road—as he had so many times before in his role as a patriot express rider—he may well have realized that he was, in the words of one of his biographers, "becoming . . . something greater than himself." Less than 60 years after Revere's death in 1818, Henry Wadsworth Longfellow, in his poem *Paul Revere's Ride*, immortalized this decisive moment in U.S. history when, "through the gloom and the light, the fate of the nation was riding that night."

On that cloudless day in April 1775, Boston was buzzing with rumor and tension. Relations between patriots and loyalists had reached an

The Paul Revere House, right, built around 1680 and owned by Revere from 1770 to 1800, is the oldest structure in downtown Boston.

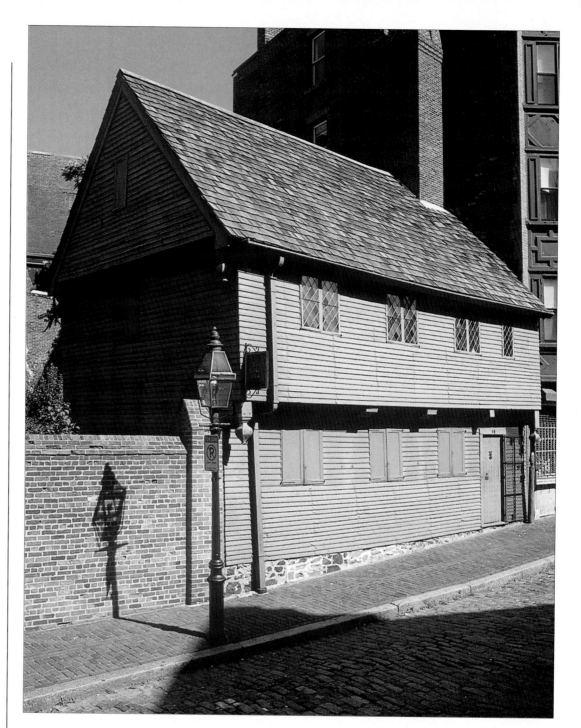

Overleaf: This tranquil section between Lexington and Concord, dubbed Battle Road, was the site of countless skirmishes between red-coats and patriots on April 19. By the time the British retreated to Charlestown, some 273 British sol-diers were dead, wounded, or miss-ing. Said Lord Percy, commander of the British 5th Regiment, "I never believed they would have attacked the King's troops, or have had the perseverance I found in them."

all-time low. The seeds of discontent had been planted in 1765, when the British Parliament passed the Stamp Act. The first direct internal tax levied on the colonies by the Crown, the act outraged colonists on two fronts: the right to tax themselves, guaranteed in their charters, had been stripped away; and the measure had been imposed by a Parliament in which they had no representation.

Rioting colonials in Boston made it clear that they considered this to be an act of tyranny. The rift only grew wider in the ensuing years, when Parliament was pressured to change the tax laws. Britain retaliated by replacing the laws with new revenue measures, including a duty on imported goods such as paint, paper, and tea.

Incidents such as the Boston Massacre in 1770—in which five patriots were killed in a violent con-frontation with British soldiers outside the Old State House—had created a deeply uneasy cli-mate. Revolution was brewing in the hearts of men such as the Sons of Liberty, whose growing patriot membership met clandestinely and called for independence from England and "Mad" King George III. After the Boston Tea Party in 1773, during which the Sons of Liberty dumped 342 chests of tea into Boston Harbor, the British gov-ernment responded with what came to be known as the Intolerable Acts. They shut down the pros-perous port of Boston and virtually annulled the Massachusetts Charter.

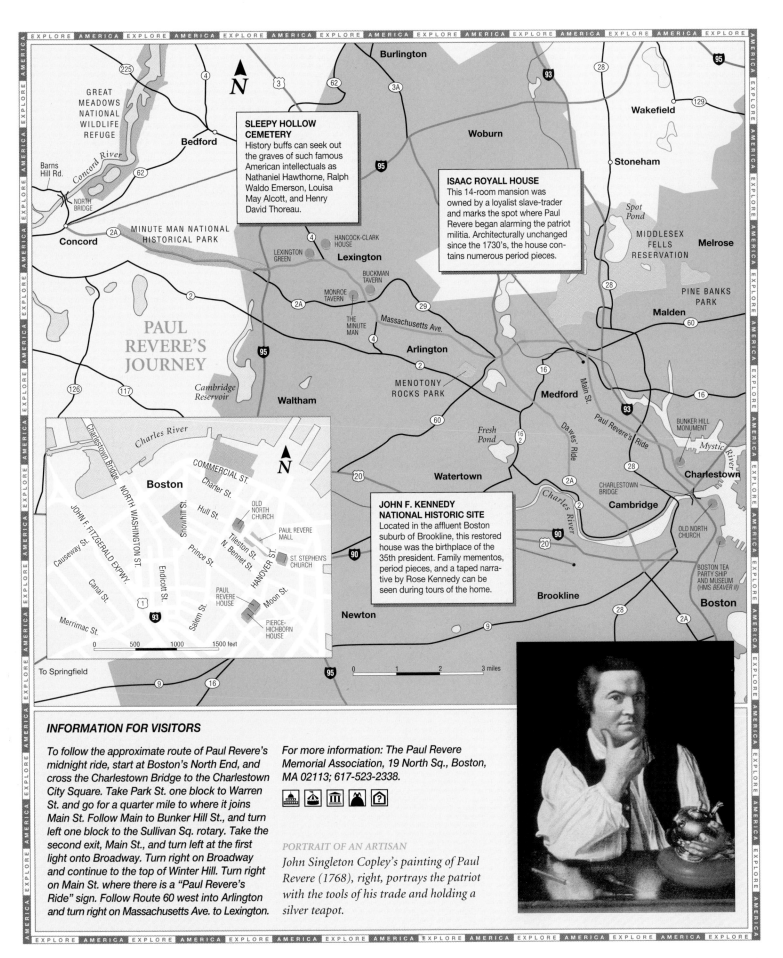

SLEEPY HOLLOW CEMETERY
History buffs can seek out the graves of such famous American intellectuals as Nathaniel Hawthorne, Ralph Waldo Emerson, Louisa May Alcott, and Henry David Thoreau.

ISAAC ROYALL HOUSE
This 14-room mansion was owned by a loyalist slave-trader and marks the spot where Paul Revere began alarming the patriot militia. Architecturally unchanged since the 1730's, the house contains numerous period pieces.

JOHN F. KENNEDY NATIONAL HISTORIC SITE
Located in the affluent Boston suburb of Brookline, this restored house was the birthplace of the 35th president. Family mementos, period pieces, and a taped narrative by Rose Kennedy can be seen during tours of the home.

PAUL REVERE'S JOURNEY

INFORMATION FOR VISITORS

To follow the approximate route of Paul Revere's midnight ride, start at Boston's North End, and cross the Charlestown Bridge to the Charlestown City Square. Take Park St. one block to Warren St. and go for a quarter mile to where it joins Main St. Follow Main to Bunker Hill St., and turn left one block to the Sullivan Sq. rotary. Take the second exit, Main St., and turn left at the first light onto Broadway. Turn right on Broadway and continue to the top of Winter Hill. Turn right on Main St. where there is a "Paul Revere's Ride" sign. Follow Route 60 west into Arlington and turn right on Massachusetts Ave. to Lexington.

For more information: The Paul Revere Memorial Association, 19 North Sq., Boston, MA 02113; 617-523-2338.

PORTRAIT OF AN ARTISAN
John Singleton Copley's painting of Paul Revere (1768), right, portrays the patriot with the tools of his trade and holding a silver teapot.

Paul Revere was near the center of the political turmoil. A silversmith by trade, he had also turned his many talents to copperplate engraving and illustrating, and he manufactured and sold false teeth—although contrary to popular legend, he did not have a hand in those worn by George Washington. Revere also used his artistic talent in the political forum. His famous engraving of the Boston Massacre, portraying the redcoats shooting down unarmed civilians in cold blood, served to stir up anti-British feelings in the city. In fact, many eyewitnesses to the incident said that the soldiers were defending themselves against an unruly mob.

A passionate defender of the colony, the young Revere fought the French at Lake George in 1756 as a second lieutenant in the colonial artillery. He joined the Freemasons and the Sons of Liberty and became an active participant in Boston's political scene, vigorously espousing the patriot cause. Some historians maintain that Revere took part in the Boston Tea Party. His quality of intellect was described by biographer Esther Forbes as "a good mind, quick and usable, but not a subtle mind."

Fortunately, subtlety was not what the revolutionary cause required of him. A leader of Boston's mechanic class, Revere was just as comfortable rubbing elbows with the city's intellectuals as he was bending an elbow with fellow artisans at a local tavern. Straddling Boston's social strata,

TEA OVERBOARD!
The Beaver II, *right, a replica of one of the three ships whose cargoes of tea were dumped into Boston Harbor on December 16, 1773, can be visited at its mooring by Boston's Congress Street Bridge.*

VIEW OF THE GREEN
Paul Revere watched the redcoats march into Lexington from an upstairs window of Buckman Tavern, right, which faces the green. The tavern houses a collection that includes 18th-century firearms.

Revere was a mediator between the classes, formulating plans, organizing resistance, and bringing diverse groups together. Most important, he was a man of action.

BUSY SPY NETWORKS With tensions mounting in the spring of 1775, the intelligence networks of both the colonials and the British were hard at work. Revere himself monitored the movements of British troops. The colonials, led by Dr. Joseph Warren, believed that the British "Regulars" from the Boston garrison intended to march on Lexington to arrest radical leaders Samuel Adams and John Hancock. On the morning of April 18, British soldiers began boarding boats to cross the Charles River. Revere wrote, "Dr. Warren sent in great haste for me, and begged that I would immediately set off for Lexington, where Messrs. Hancock and Adams were, and acquaint them of the movement, and that it was thought they were the objects."

Revere awaited the charge. He had already made arrangements for his friend Robert Newman, the sexton of Christ Church (also known as Old North Church), to signal patriots in Charlestown, across the river, as to the route the Regulars were taking to Lexington: "If the British went out by water we would show two lanterns in the North Church steeple; and if by land one as a signal, for we were apprehensive it would be difficult to cross the Charles or get over Boston Neck."

After his meeting with Warren, Revere instantly set to work. He rushed to inform Newman at his home, located on the corner of Salem and Sheafe streets, that the moment was at hand. Sneaking into the church, Newman climbed the wooden stairs up past the eight great bells in the belfry, and hung the lanterns in the steeple window—one of the highest structures in Boston—on the north side, facing Charlestown. He probably lit the lamps only for a few moments—just long enough for their glow to be spotted by the patriots who were keeping watch across the river and still escape the attention of the British soldiers on the HMS *Somerset*, anchored at the mouth of the Charles River.

Meanwhile, Revere ran to his home in North Square, where he grabbed his boots and riding coat, and "went to the north part of town where I had kept a boat; two friends rowed me across Charles River." In his hurry, according to Revere's account for his children, he forgot to take a cloth to muffle the sound of the oars. One of Revere's friends frantically knocked on the door of his sweetheart, who lived nearby. The woman came to an upstairs window, and when the men explained their plight to

AMERICAN BEAUTY
Paul Revere designed this elegant silver teapot, left, belonging to the Museum of Fine Arts in Boston, in the early 1760's. Revere signed each of his pieces with five or six different marks, including "Revere" or "PR."

STANDING HIS GROUND
Henry Hudson Kitson's statue, The Minute Man, *left, was dedicated in 1900 and now stands at the eastern point of the Lexington Green triangle. Inscribed on a nearby boulder are the words Capt. John Parker spoke to his ragtag forces on that fateful dawn: "Stand your ground. Don't fire unless fired upon. But if they mean to have a war let it begin here."*

her, threw down a flannel petticoat—still warm from her body. Wrapping the oars in the garment, the clandestine party rowed to Charlestown.

The home of this Good Samaritan no longer stands; but Paul Revere's wooden house at 19 North Square, which is maintained by the Paul Revere Memorial Association, is toured each year by 200,000 visitors. Period furnishings and Revere's memorabilia, such as his saddlebags and works of silver, evoke the world in which he lived. Massive fireplaces inside the spacious rooms protected Revere and his family against Boston's winter chill.

At the nearby Paul Revere Mall—a shady, tree-lined park located behind the Old North Church—visitors can see a statue of Revere on horseback by the 19th-century sculptor Cyrus Dallin. (Dallin's first model depicted Revere in Charlestown looking back at the Old North Church steeple.)

On landing at Charlestown at about 11 o'clock, Revere met a small group of patriots who had been alerted by the signal from the Old North Church. They gave him his mount, which Revere noted was "a very good horse." Now began the most dangerous part of his trek: the 12-mile ride to Lexington, which was thick with British patrols. Galloping through Charlestown and across the narrow Charlestown Neck, he passed the skeletal remains of a slave who had been strung up in chains

LIBERTY'S LIGHT
One of the two lanterns Robert Newman hung in the Old North Church belfry, above, is on display in the Concord Museum.

SIGNIFICANT LANDMARK
Cyrus Dallin's statue of Paul Revere, opposite page, stands near the Old North Church in Boston's North End. When Revere was 15 years old, he was one of seven bell ringers at the Old North Church, left, an Episcopal church that served a mixed patriot and loyalist congregation. In fact, Robert Newman, who hung the lanterns in its steeple, and British general Thomas Gage, commander-in-chief of the British forces in America, owned box pews on the same aisle. The church claimed America's first peal of eight bells. The bell ringers' contract, with Revere's signature, is on display in the church's museum.

GRANARY BURYING GROUND

GRANARY BURYING GROUND
One of the many headstones
still standing in Granary Burying
Ground, right, this marks the grave
of Mary Bennett. A landmark on
Boston's Freedom Trail, the ceme-
tery got its name from the grain
storage building that once stood on
the site. Paul Revere and his wives,
Sara Orne and Rachel Walker, and
three signers of the Declaration of
Independence—John Hancock,
Robert Treat Paine, and Samuel
Adams—are among the many
famous Bostonians buried here.

20 years before for poisoning his owner, a grisly display left as a warning to other rebellious slaves. Turning west toward Cambridge, Revere caught sight of two British officers on horseback waiting at a crossroads. Yanking his mount around, Revere galloped off in the opposite direction. The officers gave chase. One of them, trying to cut Revere off, became mired in an open clay pit. The other was no match for Revere's speedy mare.

The air soon crackled with warning shots and the shouts of roused colonials.

Reaching Lexington just before midnight, Revere turned right at Buckman Tavern onto Bedford Road. He dismounted at Clarke Parsonage, where Hancock and Adams were staying. (The parsonage, which is now called the Hancock-Clarke House, is located about a quarter mile north of Lexington Green on Hancock Street. It has been restored and is open to the public.) That night the sentry on duty, failing to recognize Revere, ordered him to stop making noise.

"Noise!" cried Revere as he banged on the door. "You'll have noise enough before long! The Regulars are coming out!" Hearing the voice of his compatriot, Hancock called from inside the house, "Come in, Revere. We're not afraid of *you*."

A half hour after Revere's arrival a second rider galloped up with the same urgent message. Dr. Warren had cannily hedged his bets and sent off 23-year-old Billy Dawes, a Boston cordwainer, to Lexington to give warning as well. Dawes' route, via the Boston Neck (to the south of the city), was five miles longer than Revere's.

SOUNDING THE ALARM

Galloping through the town of Mystic (the present-day Boston suburb of Medford) to Menotomy (now Arlington), Revere turned west on Bay Road in the direction of Lexington. The detour cost him precious time, but it probably saved him from being captured by the roving redcoat patrols.

In Medford, Revere woke the captain of the Minutemen. Soon a cry—"The Regulars are out!"—rang through the village as men grabbed their muskets and sent their wives and children scurrying out to hide in the swamp. Revere stopped at houses along the road, passing on the news.

FATE OF THE COLONIES
The painting at right was inspired by
Paul Revere's midnight ride through
the countryside to warn colonials
of the approaching British troops.

After delivering their warning, the two riders took to the road again, heading for Concord. Some scholars suggest that it was only after Revere and Dawes arrived in Lexington that the patriots realized the British goal was bigger than the capture of the rebel leaders. The British army's top priority was to seize the patriot store of weapons and gunpowder in Concord. Other historians believe Dr. Warren had already guessed the target of the British and had informed Revere and Dawes that the riders' ultimate destination would be Concord.

As the couriers galloped down the road that is now Massachusetts Avenue to Concord, they were joined by Dr. Samuel Prescott, just back from a late-night assignation with his sweetheart.

A British patrol descended on the riders. Revere was captured, Dawes escaped to Lexington, and Prescott jumped his horse over a stone wall and carried the alarm to Concord. After being questioned at gunpoint, Revere was released and he returned to Lexington on foot.

Back in Lexington, having collected a trunk filled with important papers for Hancock, Revere heard shots as he hurried back to the parsonage with the documents. "One gun was fired," he later said. "I heard the report, turned my head, and saw smoke in front of the troops, they immediately gave a great shout, ran a few paces and then the whole fired." The shots came from Lexington Green, where Capt. John Parker and his band of 70 colonials defied more than 700 redcoats in what was to be the opening battle of the American War of Independence.

FIRST SHOTS OF WAR

Just outside Lexington, Minute Man National Historical Park preserves the six-mile stretch of road where the first shots of the Revolutionary War were fired. Visitors can see the boulder marking the spot where Revere was captured by the redcoats, tread the historic battlefields of Lexington and Concord, and learn about the battles by perusing the displays and dioramas at the visitor center.

More than 200 years have passed since Revere's call to arms rang across the countryside and started the chain of events that forever changed the land. His voice has long been silent, but its echo resounds across the nation he helped forge.

HISTORIC HOUSE

John Hancock and Samuel Adams were staying at the Hancock-Clarke House, above, in Lexington when Revere warned them of approaching British soldiers. Now a museum, the historic building contains artifacts from the battles at Lexington and Concord, including antique British pistols and the drum that summoned the Minutemen to Lexington Green.

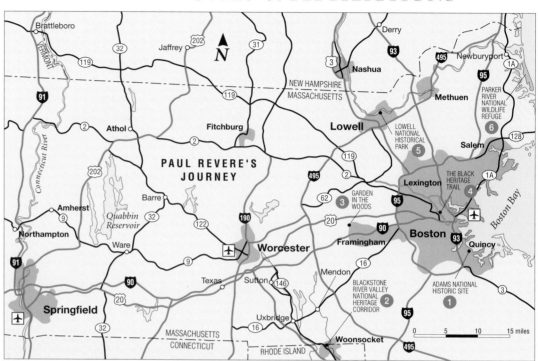

Black-eyed Susans and sneezeweed are on display along the two-mile Curtis Trail at the Garden in the Woods, below.

1 ADAMS NATIONAL HISTORIC SITE, MASSACHUSETTS

Quincy well deserves its nickname as the City of Presidents: It is the birthplace of John Adams and his son John Quincy Adams, who served as the second and sixth presidents, respectively. The site includes three historic homes: the Adams Old House and the birthplaces of John Adams and John Quincy Adams. The birthplaces are located about one and a half miles from the mansion. The Massachusetts Constitution was drafted in the John Quincy Adams birthplace, and it was here that Abigail Adams wrote many of her famous letters to John Adams during his appointment to the Continental Congress in Philadelphia. The Adams Old House displays some

30,000 artifacts reflecting the history of the family. Visitors may stroll through the 18th-century formal garden and the apple orchard. Located at 135 Adams St. in Quincy.

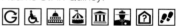

2 BLACKSTONE RIVER VALLEY NATIONAL HERITAGE CORRIDOR, MASSACHUSETTS/ RHODE ISLAND

This 250,000-acre park celebrates the industrial heritage and natural beauty of the Blackstone River Valley. It includes cities, villages, towns, canals, dams, historic buildings, and recreational areas within a 46-mile-long valley that runs between Worcester, Massachusetts, and Providence, Rhode Island. Considered the birthplace of the American Industrial Revolution, the valley became an industrial corridor in 1828 when a canal was built there, opening the river to transport. The area prospered for 15 years until the railway made the canal obsolete. Mill villages in the valley include Berkeley and Aston in Rhode Island and Hopedale and Whitinsville in Massachusetts. Typically a mill village included a dam that provided the power for the mill, and mill housing, usually duplexes or row houses made of wood or brick. In contrast, the towns of Sutton and Mendon in Massachusetts are examples of the hilltop villages that served as centers for governmental, religious, and social affairs. A towpath and sections of the canal have been restored, and a museum in Woonsocket displays machines from the industrial age. The corridor also includes Douglas and Upton state forests and parks, as well as Purgatory Chasm and Diamond Hill state parks. Visitor centers are located in Pawtucket and Woonsocket, Rhode Island, as well as Worcester, Massachusetts.

③ GARDEN IN THE WOODS, MASSACHUSETTS

Rolling hills and a meadow, pond, and sparkling stream are the setting for this 45-acre garden devoted to the preservation of temperate North American plant life. More than 1,600 species of trees, shrubs, ferns, wildflowers, and approximately 200 rare plant species grow in the glacially sculpted landscape, making the meadow an ever-changing tapestry of orange, pink, blue, white, and gold. Virginia bluebells, oconee bells, and trout lilies appear in spring, and plum-leaved azaleas and calopogon orchids in summer. Other flowers include yellow lady's slippers, great trilliums, shooting stars, and wood phlox. The garden names reflect their distinct characters: Pine Barrens, Sunny Bog, Rock Gardens, Rich Woodland Groves, and Lily Pond. Located on Hemenway Rd. in Framingham.

④ THE BLACK HERITAGE TRAIL, MASSACHUSETTS

The Black Heritage Trail links 14 historic landmark sites associated with Boston's black community. After Massachusetts outlawed slavery in 1783, many freed slaves came to the city and settled in what is now the Beacon Hill district. Two of the buildings on the trail are open to the public: the African Meeting House and the Abiel Smith School. The African Meeting House, built in 1806, is the oldest existing black church in the nation. Constructed almost entirely by black artisans, the church served as the center of the community. A school for African-American children was started in the basement of the church in 1808. Today the building serves as the Museum of Afro American History. The Abiel Smith School, constructed in 1834, replaced the Meeting House School and offered grammar and primary school education to African-American children from all over Boston. In 1855 the school closed its doors when legislation was passed that permitted black children to attend public schools in their own neighborhoods. Other highlights of the trail include the George Middleton House, built in 1797 and the oldest house erected by an African-American in the neighborhood; the Charles Street Meeting House, built in 1807 by the Third Baptist Church of Boston; and five residential structures on Smith Court that are typical of the dwellings of black Bostonians during the 19th century. Maps and information about the trail are available at the Museum of Afro American History at 46 Joy St.

⑤ LOWELL NATIONAL HISTORICAL PARK, MASSACHUSETTS

The first planned industrial city in the nation, this national historical park preserves mill complexes, boardinghouses, and a canal-and-trolley system that once served the busy region. Established in 1826, the town was named after Francis Cabot Lowell, who visited England in 1811 and toured several British textile factories to study the design of their machines. Upon Lowell's return to the United States, he began to duplicate the machines that turned raw materials into finished products. For the first 20 years of operation, the textile mills were worked by young women who were recruited by mill owners from nearby farms. Known as "mill girls,"

they worked 70 hours a week, earning wages set at a rate of $2.25 to $4.25 per week; $1.25 was deducted each week for room and board in company-owned boardinghouses. In later years large numbers of immigrants settled in Lowell, creating an ethnic mosaic. The buildings in the park include churches, social centers, and stores that served Irish, French-Canadian, Polish, Greek, and Jewish workers. Tours of the mill and canals by canal boat and a replica 1901 trolley cover five and a half miles of canal and pass 4 of the city's 10 original mill complexes. Lowell is also the hometown of writer Jack Kerouac. The park's visitor center is located on Market St. in Lowell.

⑥ PARKER RIVER NATIONAL WILDLIFE REFUGE, MASSACHUSETTS

This 4,662-acre barrier island refuge, located on the Atlantic Flyway, attracts as many as 300 species of birds a year, including many rare species. The refuge's varied terrain includes salt marshes, dense thickets, fresh to brackish wetlands, sand beaches, and dunes planted with grasses, scrub pines, and beach plum. A six-and-a-half-mile road leads visitors through the refuge, and observation towers provide commanding views of the surrounding terrain. Bird-watchers will delight in catching glimpses of the refuge's winter visitors, including snowy owls, Iceland gulls, white-winged crossbills, goldeneyes, and old-squaws. Between 200 and 300 snowy egrets flock here in the summer. The fall migration period draws as many as 15,000 ducks, 10,000 tree swallows, and 24 species of shorebirds, including pectoral sandpipers and Hudsonian godwits. Anglers will enjoy some of the region's finest surf fishing here, plumbing the depths for striped bass and bluefish. Located five miles east of Newburyport off Hwy. 1A.

Wildflowers bloom in the meadow outside the River Bend Farm Visitor Center in Uxbridge, Massachusetts, above, located within the Blackstone River Valley National Heritage Corridor.

Mico Kaufman's bronze-and-granite statue called Homage to Women, *below, was created as a tribute to the mill girls, Lowell's first labor force. It was set up in Lowell National Historical Park in 1984.*

THE FARAWAY LAND

The saga of Nantucket's seafaring past reveals its glory days as the whaling capital of the world.

A legend of the Wampanoag Indians tells of a giant named Maushop who used to sleep along the southern shore of Cape Cod. One night Maushop could not get to sleep. He tossed and turned so much his right moccasin filled up with sand. Exasperated, he stood up and threw the shoe into the ocean. It landed a short distance away and became the island of Martha's Vineyard. Maushop lay down again and tried to sleep, but it wasn't long before his other moccasin filled up with sand. This time he hurled the moccasin as far as he could, and the sand-filled moccasin became the distant island of Nantucket, which means "the faraway land" in the Massachuset dialect spoken by the Wampanoag Indians.

At least 2,500 Wampanoags lived on Nantucket when the island's first English settlers, led by Thomas Macy, made landfall at Madaket on the western shore in 1659. According to the story, Macy, his wife, Sarah, and their five children, along with their friends Edward Starbuck and 13-year-old Isaac Coleman, were forced to leave

their home in Salisbury, Massachusetts, after they offered shelter during a rainstorm to some wandering Quakers, an act that was considered a crime by their fellow Puritans. Macy, who had left England 19 years before in search of religious tolerance, departed from Salisbury for much the same reason. The stalwart Puritans set out in an open boat and traveled for 50 miles or so around Cape Cod. When a bad storm kicked up during the last leg of their voyage, Sarah Macy is said to have begged her husband to turn back and go to nearby Martha's Vineyard. But Macy responded, "Woman, go below and seek thy God. I fear not the witches on earth nor the devils in hell!"

A visitor in search of the Nantucket equivalent of Plymouth Rock will find it on a quiet strip of beach called Warren's Landing at the western end of the island. Bicycle paths lead from Madaket back to town through a rolling, pond-speckled section of the island known as Wannacomet, where the settlers lived before they moved to Nantucket Harbor. The home of one of the first settlers, Tristram Coffin, overlooked a small anchorage on the north shore called Cappamet Harbor. No longer open to the sea, and now known as Capaum Pond, this was the cradle of the island's English settlement. A stone marker indicates the spot where the Coffin house once stood, some 200 yards off present-day Madaket Road. Here the Coffins, along with the Macy, Starbuck, Folger, Swain, Bunker, Hussey, Barnard, and Gardner families, established the fundamental connections that would hold the island together for the next 200 years.

FIRST WHALE

The earliest English inhabitants raised sheep, but it wasn't long before they looked to the sea for their livelihood. Today islanders recount the story of the discovery in 1672 of a whale in Nantucket's inner harbor. The settlers herded the hapless whale by boat into shoal water and someone among them made a crude harpoon and killed the animal, cutting it up and boiling the blubber. The story may or may not be true. Certainly there is documentary evidence that, in 1672, the town hired a Cape Codder named James Loper to teach them about whale hunting and processing. And according to Obed Macy's *History of Nantucket,* published in 1835, "In the year 1690 . . . some persons were on a high hill . . . observing the whales spouting and sporting with each other, when one observed, 'there (pointing to the sea) is a green pasture where our children's grand-children will go for bread.' "

The islanders set up whale stations near the beaches at Cisco, Surfside, and Nobadeer along the southern shore of the island. From there they kept a constant watch for pods of right whales, which were the first whales to be hunted off Nantucket. Although the remorseless effects of erosion have long since washed away the last remnants of Nantucket's early outposts, the beaches look out on the waters where the island's whaling legacy began. Launching their 20-foot whaleboats through the surf, the whalers—Wampanoag and English alike—harpooned the whales and towed them back to shore where the blubber was stripped off. Then the blubber was carted by horse-drawn buggy to a try house, where it was boiled, or tried out, into oil in iron try-pots.

Several of these pots are on display at the Nantucket Whaling Museum on lower Broad Street, which also owns an excellent collection of whaling gear, such as harpoons, lances, and flensing knives, needed to kill and strip the giant beasts

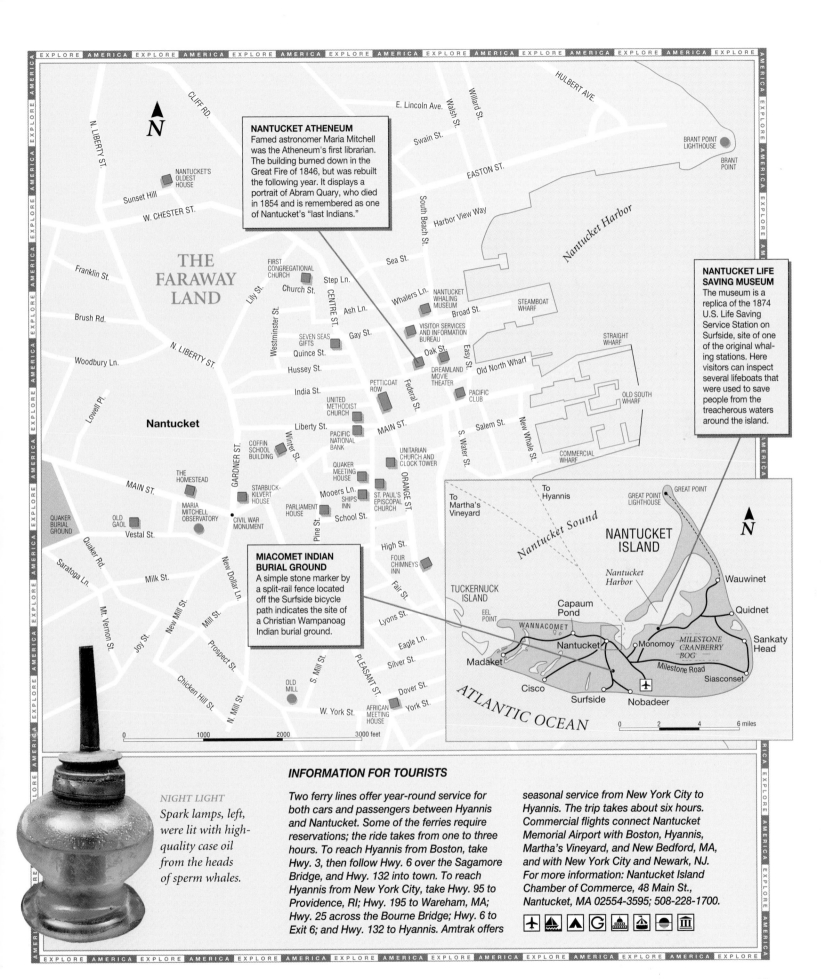

NANTUCKET ATHENEUM
Famed astronomer Maria Mitchell was the Atheneum's first librarian. The building burned down in the Great Fire of 1846, but was rebuilt the following year. It displays a portrait of Abram Quary, who died in 1854 and is remembered as one of Nantucket's "last Indians."

NANTUCKET LIFE SAVING MUSEUM
The museum is a replica of the 1874 U.S. Life Saving Service Station on Surfside, site of one of the original whaling stations. Here visitors can inspect several lifeboats that were used to save people from the treacherous waters around the island.

MIACOMET INDIAN BURIAL GROUND
A simple stone marker by a split-rail fence located off the Surfside bicycle path indicates the site of a Christian Wampanoag Indian burial ground.

THE FARAWAY LAND

Nantucket

NANTUCKET ISLAND

ATLANTIC OCEAN

NIGHT LIGHT
Spark lamps, left, were lit with high-quality case oil from the heads of sperm whales.

INFORMATION FOR TOURISTS

Two ferry lines offer year-round service for both cars and passengers between Hyannis and Nantucket. Some of the ferries require reservations; the ride takes from one to three hours. To reach Hyannis from Boston, take Hwy. 3, then follow Hwy. 6 over the Sagamore Bridge, and Hwy. 132 into town. To reach Hyannis from New York City, take Hwy. 95 to Providence, RI; Hwy. 195 to Wareham, MA; Hwy. 25 across the Bourne Bridge; Hwy. 6 to Exit 6; and Hwy. 132 to Hyannis. Amtrak offers seasonal service from New York City to Hyannis. The trip takes about six hours. Commercial flights connect Nantucket Memorial Airport with Boston, Hyannis, Martha's Vineyard, and New Bedford, MA, and with New York City and Newark, NJ. For more information: Nantucket Island Chamber of Commerce, 48 Main St., Nantucket, MA 02554-3595; 508-228-1700.

of their blubber. The museum is housed in an 1847 factory that manufactured fine candles made from spermaceti—a waxy substance refined from oil taken from the head cavity of the sperm whale. Portraits of many of the Nantucket shipmasters who commanded the 29-foot whaleboats adorn the museum's walls. On exhibit are scrimshaw, logs, and whaling memorabilia, such as a large chair made for Capt. Charles M. Fisher to commemorate a record catch. On May 4, 1884, while captaining his ship, the *Alaska*, Fisher took a 74-foot sperm whale with a head 25 feet long, which yielded an astounding 5,125 gallons of oil.

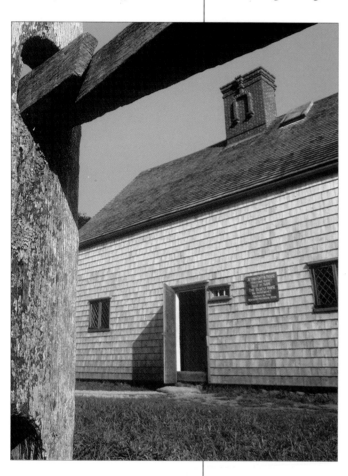

WEDDING GIFT
Nantucket's Oldest House, below, was built in 1686 on Sunset Hill as a wedding present for Jethro and Mary Gardner Coffin.

A shift from right whales in favor of sperm whales, or sparmaceti as the Nantucketers called them, began in 1712. That year, Christopher Hussey and his crew were blown out to sea in a northerly gale. As the men struggled to stay afloat, they spied a pod of whales. Even from a distance the whalers could see that the whales each had a single spout, instead of the familiar twin spouts produced by right whales. Battling the turbulent seas, the fearless whalers hurled their harpoons. When a whale's blood spilled into the rough seas, it was said to still them in almost biblical fashion.

The victim proved to be a sperm whale, which produces a much higher grade of oil than the right whale. Candles manufactured from this oil burn cleanly and give off little odor, unlike the pungent tallow candles made from animal fat. From that day on, the islanders avidly pursued the sparmaceti. In his 1851 whaling masterpiece, *Moby-Dick*, Herman Melville wrote of the sperm whale: "He is, without doubt, the largest inhabitant of the globe; the most formidable of all whales to encounter; the most majestic in aspect; and lastly, by far the most valuable in commerce."

The discovery of the sperm whale led to the construction of larger whaling vessels that could reach the whales' habitats, which were farther offshore than those of the right whale. As their populations were hunted out in the mid-1700's, whaling trips grew longer and covered far greater distances. Some whalers stayed at sea three or four years, roaming as far as the South Seas in search of the lucrative mammal. By the early 19th century whaling ships were typically about 130 feet long and transported at least six sturdy whaleboats. The try-works were set up amidships, and the measure of a trip's success was the number of barrels of oil the ship carried in the hold when it returned.

Just as whaling was becoming the island's lifeblood, the Quaker religion captured the soul of Nantucket. The founder of the Religious Society of Friends was an islander named Mary Starbuck—a descendant of Edward Starbuck—who became "convinced of the truth" at a meeting held in her home by a visiting Quaker preacher in 1702. Mary's conversion so moved witnesses that they were reduced to tears. Pine Street's Parliament House, so

named because town meetings were held here, is said to be built from the timbers of Starbuck's home. Other remnants of the island's Quaker heritage include the Quaker Meeting House on Fair Street, which is now part of the Nantucket Historical Association, and the grass hillocks of the Quaker Burial Ground, where, in keeping with the Quaker belief in simplicity in life and in death, no headstones mark the graves.

| QUAKERS WITH A VENGEANCE | Surprisingly, whaling was not viewed as a contradiction to Quaker pacifist tenets. One early 19th-century Nantuck- |

eter called whaling "an exterminating warfare against those great leviathans of the deep." Once harpooned in the head, the sperm whale did everything to escape, dragging the whaleboat along on what Chase called a "Nantucket

WHALE'S NEMESIS
Whalers used single fluke, double fluke, and toggle harpoons to hook whales. The above examples are on display at the Kendall Whaling Museum in Sharon, Massachusetts.

GRAY LADY
Most buildings on Nantucket, like those on Old North Wharf, left, are covered with Cape Cod shingles, earning the picturesque seaside community its nickname, Gray Lady of the Sea.

The flukes of a humpback whale, right, were once a common sight along the Atlantic Coast. Described by Herman Melville as "the most gamesome and light-hearted of all the whales," the humpback is now an endangered species.

Whalers passed their time on long voyages by carving scrimshaw into the lower jaws and teeth of whales. Some works, such as those below, made in the period of 1822 to 1832 by Nantucketer Edward Burdett, are very skillfully rendered.

sleigh ride." While the boat-steerer hacked at the whale's vital organs with a lance, the creature "spouted blood" and went into its tail-lashing death throes. Sometimes after being harpooned, a whale would sound, diving deep, and a huge length of line was payed out. Occasionally the whale would turn on the boat and bite a chunk out of it or smash it to pieces with its gigantic flukes. No wonder Herman Melville called the Nantucketers "Quakers with a vengeance."

Nantucket boys were brought up with a single ambition: to become whalers like their fathers. Islanders tell the story of a young lad who tried to hone his whaling skills by harpooning the family cat with a fork tied to a ball of yarn. As the pet let out a fearsome yowl, the boy's mother grabbed the ball of yarn, and the boy yelled, "Pay out, Mother! Pay out! There she sounds through the window!"

Since whalers were often away from home for years at a time, it became the responsibility of the women to run the island. Their fortitude was remarked upon as early as 1782 by St. Jean de Crèvecoeur, who visited the island and wrote of the "superior" breed of wives to be found there. The Quaker belief in the spiritual and intellectual equality of the sexes further fostered the spirit of hardy independence that characterized the island's women. One block of Centre Street is still known as Petticoat Row, after the many 19th-century businesswomen who ran shops there.

Kezia Coffin—wife, mother, and whaling merchant—lived on Centre Street. This flamboyant woman was written out of meeting, or excommunicated, by the Quakers for wearing fancy clothes and owning a piano. Coffin took over her husband's whaling interests after his death and amassed a respectable fortune. During the American Revolution, she was an ardent loyalist and her business suffered. Hoping to keep the business afloat Coffin turned to smuggling, but in the end she was forced into bankruptcy.

Near the juncture of Main Street and Straight Wharf is a brick building called the Pacific Club that served as the island's customs house at the height of the trade. When the Pacific Club was built in 1772, Nantucket's whaling ships had ventured as far north as the Arctic Circle and as far south as the Falkland Islands. In the early days the building was owned by the Rotches, the island's leading family of whaling merchants. The Rotches married into the Starbuck family. In 1773 two of the Rotch family's ships, the *Dartmouth* and the *Beaver*, laden with British tea after unloading their cargo of whale oil in London, docked in Boston. A group of patriots, dressed as Indians, boarded the ships and dumped the tea into the harbor, an act that became famous as the Boston Tea Party.

As Nantucket's whalers pushed out into the Pacific Ocean in the years after the War of 1812, the island became a very different place. The influence of the Quakers was on the wane, and the simple shingled houses of more austere times—such as the Starbuck-Kilvert House on Main Street—were replaced by more ostentatious dwellings. A prime example of this grander architecture is the Fair Street mansion of whaling captain Obed Starbuck, now called the Ships Inn, which replaced the more modest home that was the birthplace of Quaker feminist and abolitionist Lucretia Coffin Mott.

In 1830 Obed Starbuck captained what the *Nantucket Inquirer* hailed as "the greatest voyage ever made." After less than 15 months at sea Starbuck's whaleship, *Loper*, which was manned by a nearly all-black crew, returned from the Pacific with 2,280 barrels of oil worth more than $50,000. In a show of enthusiasm, the people of the town applauded the crew as they paraded up Main Street. Starbuck retired at the age of 33 and divided his time between his home in town and his farm, which stood not far from Cato Lane.

TERRIBLE VOYAGE But not all Nantucket whaling captains returned with a full hold and in record time. An especially disastrous trip in 1820 is believed to have been one of the inspirations for Melville's *Moby-Dick*. The ill-fated ship was the *Essex*, captained by George Pollard. Somewhere between the Galápagos and the Marquesa islands, the *Essex* was rammed by an enraged sperm whale and sunk. Stranded for months at sea in their frail lifeboats, the men resorted to cannibalism to survive. According to *The Essex Narrative*, written by a survivor, First Mate

DEATH THROES
Boats full of whalers advance toward a sperm whale, their harpoon guns at the ready, in a work by Robert Walter Weir, circa 1855, above. Thomas Beale, in his 1839 History of the Sperm Whale, *captures the poignant moment: "Mad with the agonies he endures from these fresh attacks, the infuriated Sperm Whale rolls over and over; he rears his enormous head, and with wide expanded jaws snaps at everything around him."*

TOWER OF LIGHT
Great Point Lighthouse, left, rises above the beaches on the northern tip of the island.

A wrought-iron gate in the shape of an anchor surrounded by a wreath, right, opens to the grave of Capt. William Whippey in the New North Burial Ground.

On a blustery day a visitor can walk along Miacomet Beach, below, and not encounter another soul.

Owen Chase, when Pollard and his fellow crew members were finally spotted by a passing ship, they were clutching "the bones of their dead messmates, which they were loth to part with."

Remarkably, Pollard captained another whaleship, only to be wrecked on an uncharted reef near the Hawaiian Islands three years later. Pollard survived, and in 1852, by now a night watchman, met Melville when the author stayed at the Ocean House, now a hotel called the Jared Coffin House on Broad Street. In Melville's words, Pollard was "the most impressive man, tho' wholly unassuming even humble—that I ever encountered." Pollard's home, on the corner of Centre and Quince streets, now houses a gift shop.

By the mid-1840's Nantucket's population had grown to 10,000, making it the third-largest port in Massachusetts. Main Street was paved with cobblestones that had once served as ships' ballast on the return voyage across the Atlantic Ocean. Two churches bracketed the town's commercial district and a row of windmills, one of which, called the Old Mill, is still there. Huge, solid-fill wharves stretched out into the harbor where marinas and art galleries now stand. Instead of the car and passenger ferries that disgorge tourists today, whaling ships were moored at the wharves, and teams of

muscle-bound men off-loaded oil casks and toiled to prepare the greasy arks for the next voyage to a distant part of the globe.

For all its outward signs of prosperity, Nantucket was beginning to decline as the mainland port of New Bedford attracted more and more whalers. Then, in 1846, Nantucket was struck by a calamity that would take the town years from which to recover. About 11:00 on the night of July 13, smoke was spotted issuing from the roof of a hat shop on the south side of Main Street. By the time the town's privately organized fire companies arrived at the scene, the blaze was out of control. The next morning more than a third of the town, including all its wooden buildings and the entire waterfront, lay in ashes. At one point, in the effort to halt the fire's spread, the fire warden and his men began to dynamite buildings. According to one version of the events that night, just as the men were about to raze the Methodist church they were stopped by Maria Mitchell, a young astronomer who would become famous the following year for her discovery of a comet from the observatory above the Pacific National Bank on Main Street. Mitchell convinced the warden that the swirling wind currents at the head of Main Street would blow the flames away from the building. Perhaps Mitchell was one of the women whom the *Nantucket Inquirer* had in mind when it later observed that, through that night, Nantucket's women "rendered more efficient service than could be obtained from the usually stronger sex."

WHALERS
TURN
PROSPECTORS

As Nantucket was recovering from the Great Fire of 1846, it took another blow—the Gold Rush of 1849. Many Nantucket men and boys, including an ambitious lad named Folger who went on to make a fortune in coffee, headed for California. Instead of being outfitted for whaling cruises, Nantucket's ships were loaded with prospectors. The crews sailed around the Horn and abandoned their ships at Golden Gate in San Francisco Bay. In 1869 Nantucket's last whaling ship, the *Oak*, left the harbor, never to return; by 1875 the island's population had fallen to 3,201.

Without whaling to sustain Nantucket's economy, the island slid into a depression that lasted until the turn of the century. There were so many widows living alone in large houses in 1888 that Benjamin F. Cleveland placed an advertisement in the island's *Inquirer and Mirror* offering to "sleep at the homes of timid ladies on stormy nights. Fifteen cents a night, or two nights for a quarter." The advertisement inspired a hilarious poem titled *Benny Cleveland's Job.*

Nantucket's economic woes did not deter visitors from enjoying its windswept beaches and quiet village life. On the eastern end of the island, an easy day's bicycle ride from the town of Nantucket, lies the fishing village of Siasconset. Here people lived by what came to be known as the "laws of 'Sconset"—a code of conduct that called for everyone, no matter whom, to be treated as equals; the laws also forbade the discussion of politics and religion. Summer visitors have been drawn to Siasconset's tiny rose-covered cottages for 150 years.

In keeping with an old island tradition, several of Nantucket's buildings have been moved to different locations and adapted to new purposes. Dreamland Theater was originally part of the Nantucket Hotel at Brant Point before it was moved to its present location on South Water Street and turned into a theater more than 70 years ago. Prior to that, the building was on Main Street and served as a Quaker meetinghouse.

Since the 1950's Nantucket has implemented a series of far-reaching regulations that have helped maintain its historic character and preserve its fabled past. Indeed, if Capt. Obed Starbuck were to steer the ferry around Nantucket's Brant Point today, he might well recognize the old gray town that comes into view as home.

HARBOR VIEW
Many of the island's older houses have lookouts built on their roofs, such as the one on Nantucket's Four Chimneys Inn, above.

NEARBY SITES & ATTRACTIONS

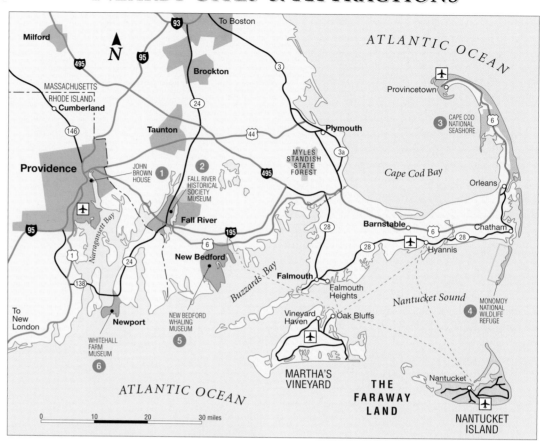

A stretch of sandy beach at Cape Cod National Seashore, below, is the perfect setting for an early evening stroll.

1 JOHN BROWN HOUSE, RHODE ISLAND

This historic house, built in 1786, is operated by the Rhode Island Historical Society. Designed by Joseph Brown for his brother John, the three-story structure is made of a combination of brownstone and brick. During the American Revolution, John Brown, a prominent local merchant, spearheaded an attack in Narragansett Bay on a British-owned ship called the *Gaspee*. Brown and a group of armed citizens over-powered the crew and set fire to the ship. Today the house that bears his name has been restored and serves as a museum. On display is an impressive collection of furniture and historical objects. Visitors can view many items that belonged to the Brown family, including a desk considered by many to be an outstanding example of American Colonial furniture because of the intricate carvings of scallop shells that adorn its doors and drawers. Located at 52 Power St. in Providence.

2 FALL RIVER HISTORICAL SOCIETY MUSEUM, MASSACHUSETTS

This imposing house was built in 1843 and remained in one location for 26 years, until it was purchased by Robert Knight Remington in 1869 and moved to its present site. Designed in the French Second Empire style, the house is made of granite from a Fall River quarry. Remington owned the house until 1878, when it was purchased by David Anthony Brayton. When Brayton's daughter died in 1935 she left the house to a nephew who then donated it to the historical society. Today the furnishings are arranged as they would have appeared in the 19th century. An interesting collection of multicolored stenciled patterns decorates many of the ceilings. Displays include artifacts relating to Fall River fami-lies, including examples of 19th-century glass and silver. One room in the house is dedicated to the Fall River Line, a steamship line that ran from Fall River to New York City. The ships traveled along the Taunton River to Narragansett Bay, then down the coast to Long Island Sound. This collection features artifacts from the steamship era, as well as an extensive display of marine paintings. Another room in the house is devoted to the painters of the Fall River School, whose works date from the mid- to late-19th and early 20th centuries. The collection includes the works of Robert Spear Dunning and Bryant Shapin. The library displays personal belongings, police photographs, and other objects from the famous murder trial of Lizzy Borden, which were donated to the museum by one of her defense attorneys. Borden was born in Fall River, and after her acquittal in 1893, she lived in the town until her death in 1927. Visitors are welcome to tour the double parlors, main front hallway, and dining room, as well as several bedrooms on the second floor—all of which look as they did when the family was in residence. Located at 451 Rock St. in Fall River.

3 CAPE COD NATIONAL SEASHORE, MASSACHUSETTS

Covering 27,000 acres and stretching for 40 miles along the 65-mile-long peninsula of Cape Cod, the national seashore protects windswept sand dunes, open heaths, thick stands of beech and pitch pine forests, and salt- and freshwater marshes. Glacial ponds, kettleholes, cliffs, and sand deposits up to 175 feet high are a legacy of the glaciers that shaped the region. There are six public beaches, all of which can be reached from Hwy. 6. Three paved bicycle trails, accessible at the Province Lands and Salt Pond visitor centers, run along sections of the seashore and lead to beaches and picnic areas. The national seashore also includes such attractions as the Marconi Station Area, White Cedar Swamp, and the Pilgrim Heights Area. Located on Hwy. 6.

4 MONOMOY NATIONAL WILDLIFE REFUGE, MASSACHUSETTS

Located along the Atlantic Flyway, this 2,750-acre refuge off Cape Cod attracts as many as 500,000 migratory and nesting birds every year. Terns, black-crowned night herons, and a colony of 20,000 herring and black-backed gulls nest here during the summer. In the autumn, as many as 9,000 roseate terns—about 80 percent of the entire northeastern population of this species—use the refuge as a stopover during their annual migration. Approximately 85,000 common terns return each May from their migration to South America. Rare species include red-necked phalaropes, Eurasian curlews, ruffs, and Hudsonian godwits. Shorebirds, such as buff-breasted sandpipers, red knots, and marbled godwits also come to the refuge, and teals, ruddies, and shovelers make up the ducks that nest here. The island is accessible by boat from Chatham.

5 NEW BEDFORD WHALING MUSEUM, MASSACHUSETTS

The museum's collection of whaling artifacts, art, and memorabilia is one of the largest in the nation. More than 150 ship models are on display, including the 89-foot-long, half-scale model of the *Lagoda,* which visitors can board. This fully rigged ship is the largest ship model in the world. A collection devoted to the whaling industry includes two full-size whaling ships and the massive skeleton of a humpback whale. Also on display are 550 harpoons, 100 navigational objects, and 2,000 pieces of scrimshaw. Two sections of a mural titled *Panorama of a Whaling Voyage Round the World*, painted in 1848 by Russell Purrington, and a 98-foot-long mural of sperm whales by marine artist Richard Ellis evoke the region's seafaring past. A film on whales and whaling plays in the museum's theater during the summer. The local history collection includes 20,000 photographs of the region, as well as 800 paintings, prints, and sketches, hundreds of pieces of locally crafted furniture, and more than 3,500 pieces of glassware. Approximately 650 household objects are also on exhibit, including many furnishings for a Victorian parlor. Located at 18 Johnny Cake Hill in New Bedford.

6 WHITEHALL FARM MUSEUM, RHODE ISLAND

In 1729 George Berkeley, then the Dean of Londonderry, Ireland, came to the New World to found a college in Bermuda with a grant from the British government. While he waited for the funds to arrive, he lived at Whitehall Farm in Rhode Island. The house, which he enlarged to accommodate his bride and an entourage, became the meeting place for scholars and clergy. By 1732 it was clear that the grant would never materialize so Berkeley returned to Ireland where he became the Bishop of Cloyne. The house passed through a series of owners and now it belongs to the National Society of the Colonial Dames who exhibit it as a memorial to the bishop. Located on Berkeley Ave. in Middletown.

A carved whale hangs above the door to the New Bedford Whaling Museum, above. New Bedford was the whaling capital of America during the 1850's.

John Quincy Adams remarked that the John Brown House, below, was "the most magnificent and elegant mansion I have ever seen on the continent."

JOHN BROWN'S RAID

The raid on Harpers Ferry came to be a symbol of the opposing views that ultimately led to civil war.

Some called John Brown a murderer, a crazed monster, and worse. Others honored him as a martyr. The writer Ralph Waldo Emerson described the legendary abolitionist as a saint whose destiny would "make the gallows glorious like the cross." Brown himself believed he was an instrument of God. More than 100 years after Brown's death, he is remembered for his role in galvanizing the national debate on the issue of slavery. The Civil War would have happened without him, but John Brown's 1859 raid on the arsenal at Harpers Ferry set in relief the profound differences between citizens of the North and South. When Northern soldiers marched off to do battle with their Southern brothers they sang, "John Brown's body lies a mould'ring in the grave, his soul goes marching on."

For as long as the question of whether freedom—or indeed any cause—justifies the use of violence, John Brown will remain a perplexing figure. Was he a prophet or a demon, a saint or a sinner, a martyr or a madman? Visitors to Harpers Ferry National Historical Park in West Virginia, Virginia, and Maryland will find much to ponder as they explore the sites connected to the event now known to the world as John Brown's Raid.

There were 21 men in Brown's band, 5 blacks and 16 whites, a diverse collection of idealists that included a lawyer and an escaped slave, a Quaker and a convict on the run. Their leader was a charismatic 59-year-old father of 20 children, who some said looked and walked "like an old man"; in keeping with the contradictory reactions he provoked, however, Brown was also described as being "quick as a cat in his movements," according to a Cleveland, Ohio, newspaper story.

By the time he led the attack on Harpers Ferry, Brown had already established a formidable reputation. During the 1850's his antislavery guerrilla activities in Kansas Territory helped establish its nickname, Bleeding Kansas. In May 1856 proponents of slavery led an attack on Lawrence, Kansas. Brown and a group of like-minded men—including four of his seven sons—retaliated by brutally murdering five settlers at Pottawatomie Creek.

Three months later the fiery Brown earned the title Old Osawatomie after a clash with proslavery Missourians at the settlement of Osawatomie.

THE NIGHT OF THE RAID

The immediate goal of John Brown's Provisional Army of the United States was to seize 100,000 rifles and muskets stored at the U.S. Armory and Arsenal in Harpers Ferry, then a part of Virginia. Their ultimate purpose was to form a republic in the Appalachians made up of fugitive slaves who would fight to rid the nation of the institution of slavery.

On Sunday night, October 16, 1859, a wagon bearing John Brown and a stash of pikes—long spears to arm the slaves once they were liberated—rolled in to Harpers Ferry. There were just a few watchmen on duty at the arsenal. Brown's men took control of the U.S. Armory on Potomac Street and the nearby Hall's Rifle Works without a shot being fired. However, as townspeople became aware of the raid near dawn, they started trading shots with Brown and his men, who took hostages and holed up in the armory's fire engine house. The hostages included Col. Lewis W. Washington (the

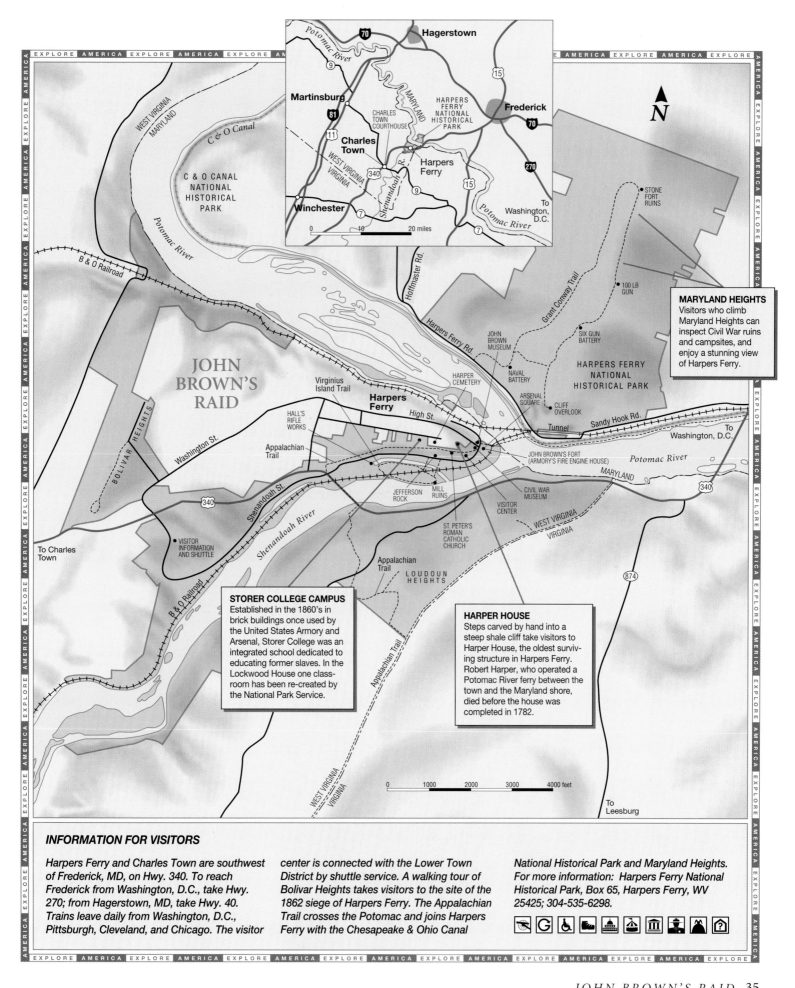

JOHN BROWN'S RAID

MARYLAND HEIGHTS
Visitors who climb Maryland Heights can inspect Civil War ruins and campsites, and enjoy a stunning view of Harpers Ferry.

STORER COLLEGE CAMPUS
Established in the 1860's in brick buildings once used by the United States Armory and Arsenal, Storer College was an integrated school dedicated to educating former slaves. In the Lockwood House one classroom has been re-created by the National Park Service.

HARPER HOUSE
Steps carved by hand into a steep shale cliff take visitors to Harper House, the oldest surviving structure in Harpers Ferry. Robert Harper, who operated a Potomac River ferry between the town and the Maryland shore, died before the house was completed in 1782.

INFORMATION FOR VISITORS

Harpers Ferry and Charles Town are southwest of Frederick, MD, on Hwy. 340. To reach Frederick from Washington, D.C., take Hwy. 270; from Hagerstown, MD, take Hwy. 40. Trains leave daily from Washington, D.C., Pittsburgh, Cleveland, and Chicago. The visitor center is connected with the Lower Town District by shuttle service. A walking tour of Bolivar Heights takes visitors to the site of the 1862 siege of Harpers Ferry. The Appalachian Trail crosses the Potomac and joins Harpers Ferry with the Chesapeake & Ohio Canal National Historical Park and Maryland Heights. For more information: Harpers Ferry National Historical Park, Box 65, Harpers Ferry, WV 25425; 304-535-6298.

JOHN BROWN'S STRONGHOLD

JOHN BROWN'S STRONGHOLD

When the raiders captured the fire engine house, above, John Brown announced to the astonished night watchman, "I want to free all the Negroes. I have possession now of the U.S. armory, and if the citizens interfere, I must only burn the town and have blood." Brown held the hostages in the building's two rooms, one of which is shown at right. Fortunately, not one hostage was killed during the siege, although Lt. Israel Green, who led the assault to recapture the engine house, described the prisoners as the "sorriest lot of people I ever saw."

great-grandnephew of George Washington), three of the colonel's slaves, and a group of armory employees who, unaware of the trouble brewing inside, showed up for work.

By noon the militia from nearby Charles Town had arrived in full force and other militias soon followed. But the troops' undisciplined attempts to recapture the engine house failed, and hysteria gripped the inhabitants of the town. Finally, late in the evening on October 17, a contingent of 90 marines under the command of Lt. Col. Robert E. Lee marched on Harpers Ferry.

Twice Brown had sought a truce and twice his attempts had been swiftly rebuffed by the townspeople. However, when Lee sent Lt. James Ewell Brown (Jeb) Stuart to the door of the fire engine house to parley with Brown on the morning of October 18, Brown refused to surrender. Stuart stepped back from the door and seconds later 12 marines led by Lt. Israel Green stormed the engine house, captured Brown and the remaining raiders, and freed the hostages.

Three Harpers Ferry citizens had been killed. Ten raiders, including two of Brown's sons, were shot dead, and five men—including John Brown—were captured and jailed in nearby Charles Town. The other raiders slipped away, and two of them were apprehended later. Tragically, the first person the raiders had mortally wounded was a free black railroad porter, Heyward Shepherd. The first raider killed was Dangerfield Newby, a former slave who had joined Brown's band in the hope of freeing his wife and children from bondage. During the weeks leading up to the raid, Newby read and reread a letter from his wife pleading with him to find a way to buy her and the children "for if you do not get me, somebody else will."

PUZZLING BEHAVIOR

Historians have asked why Brown lingered in Harpers Ferry instead of fleeing with the weapons he'd seized. Any time during the first 12 hours of the raid he and his men could probably have escaped into the mountains. Some say Brown waited in the hope that Virginia slaves would rally to his cause. Another puzzling incident concerns an eastbound Baltimore

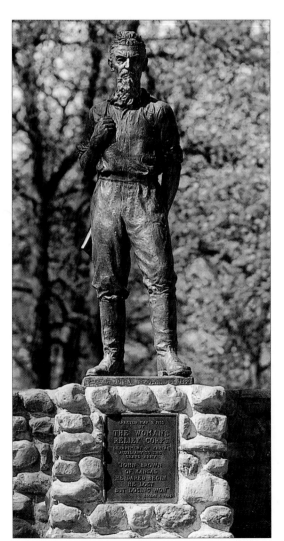

& Ohio train that stopped in Harpers Ferry during the raid. Inexplicably, Brown allowed the train to continue its trip to Baltimore. At Monocacy, Maryland, the train's crew telegraphed news of the raid to railroad officials, who alerted authorities.

Panic spread as word of the raid got out. Virginians were especially nervous because the slave rebellion of 1831 led by Nat Turner was fresh in their minds. More than 50 people, mostly women and children, were murdered in that clash, which was the subject of highly exaggerated and inflammatory news reports. Many Northerners, on the other hand, hailed Brown as a hero. A group of prominent abolitionists in the North—all white—known as the Secret Six was linked to the plot, although how much they knew of Brown's intentions before the raid remains unknown.

Only nine days after he was captured, John Brown was put on trial in the Charles Town Courthouse. Still suffering from the wounds he received in a bludgeoning given him by Lieutenant Green, Brown lay on a cot during the entire proceeding. He scorned his court-appointed attorneys and said little in his own defense although he wrote many letters from jail explaining his actions. By the end of the three-and-a-half-day trial, Brown had changed from defiant abolitionist to stoic champion of a righteous cause.

Brown was found guilty of murder, treason, and inciting a slave rebellion and condemned to die by hanging. "I am worth now inconceivably more to hang than for any other purpose," he prophesied to his brother and a would-be rescuer after his arrest. The hanging took place around 11:30 a.m. on December 2, 1859, on a gallows set up in a large field on the edge of Charles Town. A plaque on

RAILROAD DELIVERY
Replicas of wooden boxes and barrels, above, used to ship merchandise during the 19th century, stand outside the dry goods store in the Lower Town. Most outside goods arrived in Harpers Ferry by railroad.

TIMELESS HONOR
The bronze statue of John Brown, left, was erected in Osawatomie, Kansas, by the Woman's Relief Corps. The inscription at its base reads "He Dared Begin/He Lost/But Losing Won."

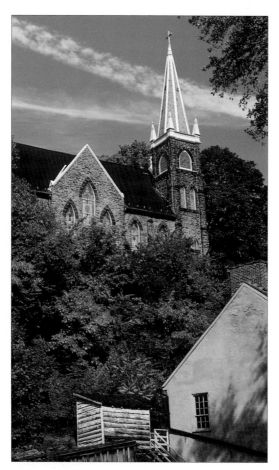

South Samuel Street marks the location. Six of his cohorts faced the same fate in the next few months.

A few prominent abolitionists were invited to speak at a private burial service for Brown in North Elba, New York. One of them likened Brown to Joseph Warren, who died leading Americans at the Battle of Bunker Hill. Songs and poems were written about Brown. Speeches were given. Some said photographs of Brown were sold to raise funds for his family, who also received a portion of the royalties from a popular biography of the time. The legend of Harpers Ferry grew.

BUILDING A LEGEND

A newspaper article published after the hanging told the story of Brown kissing a slave child in the arms of his mother as he left the jail to be executed. Various written reports of the time repeated and embellished the story, and it was the subject of a Currier & Ives lithograph and a famous painting by T. S. Noble titled *John Brown's Blessing*. But the incident probably never happened because the town was under martial law: Some 1,500 troops guarded the area and the general public was not allowed near the jail or to attend the execution. However, such tales

VIEWS OF THE PAST

The Civil War Museum, located within Harpers Ferry National Historical Park, left, displays numerous exhibits of this tumultuous period in the town's history. Most of the time this gateway to Virginia's Shenandoah Valley was controlled by Union forces, but control of the town swung between the Union and Confederate sides eight times during the war. On June 20, 1863, Virginia's western lands—including Harpers Ferry—split off from the state to form West Virginia, a Union state.

merely added to folklore that grew up around the raid and its impassioned leader. If interest in John Brown's raid ever abated, it was vigorously revived with Stephen Vincent Benét's *John Brown's Body,* an epic poem about the Civil War that was published in 1927.

Harpers Ferry National Historical Park encompasses more than 2,300 acres, including the Old Town of Harpers Ferry at the foot of Camp Hill, Maryland Heights on the other side of the Potomac River, and Loudoun Heights across the Shenandoah River. The park features several 19th-century shops and armory buildings, including the fire engine house where Brown ended his crusade. The building was dismantled and reassembled for the 1893 World's Columbian Exposition in Chicago, and then relocated close to its original site at the north end of cobblestoned Shenandoah Street. Most of the armory buildings were destroyed during the Civil War or devastated in the major flood of 1870 or by later floods. Flooding after heavy rains plagues the lower town every few years.

Along with permanent exhibits on local industries, African-American history, the Civil War, transportation, and the environment, year-round displays and audiovisual presentations given in historic buildings along Shenandoah Street and the lower part of High Street interpret John Brown's Raid for the public. The John Brown Museum contains numerous artifacts related to the history-making raid, including one of the original 1,000 pikes with which Brown intended to arm the freed slaves; a Sharp's carbine found in the fire engine house after the raid; the original gate to the armory grounds; the entrance doors to the Charles Town jail where Brown was held; and remnants of the gallows on which he was hanged.

In Jefferson County Museum in nearby Charles Town, visitors can see the wagon that carried John Brown to the gallows, his trunk, and his courtroom cot. Tours of the courthouse where Brown's trial was held give a vivid picture of the Old Man as he faced his accusers."I feel no consciousness of guilt," he said. Such was the strength of his conviction, and the growing public sentiment against the evils of slavery, that many otherwise peaceful Americans found themselves in sympathy with the actions of the raiders. "I am quite certain," Brown told his jailer, John Avis, "that the crimes of this guilty land will never be purged away but with blood."

Nearby Sites & Attractions

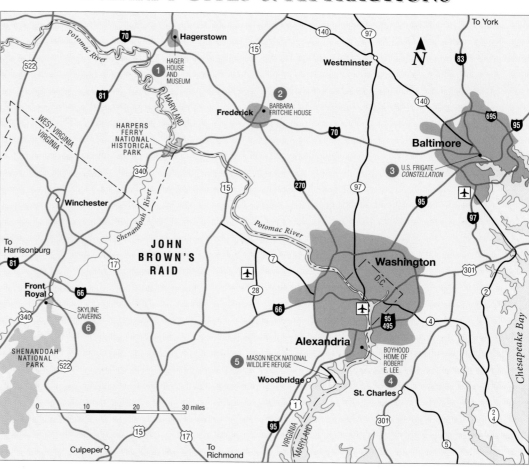

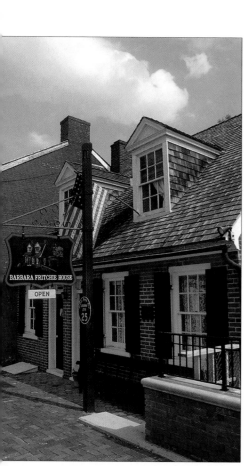

The Barbara Fritchie House, above, is a replica of the one that was devastated by a flood six years after Fritchie's death. In 1976 another flood damaged many items in this collection of memorabilia, including historic documents and books.

1 HAGER HOUSE AND MUSEUM, MARYLAND

When Jonathan Hager, a farmer and gunsmith, bought land in 1739 in what is now northern Maryland, he constructed a house sturdy enough to endure the rigors of the harsh winters. The exterior walls were made of 22-inch-thick fieldstones, and mud and straw were placed between the floors and interior walls as insulation against the cold. The three-and-a-half-story German-style building was constructed near two springs, ensuring a reliable water supply. The house was restored in 1953 and is furnished in 18th-century style. The museum, which is next to Hager's home, displays more than 500 artifacts that were unearthed during the restoration of the house. On display are 18th- and 19th-century coins, forks and combs made from bones, pottery, buttons, and ironwork. Located at 110 Key St. in Hagerstown.

2 BARBARA FRITCHIE HOUSE, MARYLAND

Barbara Fritchie was nine years old when the American Revolution began and 95 when the Civil War broke out. A staunch Unionist, she was deeply troubled by the issues of the Civil War. Legend has it that in September 1862, Fritchie defiantly waved the Union flag as Gen. Stonewall Jackson and his troops passed through Frederick. The event was immortalized by the Quaker abolitionist and poet

John Greenleaf Whittier in his 1863 poem titled *Barbara Fritchie.* The museum, in a replica of the Fritchie's home, contains a number of her personal items, including a secretary-bookcase, which Union general Reno used to write a letter to his family just two days before his death at the Battle of South Mountain; a cape and shawl that belonged to Fritchie; and the shawl of her friend Francis Scott Key, author of the *Star-Spangled Banner.* Located at 154 W. Patrick St. in Frederick.

3 U.S. FRIGATE *CONSTELLATION*, MARYLAND

The *Constellation*, built in 1854, was launched at the Gosport Navy Yard in Norfolk, Virginia. This 19th-century sloop of war, with its enormous wooden hull, is the only naval vessel to survive the Civil War era. It is also the last all-sail warship ever built by the U.S. Navy. The 179-foot-long ship has three masts and 20,000 square feet of sails, displaces about 1,400 tons, and is the largest sloop of war ever built by the navy. The *Constellation* was decommissioned in 1955 and placed in dry dock in Baltimore Harbor, where it underwent meticulous refurbishment so that it could be opened to the public. The frigate is presently undergoing work to restore it to its original condition at the beginning of the Civil War. Located at Pier One in Baltimore.

numbers have tripled in the past 10 years. Redhead and canvasback ducks have returned to the area and great blue herons have formed a large colony of 1,300 nests in the refuge. Black, mallard, and wood ducks are the refuge's most commonly sighted birds. Hikers walk the nature trails that wind through stretches of thick woodlands, dominated by 80-year-old oak and beech trees and inhabited by foxes, deer, raccoons, and a variety of bird species, including pileated woodpeckers, indigo buntings, Carolina wrens, and Acadian flycatchers. Other birds spotted in the refuge include great horned owls, turkeys, and 27 species of warblers. Located 18 miles southeast of Washington, D.C., off Hwy. 1.

6 SKYLINE CAVERNS, VIRGINIA

The caverns, which descend more than 260 feet below ground, were formed over 60 million years ago. They were discovered by Dr. Walter S. Amos, a retired geologist, in 1937 and were opened to the public in 1939. Inside the underground chambers there is a wealth of stalagmites, stalactites, anthodites (a rare crystalline formation), and flowstones, which resemble curtains. The largest anthodite is 14 to 18 inches long and estimated to be about 126,000 years old. Other underground features include three streams and 37-foot Rainbow Falls. Fairyland Lake has stalactites hanging from the ceiling and stalagmites that rise through the surface of the water. Capitol Dome resembles the dome of the Capitol in Washington, D.C. The structure is believed to be 12,000 years old and is estimated to weigh more than nine tons. The cave is home to three types of bats, as well as various fish, crayfish, spotted salamanders, and valentine beetles, found nowhere else in the world. Located one mile south of Front Royal on Hwy. 340.

The riggings of the U.S. Frigate Constellation, docked in Baltimore's Inner Harbor, left, seem to rival the World Trade Center in height.

When Robert E. Lee entered the U.S. Military Academy, known as West Point, at age 18, his home address was 607 Oronoco Street, in Alexandria, Virginia, now a museum.

4 BOYHOOD HOME OF ROBERT E. LEE, VIRGINIA

This Federal-style house was the home of Confederate general Robert E. Lee from 1811 to 1816 and 1820 to 1825. It was built in 1795 by John Potts, a friend of George Washington. Washington and the Marquis de Lafayette were both guests at the house. In 1804, the mansion, with its beautiful furnishings, was the site of the wedding between George Washington Parke Custis—the grandson of Martha Washington—and Mary Lee Fitzhugh. Their daughter, Mary Custis, married Robert E. Lee. The house has been restored to its early 19th-century appearance and is open to the public when it is not being used for private functions. Located at 607 Oronoco St. in Alexandria.

5 MASON NECK NATIONAL WILDLIFE REFUGE, VIRGINIA

Situated on a peninsula that juts into the Potomac River, this 2,277-acre refuge is located only 18 miles from the nation's capital. Its woods and marshes provide important habitats for a variety of birds. The refuge was the first to be set aside under the federal Endangered Species Act as a protected area for the bald eagle. The raptors now number 20 to 30 in the summer and 50 to 60 in the winter and their overall

THE LOST COLONY

When John White returned to Roanoke Island after a three-year absence, all that remained of the colony's 117 inhabitants was the mysterious word Croatoan.

The image is one of the most haunting in American folklore: colonist Eleanor Dare cradling her infant daughter amid a vast wilderness, seemingly forgotten by Eleanor's father, John White, who brought them to the unfamiliar land and left them to fend for themselves.

In the four centuries since their disappearance, Eleanor and Virginia Dare have become symbols of an epic unsolved mystery that challenges historians and archeologists to this day. In 1587 more than 100 men, women, and children left Plymouth, England, and traveled to Chesapeake Bay with the intention of establishing the first settlement of English families in America. Within three years the colonists had vanished with scarcely a trace—117 English subjects seemed to have been swallowed up by the New World frontier.

Roanoke Island appears much as it did at the time of the colonists' arrival. The low, narrow strip of land, which lies between North Carolina's treacherous Outer Banks and the mainland, is characterized by vast tracts of marshland, thick stands of twisted live oak trees, and scuppernong grapevines. This was a seemingly hospitable site for settlement. But fate and the sometimes harsh environment conspired to thwart the earliest settlers.

The famed Lost Colony of Roanoke Island represented the second attempt by England to colonize North America. In March 1584, Queen Elizabeth I granted Sir Walter Raleigh a patent to all the lands he could occupy in the New World. Raleigh—a soldier, man of letters, and favorite of the queen—dispatched explorers to the Outer Banks of North Carolina, where they spent several months scouting the broad sounds and barrier islands for potential colony sites. The men returned to England later that year, full of glowing reports of lush virgin forests, rivers brimming with fish, and friendly Indians.

In July 1585 a party of nearly 400 soldiers, craftsmen, and scholars sent by

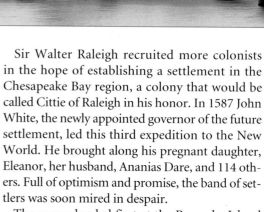

SAILING BACK IN TIME

The Elizabeth II, *right, moored at the* Elizabeth II State Historic Site, *is a colorful reproduction of the type of boat that carried British settlers to North Carolina. The vessel is 69 feet long, and the main mast measures 65 feet high. Visitors can tour the captain's cabin, below, whose cramped quarters show how uncomfortable long voyages at sea in these vessels could be.*

Raleigh landed at Roanoke Island to build a military outpost, and 108 soldiers remained at the site to construct the garrison. But the outpost was doomed from the start. The men had arrived too late in the season for planting, and relations with the Roanoke Indians rapidly deteriorated. In the summer of 1586, strapped for supplies, all but 15 soldiers abandoned the fort and sailed back to England with Sir Francis Drake and his men.

Sir Walter Raleigh recruited more colonists in the hope of establishing a settlement in the Chesapeake Bay region, a colony that would be called Cittie of Raleigh in his honor. In 1587 John White, the newly appointed governor of the future settlement, led this third expedition to the New World. He brought along his pregnant daughter, Eleanor, her husband, Ananias Dare, and 114 others. Full of optimism and promise, the band of settlers was soon mired in despair.

The group landed first at the Roanoke Island military outpost in July to resupply the 15 soldiers before continuing on to Chesapeake Bay. But, by White's account, the ship's captain felt it was too late in the season to proceed. The colonists had misgivings about remaining in Roanoke for the winter when they found the bones of a British soldier there, and detected no signs of the other 14 men. Nevertheless, they unloaded their belongings, and repaired to the abandoned village.

On August 18, 1587, Eleanor Dare gave birth to a daughter, Virginia, earning the baby the distinction of being the first English child born on American soil. A few days later, a second baby was born on the island. With winter approaching and their supplies dwindling, White decided to return to England to fetch provisions. But upon his arrival

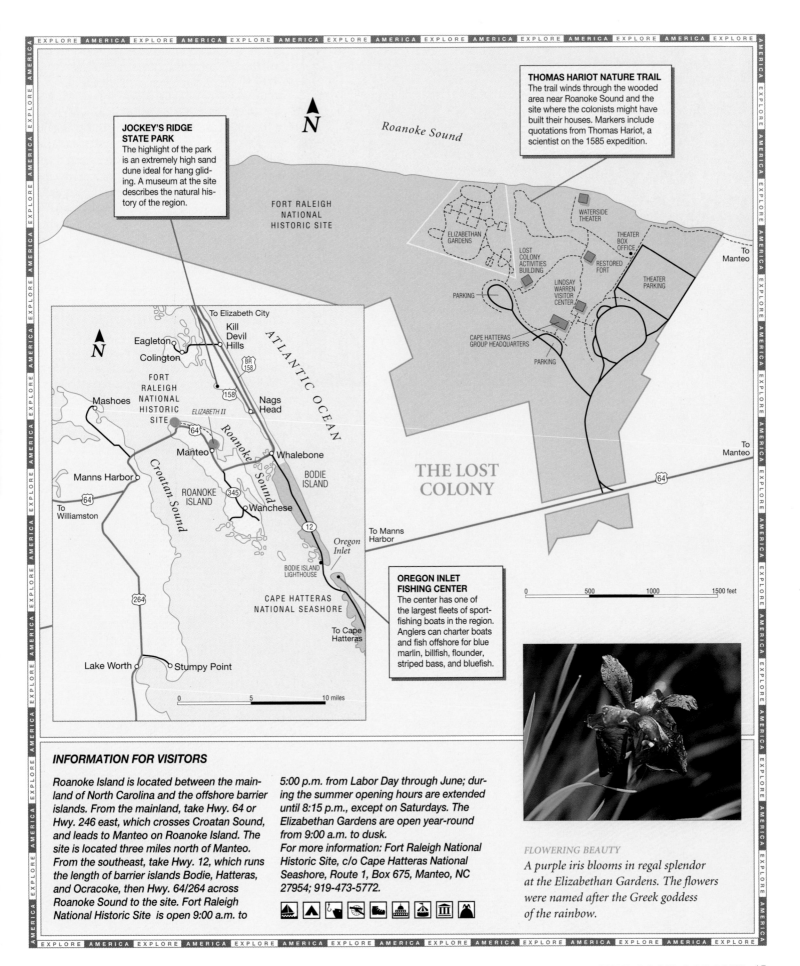

JOCKEY'S RIDGE STATE PARK
The highlight of the park is an extremely high sand dune ideal for hang gliding. A museum at the site describes the natural history of the region.

THOMAS HARIOT NATURE TRAIL
The trail winds through the wooded area near Roanoke Sound and the site where the colonists might have built their houses. Markers include quotations from Thomas Hariot, a scientist on the 1585 expedition.

Roanoke Sound

FORT RALEIGH NATIONAL HISTORIC SITE

WATERSIDE THEATER
ELIZABETHAN GARDENS
LOST COLONY ACTIVITIES BUILDING
THEATER BOX OFFICE
RESTORED FORT
THEATER PARKING
LINDSAY WARREN VISITOR CENTER
PARKING
CAPE HATTERAS GROUP HEADQUARTERS
PARKING
To Manteo

THE LOST COLONY

To Manteo

64

To Elizabeth City
Kill Devil Hills
Eagleton
Colington
BR 158
158
ATLANTIC OCEAN
FORT RALEIGH NATIONAL HISTORIC SITE
Mashoes
ELIZABETH II
Nags Head
64
Manteo
Roanoke Sound
Whalebone
Manns Harbor
BODIE ISLAND
ROANOKE ISLAND
345
Croatan Sound
Wanchese
64
To Williamston
12
To Manns Harbor
Oregon Inlet
264
BODIE ISLAND LIGHTHOUSE
CAPE HATTERAS NATIONAL SEASHORE
Lake Worth
Stumpy Point
To Cape Hatteras

0   5   10 miles

OREGON INLET FISHING CENTER
The center has one of the largest fleets of sport-fishing boats in the region. Anglers can charter boats and fish offshore for blue marlin, billfish, flounder, striped bass, and bluefish.

0   500   1000   1500 feet

INFORMATION FOR VISITORS

Roanoke Island is located between the mainland of North Carolina and the offshore barrier islands. From the mainland, take Hwy. 64 or Hwy. 246 east, which crosses Croatan Sound, and leads to Manteo on Roanoke Island. The site is located three miles north of Manteo. From the southeast, take Hwy. 12, which runs the length of barrier islands Bodie, Hatteras, and Ocracoke, then Hwy. 64/264 across Roanoke Sound to the site. Fort Raleigh National Historic Site is open 9:00 a.m. to 5:00 p.m. from Labor Day through June; during the summer opening hours are extended until 8:15 p.m., except on Saturdays. The Elizabethan Gardens are open year-round from 9:00 a.m. to dusk.
For more information: Fort Raleigh National Historic Site, c/o Cape Hatteras National Seashore, Route 1, Box 675, Manteo, NC 27954; 919-473-5772.

FLOWERING BEAUTY
A purple iris blooms in regal splendor at the Elizabethan Gardens. The flowers were named after the Greek goddess of the rainbow.

EXPLORE AMERICA EXPLORE AMERICA EXPLORE AMERICA EXPLORE AMERICA EXPLORE AMERICA EXPLORE AMERICA EXPLORE AMERICA EXPLORE AMERICA EXPLORE

THE LOST COLONY 45

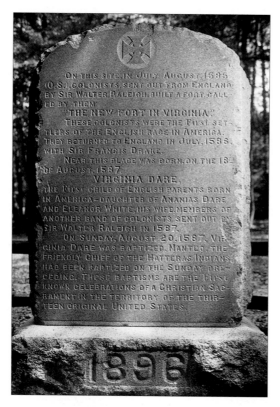

there, his ship was immediately pressed into service in the war with Spain. He was unable to go back to the colony until August 18, 1590—his granddaughter Virginia's third birthday. He found the site deserted, plundered, and surrounded "with a high palisado of great trees, with cortynes and flankers, very Fort-like." On one of the palisades, the single word CROATOAN was carved, and the letters CRO had been gouged into a nearby tree.

White did not become alarmed. The words were part of a prearranged sign to indicate that the colonists had relocated. White had also instructed the group to carve a Maltese cross as a sign should they be forced to leave under duress. Finding no cross, White assumed that the colony had moved safely to Croatoan, a part of present-day Hatteras Island. There, White assured himself, the colonists would be safe with friendly Chief Manteo and his Croatoan tribe.

Before White could explore any further, a hurricane arose that damaged his ships, forcing him back to England. Despite repeated attempts, he

never again made the journey across the Atlantic. White died some years later, ignorant of the fate of his family and the colony.

Upon his arrival in Jamestown, Virginia, in 1607, British captain John Smith renewed the search for the lost colonists. Smith met with the hostile Indian chieftain Powhatan, who, to Smith's dismay, said that he had attacked the Roanoke settlement and slaughtered most of its inhabitants. As proof that he was speaking the truth, Powhatan showed the Englishman "a musket barrel and a brass mortar,

A North Carolina man, Hamilton McMillan, published a pamphlet in 1888 stating that the Pembroke Indians of North Carolina's Robeson County claimed their ancestors came from "Roanoke in Virginia." According to McMillan, the Pembrokes spoke a dialect of British English and many of them bore the last names of lost colonists. Furthermore, Raleigh and his contemporaries had called the Roanoke Island settlement "Roanoke in Virginia." The Pembrokes exhibited strikingly European physical features, including

Virginia Dare

An infant born August 18, 1587, at Roanoke Island, was the first English child born in the New World. The following Sunday, "because this child was the first Christian borne in Virginia, she was named Virginia."

FAMOUS CHILD
A historic marker at the Fort Raleigh National Historic Site, left, commemorates the birth of Virginia Dare. She was baptized Virginia in honor of England's Queen Elizabeth I, the Virgin Queen.

and certain pieces of iron that had been theirs." By 1612 rumors placed the surviving colonists in the Chesapeake Bay area. But, as each successive search party failed to turn up any traces of the lost colonists, the hunt was eventually abandoned. The 117 pioneers of Roanoke Island had been erased forever from existence.

THEORIES AND HOAXES

Over the years, the fate of the Lost Colony fueled the fires of speculation. In 1709 English explorer John Lawson went to Roanoke Island and spent time among the Hatteras Indians, descendants of the Croatoan tribe. "Several of their ancestors were white people," Lawson wrote, "and could talk in a book [read] as we do, the truth of which is confirmed by gray eyes being found infrequently among these Indians." This comment was taken by some to mean that the remaining colonists, or other early European explorers, had been assimilated by the tribe.

fair eyes, light hair, and Caucasian bone structure.

In 1937 a traveler discovered a mysterious rock lying in a swamp 60 miles west of Roanoke Island. Dubbed the Eleanor Dare Stone, the rock was covered with strange carvings, which, when deciphered, appeared to be a message from Eleanor Dare to her father, indicating that she and the other settlers had fled Roanoke Island after an Indian attack.

Over the next three years, nearly 40 similar stones were found in places from North Carolina to Georgia. When their inscriptions were pieced together, they gave a dramatic account of the colonists' overland journey through the southeast that culminated in the death of Eleanor Dare in 1599. With the exception of the Eleanor Dare Stone, the trail of evidence was exposed by an investigative reporter in 1940 as an elaborate hoax.

Many local residents believe that the colonists relocated inland. In the 1950's, the West Virginia Pulp and Paper Company ran logging operations in a remote section of Dare County known as

Beechland. Digging into a large mound, they uncovered Indian artifacts and several caskets fashioned from cypress trees. The coffin lids were carved with a Christian cross and the letters "INRI," the Latin abbreviation for "Jesus of Nazareth, King of the Jews." But the loggers, unfamiliar with the area's history, failed to understand the value of their find and most of the artifacts were destroyed.

In the past 40 years researchers have combed through documents in Spanish and British archives, such as ships' logs, court records, and letters to King James, which may point to a logical explanation for the colonists' disappearance. Circumstantial evidence suggests that after White left Roanoke for England in 1587, the colony split into two factions, with the largest group departing for Chesapeake Bay. The rest of the colonists stayed behind to await White's return. Sometime in the spring of 1588, however, this group fled to Croatoan, carving the mysterious inscriptions upon their departure.

Roanoke Island has not forgotten the colonists, and the residents' pride in their heritage is evident. In the 1890's islanders began an annual celebration in honor of the colonists, which takes place on Virginia Dare's birthday. The tradition continues today: Each August 18 the 513-acre park hosts an Elizabethan street party in which costumed interpreters celebrate the baby's birth.

In 1937 the residents commissioned Pulitzer Prize–winner Paul Green to write a play about Raleigh's colony in commemoration of its 350th anniversary. Green's outdoor drama, *The Lost Colony,* which combines dance, drama, and music, opened in a specially built theater near the Fort Raleigh site on July 4, 1937.

HISTORIC FORT RALEIGH

The northern end of Roanoke Island is acknowledged as the birthplace of English America, and in 1941 the federal government purchased the grounds to create the Fort Raleigh National Historic Site. Several years later archeologists restored the old earthen fort and the moat thought to have been built by Raleigh's party of English soldiers in 1585.

The history of Fort Raleigh is interpreted through a film on the story of the Lost Colony and exhibits of items recovered at the fort site. These artifacts include an Indian pipe, Algonquian pottery, a wrought-iron sickle, and metal counters used in accounting. So far, however, archeologists cannot confirm that any of the items recovered near the fort came from the Lost Colony, deepening the mystery of the colonists' fate.

Sir Walter Raleigh Street and Eleanor Dare Avenue in the nearby town of Manteo hark back to the past. The quaint downtown area is centered on a beautifully restored waterfront with docks reaching into Shallowbag Bay. A paved bicycle path runs the length of the north end of the island, from Manteo to Fort Raleigh.

To mark the 400th anniversary of the first Roanoke voyage, in 1984, the state of North Carolina commissioned the *Elizabeth II.* When she is not sailing the majestic waters of North Carolina's rivers and sounds, the ship graces Manteo's harbor, offering visitors a glimpse of shipboard life

SECOTON

during the Elizabethan era. Costumed interpreters give living history demonstrations throughout the summer.

At the southern end of Roanoke Island, visitors can walk along the sandy lanes of Wanchese, an active fishing village. Generations of Outer Banks fishing families have called the village home.

Though the post and tree bearing the signal to John White are long gone, many of the oaks that cast their shadows over the park now were seedlings during the colonists' tenure. A nature trail wends its way through a forest of moss-draped oaks and pines and approaches the spot where the courageous pioneers first set foot on the narrow island.

The lovely Elizabethan Gardens, located next to the park, stand as a living memorial to the ill-fated colonists. Founded by the women's Garden Club of North Carolina in 1952, the gardens are

abloom with camellias, azaleas, dogwoods, roses, and hundreds of other varieties of trees and flowers. At the heart of this landscape is a sunken garden, which features an antique fountain. A statue in alabaster of an adult Virginia Dare, created by American artist Maria Louisa Lander, graces the gardens.

On summer nights, as the woods around the Waterside Theater gradually grow dark and the lights slowly go up on Green's *The Lost Colony*, visitors are transported 400 years into the past. These adventures are taking place in an Indian village on Roanoke Island; in Queen Elizabeth's English garden; dockside in Plymouth, England; and, finally, in the North Carolina woods, where the original colonists, frightened and starving, vanish in the deepening gloom, leaving audiences alone with their own thoughts on the fate of Roanoke's Lost Colony.

FISHING VILLAGE

The picturesque town of Manteo, above, named after the Algonquian chief who befriended the region's first settlers in 1585, hugs the tranquil shores of Shallowbag Bay.

IMMORTALIZED IN STONE

The statue of Virginia Dare in the Elizabethan Gardens, left, is an imagined portrait of the first English child born on North American soil.

NEARBY SITES & ATTRACTIONS

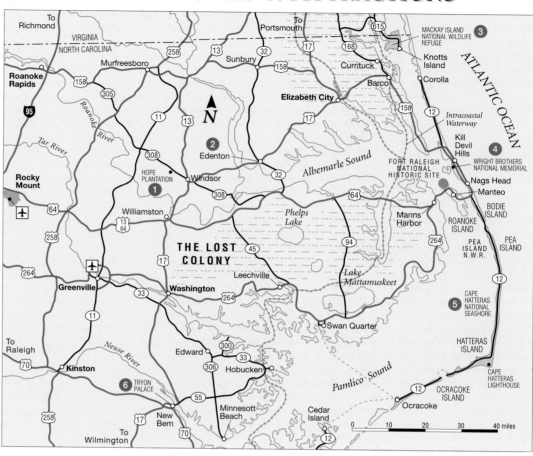

A 60-foot monument, below, stands at the top of Big Kill Devil Hill, the grassy sand dune where the Wright brothers made hundreds of glider flights before they attempted their first powered flight.

1 HOPE PLANTATION, NORTH CAROLINA

In addition to the original 1803 Hope Mansion, two other historic homes, the Samuel Cox House and the King Bazemore House, were moved to this 18th-century plantation. The houses and their outbuildings have been restored and furnished in period styles and offer insight into life in rural North Carolina between 1760 and 1840. Hope Mansion is a Georgian-style plantation house that was once owned by David Stone, North Carolina's first governor. The self-sustaining plantation included a black-smith's shop, gristmill, and saw mill. More than 100 slaves worked in the fields planting and harvesting wheat, cotton, and corn. Located four miles west of Windsor on Hwy. 308.

2 EDENTON, NORTH CAROLINA

Edenton was incorporated as a city in 1722 and became the first capital of the colony of North Carolina the same year. Walking tours of the town's historic sites begin at the visitor center, which offers exhibits and an audiovisual program about Edenton history. The 1758 Cupola House was once the home of land agent Francis Corbin and is now a National Historic Landmark. Construction of St. Paul's Episcopal Church began here in 1736, making it the second-oldest church in the state. Communion silver from the early 18th century is still used during church services. The Barker House was built around 1782

for Thomas and Penelope Barker. Penelope organized the Edenton Tea Party of October 25, 1774, in which 51 women signed a declaration in support of the colony's refusal to buy highly taxed British imports, such as tea and cloth. Located on Hwy. 17.

3 MACKAY ISLAND NATIONAL WILDLIFE REFUGE, NORTH CAROLINA/VIRGINIA

A visit to this 8,646-acre bird refuge inspired Joseph Knapp to create Ducks Unlimited, a volunteer organization dedicated to protecting wildlife. Great egrets, great blue herons, tundra swans, 30,000 snow geese, and up to 20,000 ducks visit or live in the island's marshlands. The ducks can be viewed from either the visitor center or a causeway that connects the mainland and the island, or by canoe. Walking and bicycle trails wind through the refuge's woodlands where visitors can spot pileated woodpeckers and prairie and prothonotary warblers. Located 19 miles northeast of Elizabeth City on Hwy. 615.

4 WRIGHT BROTHERS NATIONAL MEMORIAL, NORTH CAROLINA

This 431-acre memorial pays tribute to the achievements of Orville and Wilbur Wright, inventors of the first manned heavier-than-air flying machine. The historic flight took place on December 17, 1903.

With Orville at the controls, the aircraft flew for 12 seconds and traveled 120 feet. The aircraft was flown three more times in the next few hours, with the final flight—Wilbur at the controls—lasting 59 seconds and covering a distance of 852 feet. Replicas of a glider built by the Wrights in 1902 and the *Flyer* that was used in their historic flights of 1903 are on display at the memorial site. A replica of their workshed and living quarters is open to the public. Tools, propellers, and drafting equipment are on display at the visitor center. A large granite boulder near the visitor center indicates the spot where the first airplane left the ground. The marker is inscribed with the words, "conceived by Genius, achieved by Dauntless Resolution and Unconquerable Faith." Other markers on the dunes indicate the lengths of the four other flights. A 3,000-foot paved airstrip at the site can be used by small private planes. Located one mile south of Kill Devil Hills off Hwy. 158.

5 CAPE HATTERAS NATIONAL SEASHORE, NORTH CAROLINA

This national seashore stretches the length of the barrier islands of Bodie, Cape Hatteras, and Ocracoke. The islands are connected by Highway 12 and by the Hatteras Inlet ferry. More than 600 ships have been wrecked in the treacherous offshore shoals, once known as the Graveyard of the Atlantic. Lighthouses were built on the islands to warn ships of the hazards. At 208 feet in height, Cape Hatteras Lighthouse, built in 1870, is the tallest brick lighthouse in the nation, and Ocracoke Lighthouse, erected in 1823, is the oldest. The lighthouse on Bodie Island was erected in 1872. The town of Ocracoke on Ocracoke Island is said to have been a favorite hideout of Edward Teach, better known as the infamous Blackbeard. The pirate and his crew were killed here in 1718. The islands encompass 72 miles of sandy beach and a maritime forest of yaupon holly, oak, and cedar trees. A four-mile-long nature trail along a boardwalk on Bodie Island takes visitors through a salt marsh. The Pea Island National Wildlife Refuge offers numerous walking trails and observation platforms, from which 250 species of native and migratory birds can be observed. Located 13 miles southwest of Fort Raleigh on Hwy. 12.

6 TRYON PALACE, NORTH CAROLINA

Tryon Palace was designed by the English architect John Hawks and constructed between 1767 and 1770. It served as the state house for the colony and then for the state of North Carolina. Royal governor William Tryon and his successor Josiah Martin lived in the mansion. In 1774 the first provincial congress met in Tryon Palace to elect delegates to attend the First Continental Congress, and Richard Caswell was sworn in here as the first governor of the state of North Carolina in 1777. In 1798, four years after the state capital was moved to Raleigh, the building burned to the ground, except for one wing. The wing was restored in 1959, and the rest of the building was reconstructed on the site of the original foundation. Period furniture decorates the many rooms, and portraits of George I, George III, and Queen Charlotte hang on the walls. A library

on the first floor contains books that belonged to William Tryon. Costumed interpreters demonstrate candlemaking, basket weaving, and blacksmithing. Visitors are welcome to explore the palace gardens. Located on Pollock St. in New Bern.

The Chowan County Courthouse in Edenton, above, was built in 1767, making it one of the oldest courthouses in the country.

The Atlantic Ocean dominates the sandy coastline of Cape Hatteras National Seashore, left. Strong littoral rip, tidal currents near inlets, and shifting sand help shape the three barrier islands located off the coast of North Carolina.

DANIEL BOONE'S KENTUCKY

A stout and resourceful frontiersman, Daniel Boone blazed a trail deep into the Kentucky wilderness and helped open the doorway to the West.

An admirer once asked Daniel Boone if he had ever been lost in the woods. "No," America's most famous frontiersman replied, "I can't say as ever I was lost, but I was *bewildered* once for three days." Searching for the real Daniel Boone behind the folklore that has grown up around him can be equally bewildering. Those who have tried encounter a man greater, and more flawed, than the myth.

Unlike the tall, strapping adventurer created by Hollywood, the true-life Boone was of average build, a devoted husband and father, and middle aged at the height of his explorations. He also probably never wore a coonskin cap—his preferred headwear was a wide-brimmed hat, which gave him shelter from sun and rain. He did indeed fight Indians, but he killed few and generally tried to avoid confrontations with them. In fact, Boone befriended a number of Native Americans, and in many respects

he modeled his life after them. Boone was an expert shot and a superb tracker, but his skills did not prevent him from being ambushed, robbed, and captured—on more than one occasion.

Folklore depicts Boone as most content wandering in the wilderness. In his epic work *Don Juan*, British poet Lord Byron says: "Of the great names in which our faces stare/ The General Boon, back-woodsman of Kentucky/ Was happiest amongst mortals any where." Indeed, Boone did seem at home in the woods. But his happiness was colored by tragedy: two of his sons and many of his friends were killed brutally by Native Americans. The threat of Indian attack was unrelenting.

Although Boone was not the first white man to explore Kentucky, it was his tireless effort to blaze a trail through the Cumberland Gap that opened the floodgates for a stream of westward immigrants.

A LEGEND AND HIS LAND
A steady-eyed Daniel Boone is captured in a portrait, right, at the Historic Daniel Boone Home in Defiance, Missouri. The painting shows Boone in his sixties, around 1797, when he moved his family to Missouri. Some 30 years earlier, the legendary frontiersman had blazed a trail through the Cumberland Gap, below.

But perhaps Boone's greatest contribution to the burgeoning nation was his indomitable spirit of exploration and the example it set for those who would follow in his footsteps. If the myth fails to match reality, no matter: by any measure the Boone of history was a man of heroic stature.

FRONTIER CHILDHOOD One of 11 children, Daniel Boone was born in 1734 near Reading in Berks County, Pennsylvania. His parents, Squire and Sarah Boone, were English-born Quakers. Squire Boone was a farmer and blacksmith content with his station in life. But young Daniel suffered pangs of wanderlust. Given a rifle at age 12, the boy prowled the forests for weeks at a time. "Let the girls do the spelling," his father would say, "and Dan will do the shooting." In 1750 the Boones moved south to Virginia's Shenandoah Valley where they lived for a year before settling on the edge of the North Carolina frontier in the upper reaches of the Yadkin River. North Carolina's rolling piedmont was rich in game, and Boone stayed there longer than he would anyplace else. He might have remained a competent but unknown Carolina frontiersman had he not signed up for his first great adventure.

In 1755 Gen. Edward Braddock assembled a force of 1,500 British troops and colonial militia to march against the French at Fort Duquesne, located on the site of modern Pittsburgh. A contingent of North Carolinians rushed to join the expedition. Daniel, not yet 21, was among them, serving as a teamster and blacksmith. During the march, Boone met John Finley, a long hunter (so named for months'-long hunts) whose tales of faraway Kentucky and the forested paradise found there left his companions open-mouthed.

Braddock marched his troops straight into a deadly ambush, rigged by the French with their Indian allies, and much of his command was slaughtered. Boone escaped, but his brush with death taught him a valuable lesson in the wages of Indian warfare. However, the harrowing experience failed to dampen his newfound yearning to see the wonders of Kentucky.

Boone's itch for adventure would send him across much of early America—southward to Florida and westward to Missouri—but it was Kentucky that retained a fascination for him. In Boone's day, Native Americans called the region *ken-ta-ke* (a word that means meadowlands). American frontiersmen knew it as Cain-tuck or Kentuck. As the prime hunting land of the Cherokees and Shawnees, most of the region was devoid of Indian settlements. Early probes by explorers yielded tales of deer at every salt lick, mighty herds of buffalo, and flocks of carrier pigeons so thick they blocked out the sun. In 1768 Boone was still dreaming of Kentucky but had not yet been to the place that would come to be known as Daniel Boone country. He had married Rebecca Bryan, after returning from Braddock's defeat, fathered several children, and was living in a cabin on Sugartree Creek near North Carolina's Yadkin River.

One day Boone's old companion Finley showed up on his doorstep. Now a peddler and fur trader, Finley yearned to return to Kentucky. More than a decade before, the explorer Dr. Thomas Walker

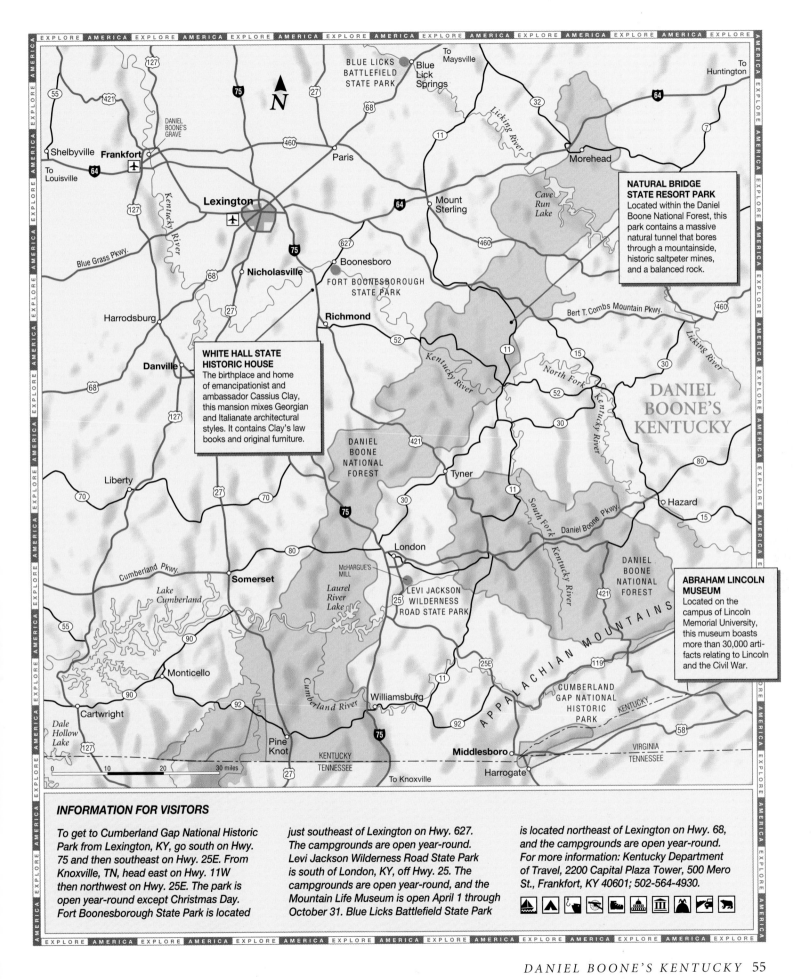

EXPLORE AMERICA EXPLORE AMERICA EXPLORE AMERICA EXPLORE AMERICA EXPLORE AMERICA EXPLORE AMERICA EXPLORE AMERICA EXPLORE

To Maysville

To Huntington

BLUE LICKS BATTLEFIELD STATE PARK

Blue Lick Springs

Licking River

Morehead

Cave Run Lake

NATURAL BRIDGE STATE RESORT PARK
Located within the Daniel Boone National Forest, this park contains a massive natural tunnel that bores through a mountainside, historic saltpeter mines, and a balanced rock.

DANIEL BOONE'S GRAVE

Shelbyville

Frankfort

To Louisville

Paris

Mount Sterling

Bert T. Combs Mountain Pkwy.

Licking River

Kentucky River

Lexington

Blue Grass Pkwy.

Nicholasville

Boonesboro

FORT BOONESBOROUGH STATE PARK

Richmond

Kentucky River

North Fork

Kentucky River

DANIEL BOONE'S KENTUCKY

Harrodsburg

WHITE HALL STATE HISTORIC HOUSE
The birthplace and home of emancipationist and ambassador Cassius Clay, this mansion mixes Georgian and Italianate architectural styles. It contains Clay's law books and original furniture.

Danville

DANIEL BOONE NATIONAL FOREST

Tyner

Hazard

Liberty

DANIEL BOONE NATIONAL FOREST

South Fork Kentucky River

Daniel Boone Pkwy.

Cumberland Pkwy.

Somerset

Lake Cumberland

Laurel River Lake

McHARGUE'S MILL

London

LEVI JACKSON WILDERNESS ROAD STATE PARK

ABRAHAM LINCOLN MUSEUM
Located on the campus of Lincoln Memorial University, this museum boasts more than 30,000 artifacts relating to Lincoln and the Civil War.

Monticello

Cumberland River

Williamsburg

APPALACHIAN MOUNTAINS

CUMBERLAND GAP NATIONAL HISTORIC PARK

KENTUCKY

Dale Hollow Lake

Cartwright

Pine Knot

KENTUCKY TENNESSEE

Middlesboro

VIRGINIA TENNESSEE

0   10   20   30 miles

To Knoxville

Harrogate

INFORMATION FOR VISITORS

To get to Cumberland Gap National Historic Park from Lexington, KY, go south on Hwy. 75 and then southeast on Hwy. 25E. From Knoxville, TN, head east on Hwy. 11W then northwest on Hwy. 25E. The park is open year-round except Christmas Day. Fort Boonesborough State Park is located

just southeast of Lexington on Hwy. 627. The campgrounds are open year-round. Levi Jackson Wilderness Road State Park is south of London, KY, off Hwy. 25. The campgrounds are open year-round, and the Mountain Life Museum is open April 1 through October 31. Blue Licks Battlefield State Park

is located northeast of Lexington on Hwy. 68, and the campgrounds are open year-round. For more information: Kentucky Department of Travel, 2200 Capital Plaza Tower, 500 Mero St., Frankfort, KY 40601; 502-564-4930.

had discovered a pass through the rugged mountains called the Cumberland Gap. From that point, it was said, a hunter's trace cut deep into the heart of Kentucky. With an expert tracker like Daniel, a party could likely find the trace and come home laden with furs. It was all Boone needed to hear: on May 1, 1769, he bid good-bye to his indulgent wife, braced his brood of offspring for his departure, and, accompanied by Finley and four others, headed for Kentucky. The party got to the Cumberland Gap, where they encountered a trail leading into the wilderness just as rumored.

DOORWAY TO THE WEST

The Appalachian Mountains were a mammoth barrier to the expansion of American settlements westward. Even after the natural passage through the mountains was found, the French and Indian War prevented exploration of the territory. When Boone and his companions crossed the Gap in 1769, the route was still largely unknown to white settlers.

Today the National Park Service operates the 21,000-acre Cumberland Gap National Historic Park, situated near Middlesboro, Kentucky, where the borders of Tennessee, Virginia, and Kentucky meet. The park features a sprawling, tree-shaded campground, picnic sites, and 55 miles of hiking trails. Interpretive programs provide visitors with information on the region's history and mountain culture. Historical signs and artillery pieces mark the site of fortifications erected during the Civil War to protect the strategic position.

Highway 58 enters the park from the east along the route of the colonial-era Wilderness Road. Numerous trails offer hikers different perspectives on the lush landscape that greeted Boone and the later immigrants who passed through the Cumberland Gap on their way west in the late 18th century. A brief climb from the parking lot takes modern travelers to a high overlook.

In 1904, more than 200 years after traffic through the Cumberland Gap reached a peak, a group of people established the Hensley Settlement in what is now the center of the park. Restored split-rail fences, chestnut-log houses, and barns with shake-shingle roofs are fine examples of the Appalachian structures built here in the early 20th century. Several fields are maintained using traditional farming techniques.

TRAILBLAZER
An engraved stone marker along Boone's Trace, above, marks a path blazed by Daniel Boone when he explored the Kentucky wilderness in 1775.

Beautiful Wilderness Road, left, which was commissioned by the state of Kentucky in 1796, leads hikers on a historic trek through the Cumberland Gap.

BOUNTIFUL HUNTING

Kentucky proved to be all that Boone had hoped for. In six months of hunting, he and his companions had accumulated a huge cache of deerskins. Then they encountered the dark side of paradise: Shawnee warriors captured Boone and another hunter and confiscated the pelts. A few days later the pair were released and ordered out of Kentucky. Instead, they crept into the Shawnee camp and made off with some horses. They were recaptured and escaped again without suffering serious harm. Their lives had been spared, but a half-year's work was gone. Most of the party went home, but Boone, joined by his brother, Squire, remained. Two years later, the pair were almost out of Kentucky with another store of pelts when they were robbed again. Boone went home empty-handed but with a burning desire to go back to the abundant hunting ground.

He did return in 1773, this time at the head of a party of settlers. The group, jointly commanded by another frontiersman named William Russell, included Boone's wife and eight children. Early in the journey, a Native war party attacked one of the settlers' camps and killed Boone's 16-year-old son James and five other people. A grieving Boone buried his son in the linen bedsheet his wife had brought along for their new home.

A reminder of the violent events that befell Kentucky's aspiring settlers is found at Levi Jackson Wilderness Road State Park. Located southeast of

PIONEER SETTLEMENT
Tranquility now reigns in reconstructed Fort Boonesborough, left, belying the sporadic violence that broke out there. In 1778, during the Great Siege of Boonesborough, Native American warriors tried to set fire to the fort by shooting volleys of flaming arrows onto the roofs of the cabins. As women and children doused the flames, the men of Boonesborough repelled the attackers.

London, just off Daniel Boone Parkway, the lush 800-acre park contains campgrounds, picnic areas, an amphitheater, hiking trails, a museum, and a reproduction of a typical pioneer gristmill on the Little Laurel River. Just inside the park near the mill, lies a shady patch of riverside bottomland with a scattering of river-rock gravestones. The stones commemorate the victims of a pioneer massacre, similar to the one suffered by Boone's party in 1773, which took place on a nearby hillside.

On October 3, 1786, a group of some 60 settlers made camp at this site. They neglected to post guards, and that night Chickamauga warriors attacked the camp, captured the party's horses and cattle, kidnapped five women, and killed some 24 people. One pregnant woman is said to have escaped by hiding in a hollow tree, where she promptly gave birth. Today the tiny collection of markers is a mute memorial to the sacrifices of those early Americans who risked their lives on what Boone's Cherokee acquaintance Dragging Canoe called Kentucky's bloody ground.

The settlers buried at the park had been following Boone's Trace, a trail he blazed in 1775. That year, undeterred by the disaster that had marred his first attempt to lead settlers into the region, Boone returned as an agent of Col. Richard Henderson, an affluent developer who planned to establish a colony named Transylvania. Recruiting woodcutters, Boone set off through the thick Kentucky forests. The route they blazed roughly followed an ancient Indian hunting trail that emerged from the Cumberland Gap. The Wilderness Road, commissioned by the young state of Kentucky in 1796, paralleled Boone's Trace, and portions of all three trails pass through Levi Jackson Wilderness Road State Park today. Sections of the trail are open to hikers and horseback riders.

Boone's trailblazing expedition faced a daunting challenge: to carve a 100-mile path through the dense growth and rugged terrain of a virgin forest in Indian territory. Several of Boone's axmen were killed in Indian attacks. Boone's Trace, perhaps his greatest achievement, provided a narrow lifeline for pioneers plunging into Kentucky.

On April 1, 1775, Boone and his men began to build log cabins on the south bank of the Kentucky River, which they christened Fort Boone. A few weeks later, Henderson arrived and ordered work to begin on a larger settlement several hundred yards upriver. By the summer, the settlement consisted of 26 cabins protected by four blockhouses. Henderson declared that the fledgling colony's existence "was owing to Boone's confidence in us and the people's in him." Fittingly, the community was named Boonesborough and became the capital of the new settlement. Although the colony didn't last very long, Boonesborough was a vital outpost for western expansion and the place where the first official Christian service in Kentucky took place.

RE-CREATING THE COLONY

Fort Boonesborough State Park, southeast of Lexington, preserves a sense of frontier life. The park offers spacious campgrounds and recreational facilities, and boasts a full-scale reproduction of Boonesborough. Built in 1974, the colony is reconstructed from the original plans, which feature a walled village of log cabins. It is perched on a bluff above the original site to avoid the flooding that plagued the historic settlement. The structures at Boonesborough are

EXPLORING A WONDERLAND
Cloaked in an ethereal mist and carpeted by the brightly colored leaves of fall, a path through the Cumberland Gap, below, provides a rewarding look at the natural beauty that first attracted Boone to the region.

equipped with period furnishings. Living history specialists demonstrate colonial-era crafts, including pottery, weaving, and soap making. The scent of smoke from the blacksmith's forge wafts across the scene, imbuing it with authenticity.

As might be expected, Native Americans eyed the original post with hostility. The settlers repelled numerous attacks and suffered frequent scares. On a summer afternoon in 1776, Boone's 14-year-old daughter Jemima and two other girls were captured by a group of Shawnees and Cherokees while canoeing. Legend says that Boone led a party of frontiersmen in relentless pursuit, following small pieces of clothing left along the trail by the girls. Two days later he and his men snuck up on the kidnappers' camp, catching them by surprise. One account has it that when two Shawnee warriors fell beneath the rifle fire, Jemima Boone joyfully shouted, "That's Daddy!" The Indians fled, and Boone and his men rescued the girls unharmed.

RELICS OF A BYGONE ERA
Water tumbles past McHargue's Mill, above, in Levi Jackson Wilderness Road State Park. The old mill, located on the banks of the Laurel River where it intersects Boone's Trace, displays the largest collection of millstones in the country. Boone used the macramé-and-leather satchel at left to carry the game he bagged during his hunting expeditions. The satchel is displayed at the Carnegie Museum of Natural History in Pittsburgh.

The Boone name has inspired many forgeries. A tree in Kentucky bears his initials, right, but, like similar carvings in the region, is probably a fake. Likewise, two antique rifles, below, which bear whimsical carvings, such as "Boons best fren," probably never belonged to the frontiersman.

As a captain in the Virginia militia in February 1778, Boone was captured by Shawnee raiders while leading a salt-making expedition to Blue Licks. After Boone persuaded his captors not to launch a planned attack on the colony, the Shawnees took him to Detroit as a prize to impress their British allies. But en route, Boone befriended his enemies and avoided being sold to the British. In fact, the Shawnees grew to admire him so much, he was given an Indian name and became an adopted son of their chief, Blackfish. During his more than four months in captivity, Boone learned of British plans to sponsor a major Shawnee attack on Boonesborough. At the first chance, he escaped and rode 160 miles through the wilderness to warn the unsuspecting colonists. With Boone's help, the Boonesborough settlers withstood a nerve-jangling 13-day siege by more than 100 Shawnee warriors.

DEATH OF A SON

In August 1782 a force of 182 armed settlers marched toward Blue Licks, Boone's salt-making site on the Licking River. The 47-year-old Boone, at the time a lieutenant colonel in the militia, was in command of a large part of the force. At his side was his 23-year-old son Israel. As the riflemen approached the Licking River, they saw Native Americans gathering in force on the thickly wooded bluffs above.

When the militia arrived at the Licking River ford, Boone sensed impending danger and urged caution. But Hugh McGary, another leader of the group, led his horse into the river shouting, "Them that ain't damned cowards follow me, and I'll show you where the yellow dogs are." The eager soldiers splashed across the river and rushed up the opposite bluff—straight into a deadly ambush. At least 60 militiamen were killed and more than 80 others were wounded. When the chaos erupted, Boone steadied a horse for his son so he could join the others; but Israel refused, saying, "Father, I won't leave you." Then he fell—shot to death. Kentucky had claimed another of Boone's children.

The site of the bloody confrontation has been dedicated as Blue Licks Battlefield State Park. It is located in northeastern Kentucky between Paris and Maysville. Along with woodland and riverside hiking trails, campgrounds, and recreational attractions, the park includes the Pioneer Museum, complete with Native American artifacts and fossilized prehistoric remains. Weapons from Boone's day, period dress and implements, and two battered salt-making kettles perhaps used by Boone himself are among the displays. On a wooded bluff facing the Licking River is the site's principal landmark: a granite monument that memorializes the Kentucky frontiersmen who were killed on August 16, 1782, at the Battle of Blue Licks.

Spurred by the disaster at Blue Licks, a huge force of frontiersmen led by George Rogers Clark set upon the Shawnee town of Chillicothe and five other Indian villages north of the Ohio, and destroyed them, adding another tragic chapter to Kentucky's bloody Indian warfare. Within a decade more than 100,000 pioneers had passed through the Cumberland Gap and settled in Kentucky, and the state was admitted to the Union in 1792. By 1800 more than 300,000 people had followed Boone's route on their westward trek.

For Boone, the end of the century was a trying time. He served in a variety of public posts in Kentucky in the 1780's—county lieutenant, deputy surveyor, legislator—yet seemed unable to hold on to the bluegrass soil he loved. Boone once owned 100,000 Kentucky acres, but the devious practices of land agents, who sold parcels of land that overlapped other plots, left him landless and in debt.

In 1788 Boone moved to Virginia's Kanawha River region, now in West Virginia, where he lived for 10 years and became a Virginia legislator. Still seeking adventure, Boone led a band of pioneers to the Spanish-held lands west of St. Louis in 1799. He was granted a huge tract of land, which he lost when the territory was claimed by the United States as part of the Louisiana Purchase. Eventually, Congress restored 840 acres in Missouri to him. By this time, Boone was internationally famous.

His life's story had been published in John Filson's *The Discovery, Settlement and Present State of Kentucke*, and the Hawkeye character in James Fenimore Cooper's *Last of the Mohicans* was probably modeled on the living legend.

Boone was living back in Kentucky in his mid-seventies, and by 1810 had paid off the last of his debts, reportedly leaving him with a surplus of 50 cents. In 1813, after 56 years of marriage, Boone's devoted wife, Rebecca, died and he moved in with his children. On September 26, 1820, Boone died at the age of 85. He did not spend his final years with his feet propped up on the porch. The frontier was pushing ever westward and the pull proved irresistible to him. A wanderer to the end, the elderly Boone may have explored as far west as modern Iowa, or even farther. Some legends say that a weathered and white-headed Boone told tales of gazing upon the snowcapped mountains and steaming geysers in the wildest reaches of Yellowstone country.

IMMORTALIZED ON CANVAS
Painted by American artist George Caleb Bingham, Daniel Boone Escorting Settlers Through the Cumberland Gap, *below, portrays Boone and his party in a romantic light. The woman on the white horse is Boone's wife, Rebecca. Paintings and written accounts of Boone's exploits helped spread his fame worldwide.*

NEARBY SITES & ATTRACTIONS

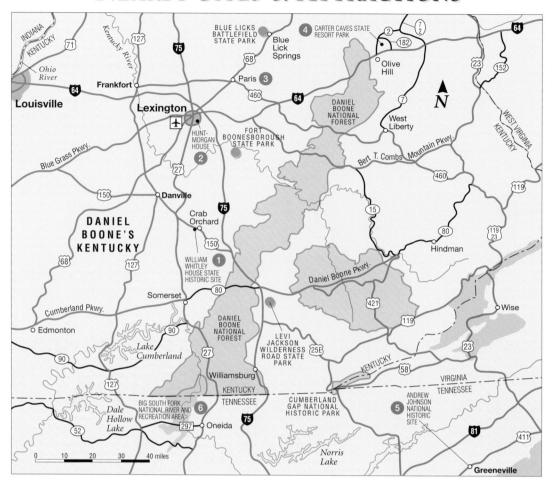

The handsome Andrew Johnson Homestead, below, was bought by the federal government in 1941 and restored in 1958.

1 WILLIAM WHITLEY HOUSE STATE HISTORIC SITE, KENTUCKY

Set atop a hill with a commanding view, this 18th-century structure, built between 1785 and 1792 by Kentucky pioneer William Whitley, served as a home, prison, fortress, and meetinghouse for colonists in the area. The house was dubbed the Guardian of the Wilderness Road due to Whitley's reputation as an Indian fighter and because its basement was used as a prison for captured enemies. George Rogers Clark, Daniel Boone, and Isaac Shelby are among the famous frontiersmen Whitley entertained here. In 1788 Whitley built Kentucky's first horse track on the property. To demonstrate his anti-British sentiments, he had the races run counterclockwise rather than clockwise as was the tradition in England. This solid house has two-foot-thick brick walls, poplar floors, walnut and pine interior paneling, and dentil molding on the roof. The initials of Whitley and his wife were carved on the front and back of the house more than two centuries ago. Located two miles west of Crab Orchard off Hwy. 150.

2 HUNT-MORGAN HOUSE, KENTUCKY

This museum, the home of generations of famous Kentuckians, contains fine examples of 19th-century art and furniture. Built in 1814 by John Wesley Hunt—one of the first millionaires west of the Allegheny Mountains—the stately mansion includes a walled courtyard, a cantilevered staircase, and an elaborate garden. Later the house was the residence of Hunt's grandson Gen. John Hunt Morgan, known as the Thunderbolt of the Confederacy, and it was the birthplace of his nephew, Thomas Hunt Morgan, who won the Nobel Prize for medicine in 1933 for his work on genetic research. The museum displays paintings, antique furniture built in Kentucky, and a

Bridge—the only natural bridge in the state crossed by a paved highway. Eleven miles of trails wind through the park so that visitors can explore the region's aboveground beauty. Carter Caves Lake is popular with anglers. Located eight miles northeast of Olive Hill off Hwy. 182.

⑤ ANDREW JOHNSON NATIONAL HISTORIC SITE, TENNESSEE

This 17-acre site includes two homes owned by Andrew Johnson, the 17th president of the United States. Best known for his successful defense against impeachment in 1868, Johnson is also remembered for negotiating the purchase of Alaska. He started out as a tailor, and his shop at the site contains his tools and a wedding coat he made. Johnson lived in the Andrew Johnson Homestead from 1851 to 1875. His grave is located in the national cemetery, also on the grounds. Located in Greeneville.

Built by John Wesley Hunt, who made his fortune selling supplies to pioneers heading west, the Federal-style Hunt-Morgan House, left, includes a doorway with an overarching Palladian window.

collection of the Hunt family's porcelain. On the second floor of the house, the Alexander T. Hunt Civil War Museum displays a variety of Civil War memorabilia. Located on North Mill St. in Lexington.

③ PARIS, KENTUCKY

The residents of this picturesque town, which was called Hopewell when it was incorporated in 1789, changed its name to Paris as a sign of their gratitude for French assistance during the Revolutionary War. The Duncan Tavern Historic Shrine, frequented by Daniel Boone and other frontiersmen, is located on the public square. The tavern is constructed of native limestone and contains many period furnishings. Erected in 1822, the famous drinking establishment now contains historical and genealogical information, including the original manuscript of the novel *The Little Shepherd of Kingdom Come* by John Fox Jr., a local author. The book, which describes rural life in Kentucky during the Civil War period, was the first American novel to sell 1 million copies. The adjoining Anne Duncan House, built about 1801, has been fully restored and is open to the public. Located at 323 High St. in Paris.

④ CARTER CAVES STATE RESORT PARK, KENTUCKY

The 1,600-acre park's geological formations include several caves, natural bridges, steep cliffs, and a pristine mountain lake. Long before settlers came to the region in the 1780's, Cherokee Indians used the caves to store pelts. Tours are given of Cascade Cave, with its underground river and 30-foot-high waterfall; X Cave with its twisting maze of passageways; and Saltpeter Cave, which was mined during the War of 1812 for the ingredients of gunpowder. During the summer, guides lead tours of Bat Cave, where thousands of endangered Indiana bats hibernate in the winter. One of the park's most distinctive features is the 180-foot-long Carter Caves Natural

Massive sandstone boulders, above, line the banks of the Big South Fork National River and Recreation Area.

⑥ BIG SOUTH FORK NATIONAL RIVER AND RECREATION AREA, KENTUCKY/ TENNESSEE

Encompassing some 80 miles of the Big South Fork River and covering more than 100,000 acres, the recreation area is ideal for canoeing, camping, hunting, and fishing. The river and its tributaries were once the center of extensive mining and logging activities, and remnants of mine entrances, camps, and homesteads can be seen here. The river cuts through the sandstone of the Cumberland Plateau, where visitors can view gorges, spires, natural arches, and overhanging rocks. There are more than 300 miles of old roads and trails, including a section of the John Muir National Recreation Trail. Located six miles west of Oneida off Hwy. 297.

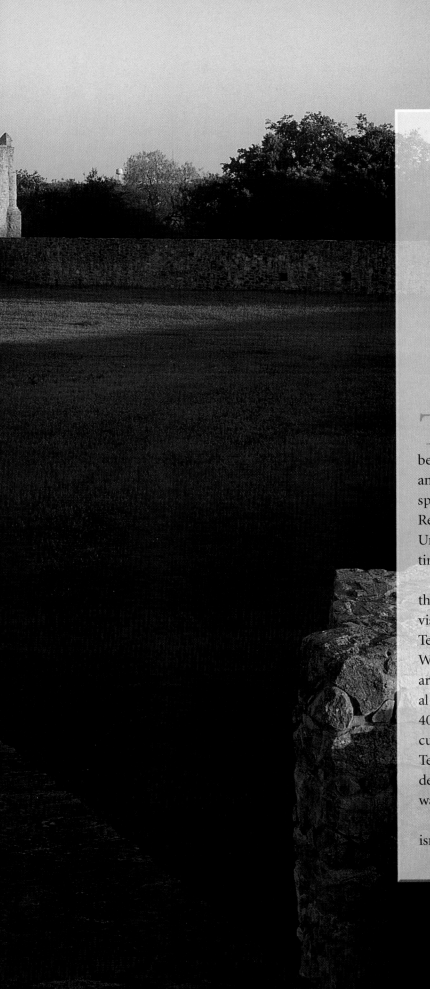

TEXAS REVOLUTION

*Larger-than-life characters played
central roles in the liberation of
Texas from Mexico.*

The war that created the Republic of Texas in 1836 was short—scarcely seven months between the firing of the first and last shots—and involved relatively small armies at odds over sparsely populated territories. But the Texas Revolution altered the political portrait of the United States and propagated legends that continue to baffle historians and engage storytellers.

Of the war's dozen or so military engagements, three define its character, and their sites can be visited today: the Alamo, a walled fort where 188 Texans, including Davy Crockett, Jim Bowie, and William Travis, fought to the death against an army of some 2,500 men led by Mexican general Santa Anna; Presidio La Bahía at Goliad, where 400 or so Texans were taken prisoner and executed; and the Plain of San Jacinto, where the Texan army, commanded by Samuel Houston, defeated the Mexicans and, in effect, where Texas was ceded to the colonists.

By any measure this was a war of epic heroism and savage vengeance, waged on one side by

NEVER TO BE FORGOTTEN
The life-size statues in Pompeo Coppini's 1940 cenotaph in Alamo Plaza in San Antonio, right, honor the men who died at the Alamo, among them Davy Crockett, William B. Travis, and Jim Bowie.

REMEMBER GOLIAD!
Overleaf: Colonel Fannin and his men were summarily executed somewhere in the woods around the Presidio La Bahía. The colonel's body is believed to be buried where the Fannin Monument now stands, just southeast of the presidio.

PRESIDENT'S HOME
The home of Anson Jones, below, last president of the Republic of Texas (1844–46), was moved to Washington-on-the-Brazos State Historical Park in 1936. The park commemorates the formal signing of the Texas Declaration of Independence on March 2, 1836.

the Mexican army, whose leader was described as a cruel, opium-addicted despot, and on the other by an odd assortment of American adventurers, frontiersmen, brawlers, hotheads, misfits, and eccentrics—most of whom, it seems, had gone to Texas one step ahead of personal misfortune, debt, or legal problems. Of this handful of men who would etch their names into the annals of history, perhaps none was more charismatic than the one who commanded the Texas forces: Sam Houston.

THE RAVEN

By the time the American settlers took up arms against Mexico in 1836, Sam Houston had been a citizen of three nations: the United States, the Cherokee, and Mexico. In each he had been an influential leader. Born in 1793 in Rockbridge County, Virginia, Houston ran away from home when he was 17 and lived for almost three years with the Cherokees, who called him Co-lo-neh, or the Raven. At 21 he fought at the Battle of Horseshoe Bend in Alabama during the War of 1812, under his commanding officer, Andrew Jackson. Later he served as a U.S. congressman and was a two-term governor of Tennessee. By all accounts, Houston was a born leader. "Old Sam was a man commissioned for leadership by God," said a contemporary.

Then, at the age of 36, Houston married Eliza Allen, a woman 16 years his junior; but less than three months later, for reasons that have never been recorded, she left him. Apparently shattered by the event, Houston resigned his office as governor of Tennessee and moved west to Indian Territory (now Oklahoma). There he lived among the Cherokees again, this time with a Cherokee woman, Tiana Rogers. Always a hard-drinking, profane man, he earned a new Cherokee name at this time: Oo-tse-tee Ar-dee-tah-skee, or Big Drunk. Still, over the next few years, he represented the Cherokees twice in Washington, D.C., defending their interests against corrupt land agents.

In 1832 Houston was recruited by Pres. Andrew Jackson to go to Texas—ostensibly to negotiate peace treaties with various Native American tribes who were hostile to settlers on the frontier. The true purpose of Houston's mission in Texas is still debated by historians a century and a half later. Some contend that Houston agreed to go to Texas to make a fresh start for himself; others believe that President Jackson, who had been attempting to purchase Texas from Mexico, sent Houston to lead its residents in a revolt. Certainly, the province was ready to throw off the yoke of Mexican rule.

Mexico was in a state of turmoil, and not only because of its intractable, American-dominated province of Texas. In 1821 the country had gained its independence from Spain. A year later, a revolt against the new centralist Mexican government was ignited by an ambitious young general named Don Antonio López de Santa Anna—known to history simply as Santa Anna. Liberals rallied to Santa Anna's cause, and a new constitution was hammered out to establish a federalist government similar to that of Mexico's neighbor, the United States. Over the next decade, thousands of Americans poured into Texas and settled on generous land grants given by the Mexican Congress.

Despite the settlers' qualms about certain provisions in the 1824 democratic constitution, particularly the one that forbade them to keep slaves, they were content with it. But soon trouble was brewing. The Texans wanted good roads, post offices, and schools of the caliber of those in the United States. They also objected to the interminable justice system. With each demand by the colonists, the government tightened its grasp, becoming more repressive and centralist. For a while some colonists believed that the solution to these problems lay with Santa Anna, who was

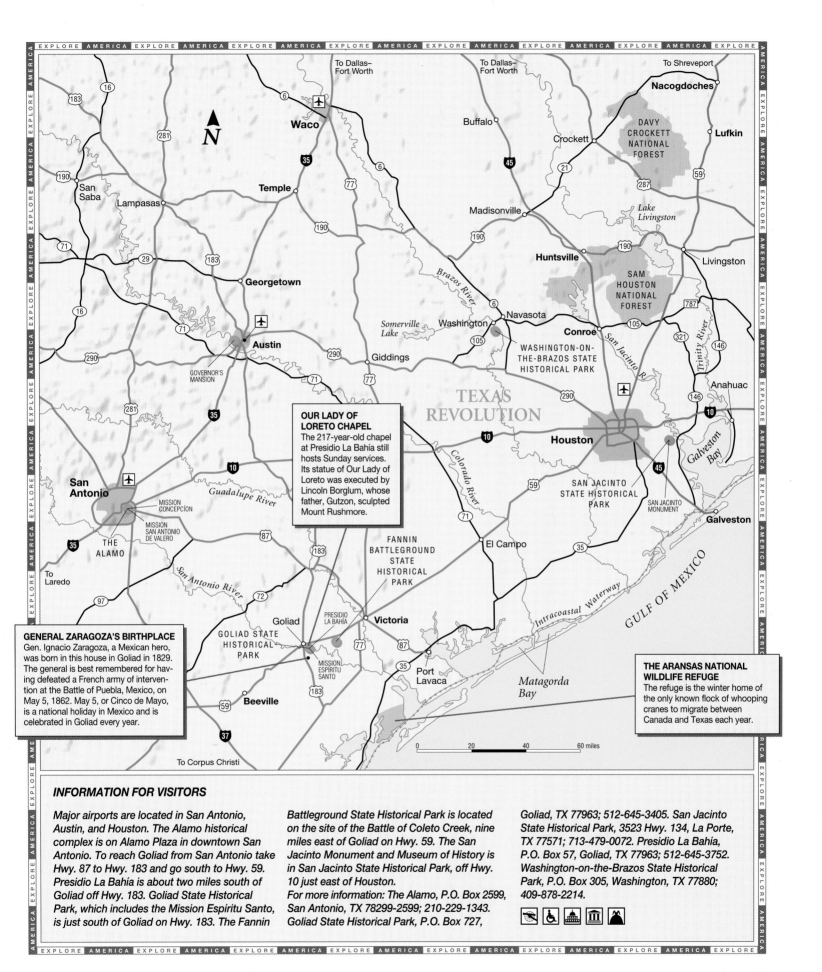

To Dallas–
Fort Worth

To Dallas–
Fort Worth

To Shreveport

Nacogdoches

16

183

6

Waco

281

N

DAVY CROCKETT NATIONAL FOREST

Buffalo

Crockett

Lufkin

45

21

59

35

287

190

San Saba

Lampasas

Temple

6

77

190

Madisonville

Lake Livingston

190

71

190

29

183

Brazos River

Huntsville

Livingston

SAM HOUSTON NATIONAL FOREST

787

16

Georgetown

6

105

321

Trinity River

146

71

Somerville Lake

Washington

Navasota

Conroe

105

Austin

290

Giddings

945

WASHINGTON-ON-THE-BRAZOS STATE HISTORICAL PARK

290

Anahuac

146

GOVERNOR'S MANSION

71

77

TEXAS REVOLUTION

10

35

OUR LADY OF LORETO CHAPEL
The 217-year-old chapel at Presidio La Bahía still hosts Sunday services. Its statue of Our Lady of Loreto was executed by Lincoln Borglum, whose father, Gutzon, sculpted Mount Rushmore.

10

Colorado River

Houston

Galveston Bay

San Antonio

10

Guadalupe River

59

SAN JACINTO STATE HISTORICAL PARK

SAN JACINTO MONUMENT

45

MISSION CONCEPCÍON

MISSION SAN ANTONIO DE VALERO

87

183

FANNIN BATTLEGROUND STATE HISTORICAL PARK

El Campo

35

Galveston

35

THE ALAMO

San Antonio River

To Laredo

97

72

PRESIDIO LA BAHÍA

Victoria

77

87

Intracoastal Waterway

GULF OF MEXICO

GENERAL ZARAGOZA'S BIRTHPLACE
Gen. Ignacio Zaragoza, a Mexican hero, was born in this house in Goliad in 1829. The general is best remembered for having defeated a French army of intervention at the Battle of Puebla, Mexico, on May 5, 1862. May 5, or Cinco de Mayo, is a national holiday in Mexico and is celebrated in Goliad every year.

Goliad

GOLIAD STATE HISTORICAL PARK

MISSION ESPÍRITU SANTO

35

Port Lavaca

Matagorda Bay

THE ARANSAS NATIONAL WILDLIFE REFUGE
The refuge is the winter home of the only known flock of whooping cranes to migrate between Canada and Texas each year.

59

Beeville

183

37

0   20   40   60 miles

To Corpus Christi

INFORMATION FOR VISITORS

Major airports are located in San Antonio, Austin, and Houston. The Alamo historical complex is on Alamo Plaza in downtown San Antonio. To reach Goliad from San Antonio take Hwy. 87 to Hwy. 183 and go south to Hwy. 59. Presidio La Bahía is about two miles south of Goliad off Hwy. 183. Goliad State Historical Park, which includes the Mission Espíritu Santo, is just south of Goliad on Hwy. 183. The Fannin

Battleground State Historical Park is located on the site of the Battle of Coleto Creek, nine miles east of Goliad on Hwy. 59. The San Jacinto Monument and Museum of History is in San Jacinto State Historical Park, off Hwy. 10 just east of Houston.
For more information: The Alamo, P.O. Box 2599, San Antonio, TX 78299-2599; 210-229-1343. Goliad State Historical Park, P.O. Box 727,

Goliad, TX 77963; 512-645-3405. San Jacinto State Historical Park, 3523 Hwy. 134, La Porte, TX 77571; 713-479-0072. Presidio La Bahía, P.O. Box 57, Goliad, TX 77963; 512-645-3752. Washington-on-the-Brazos State Historical Park, P.O. Box 305, Washington, TX 77880; 409-878-2214.

THE ALAMO

The Alamo church, right, was used by the Spanish, Revolutionary, and Mexican military from the early 1800's until the Texans captured it in 1836. Its exterior was altered around 1849 when a distinctive parapet was added to the church facade. Operated by the Daughters of the Republic of Texas, the Alamo grounds still contain the Long Barrack, now a museum, where some of the defenders took shelter, until the Mexicans blasted its massive doors with cannon shot. Also on the grounds is the Sales Museum, which displays portraits, rare documents, and artifacts of the war and the history of Texas.

styling himself as a federalist. A popular leader, particularly after having defeated an attempt by Spain to reconquer Mexico at Tampico, Santa Anna was also admired by many Americans, including Andrew Jackson, who praised him as the "pride of all Mexican soldiers and the idol of the priesthood."

NAPOLEON OF THE WEST

Time revealed Santa Anna to be a man of no particular ideology. He was possessed of an arrogant and volatile nature, exacerbated, according to some historians, by his addiction to opium. After gaining the presidency in 1833, the Hero of Tampico not only betrayed his federalist stance but also scrapped the constitution entirely. Dubbing himself the Napoleon of the West, Santa Anna ruled by a doctrine inherited from royalist general Joaquín de Arredondo, under

whom he had served during the Mexican war for independence: "If you execute your enemies it saves you the trouble of having to forgive them."

By the time Houston arrived in Texas, Santa Anna's enemies were legion. The president had banned further Anglo immigration and imposed new taxes on imported goods—measures that enraged independent-minded citizens. Hostilities flared. Santa Anna responded by building up his military presence in the Texas territory.

On October 2, 1835, Mexican troops rode into the town of Gonzales, near the Guadalupe River, west of San Antonio, to confiscate a cannon and thus prevent its possible use against the government. The townspeople stuffed the cannon with scrap metal and fired upon the soldiers. It was the first shot of the war. In the skirmishes that were to follow, Texans proved themselves superior in combat against the larger and better-armed Mexican forces. At Mission Concepción, one of four missions now within San Antonio Missions National Historical Park, 90-odd Texans defeated some 400 Mexican soldiers, losing only one man and killing perhaps as many as 60 of the enemy in a 30-minute battle. Two months later, about 400 colonists stormed San Antonio, forcing the Mexican soldiers to pull back to the border, where Santa Anna met them with a massive army, intent upon crushing the rebellion.

Santa Anna and his men marched to San Antonio, encountering no armed resistance. Most Texas citizens had scattered into the countryside. The remainder withdrew into the Alamo, the roofless ruin of a mission church surrounded by a high rock wall.

Their leader, Col. William B. Travis, was a lawyer who had journeyed to Texas by wagon train from Alabama and settled in Anahuac, the principal port on Galveston Bay. Travis is credited with precipitating the war against Mexico by running Mexican tax collectors out of Anahuac in January 1835. Some researchers believe that the defenders of the Alamo initially consisted of about 150 men, along with a few women and children; another 32 men sneaked through enemy lines after the siege began, boosting the number of defenders to at least 188. Other scholars, still combing through archival documents, believe the actual number inside the church was closer to 250.

Among the defenders were Col. Jim Bowie—best known for the knife that bears his name (designed either by him or his brother Rezin)—and Davy Crockett. Crockett had entered the mission along with 12 volunteers from Tennessee just days before Santa Anna arrived. A former U.S. congressman from Tennessee, Crockett has been immortalized in books and films. A more accurate description of him, however, may be contained in a recent *Texas Almanac*: "At his best he was honest, brave, noble, resourceful, blessed with abundant horse sense, independent to a fault and able to tell a good story; at his worst, uneducated, crude, violent, boastful, drunken, and even clownish."

By any account, the battle of the Alamo was lopsided. Santa Anna's army probably numbered between 2,500 and 4,000, but it was held at bay for 13 days while a convention of Texans worked on the wording of a declaration of independence at Washington-on-the-Brazos and commissioned Sam Houston to organize an army. Day after day the Mexicans bombarded the Alamo with cannon fire, but no Texan lives were lost.

As the standoff continued, Travis became convinced that reinforcements were not forthcoming and gave his men the choice of staying and fighting to the death or leaving. According to the legend, he drew a line on the ground and said, "Those prepared to give their lives in freedom's cause come over to me." Only one person, Lewis "Moses" Rose, left. He climbed the wall and escaped through Mexican lines. Historians have little doubt that all the men could have escaped the same way.

Finally, on the morning of March 6, the Mexican forces moved against the Alamo. Within 90 minutes, 600 Mexican troops and all the defenders of the Alamo were killed. A few sick and wounded survived the battle, but were hastily executed. Santa Anna ordered the bodies to be tossed in a pile and

PEACEFUL MISSION
The Mission Espíritu Santo, above, was founded in 1722 to serve the Karankawa Indians. The mission and its fort, the Presidio La Bahía, were originally built near the ruins of the French fort of St. Louis on Matagorda Bay. In 1749 the structures were moved to their present sites in Goliad on the banks of the San Antonio River. The mission has been largely restored and is now open to the public.

TEXAN HERO
The engraving at left shows Sam Houston as every bit the politician—a far cry from the days when his preferred dress was buckskins, moccasins, and feathers. A self-educated man and an orator of some distinction, Houston quoted liberally from classic literature and delivered his speeches in a booming voice.

burned. Thirteen noncombatants, most of them women and children, were spared.

While the Alamo was under siege, Col. James Fannin and about 400 volunteers had withdrawn from the Presidio La Bahía in Goliad. A few miles away from Goliad they were pinned down by another of Santa Anna's armies, about 2,000 strong. The Texans surrendered near Coleto Creek and were taken back to the presidio. Santa Anna, furious when he learned that the Texans had not been killed outright, ordered that they be executed. His order was carried out on March 27—Palm Sunday.

The shattering losses at Goliad and the Alamo precipitated a flight toward Louisiana—called the Runaway Scrape—and the safe haven of the United States. The three prongs of Santa Anna's army swept undeterred toward the San Jacinto River. At the same time, Houston was marshaling and training his army of 750. So far he had managed to avoid combat, a fact that caused some of his men to question his motives and even his courage. But as Santa Anna drove eastward, Houston mobilized his troops and overtook the Mexican army on the Plain of San Jacinto on April 20.

For reasons lost to history, the Mexican encampment was virtually unguarded when Houston made

GOVERNOR'S STUDY
Much of the interior of the Governor's Mansion in Austin, Texas, including the study, right, looks as it did when Sam Houston lived there with his second wife, Margaret Lea, and their eight children. Houston served as president of the Republic of Texas (1836–38; 1841–44) and senator from the state of Texas (1846–59) before he became governor. He resigned as governor and quit the mansion in 1861 when he refused to take the oath of allegiance to the Confederate States of America.

his move. Santa Anna may have felt confident that the field was his, since his better-equipped army had only that morning received reinforcements that gave them a two-to-one advantage. The Texans spread out in a long line behind the tall grass that partially concealed the Mexican bivouac, then moved out across the rising plain, first at a walk, then at a trot. Some of Santa Anna's men were napping, others were cooking or playing cards. Their muskets were stacked, their cannons unmanned, and the general was in his tent. By the time someone noticed the advancing Texans and sounded an alarm, they were within several hundred yards of the Mexican barricades. Once the shooting started, the battle became a free-for-all with no fronts.

"Remember the Alamo!" and "Remember Goliad!" cried the Texans as they slashed through the Mexican camp. Mexican soldiers dropped to their knees and pleaded in broken English, "Me no Alamo, me no La Bahía," but were run through

MONUMENT TO FREEDOM
A 34-foot-high, 220-ton Star of Texas tops the San Jacinto Monument, above, which was built between 1936 and 1939 in memory of the men who had died for independence a century before. An elevator takes visitors to the observation tower, and historical displays are housed in a museum in the base.

with sabers, shot, or bludgeoned to death with musket butts. "The most awful slaughter I ever saw," wrote Sgt. Moses Ryan, an eyewitness to the bloodbath, "killing on all sides, even the wounded." When the 18 minutes of ferocious fighting ended, only 8 Texans lay dead, but the plain was strewn with 630 dead or dying Mexican soldiers.

CAPTIVE DICTATOR Santa Anna escaped into the swamps disguised as a Mexican private, and was captured the next day. For a short while he went unrecognized, until his fine shirt and the cries of "El Presidente!" from his fellow prisoners betrayed his identity to his captors. The general was taken to Sam Houston, who allowed him to ingest opium to calm his nerves. Then Santa Anna was compelled to recognize the Republic of Texas. A treaty between the new republic and Mexico was signed three weeks later. From that day until 1845,

when it was annexed to the United States, Texas remained an independent republic. Santa Anna was forbidden to leave Texas for several months after his defeat, until he was sent to meet Pres. Andrew Jackson, who returned him to Mexico, where he was forced to retire.

Historians still debate gaps and contradictions in the various accounts of the war, but the legends that have grown up around the men who liberated Texas keep their exploits alive. Cities, counties, rivers, parks, and national forests in southeastern Texas bear the names and signs of these distant battles, so rich with mystique. But perhaps none of these is more evocative than San Jacinto Monument in San Jacinto Battleground State Historical Park. Like the long barrel of a cannon aimed at the heavens, the monument stands on the rise of land where the armies faced off, a stark reminder of the lives that were lost and the land that was won there.

NEARBY SITES & ATTRACTIONS

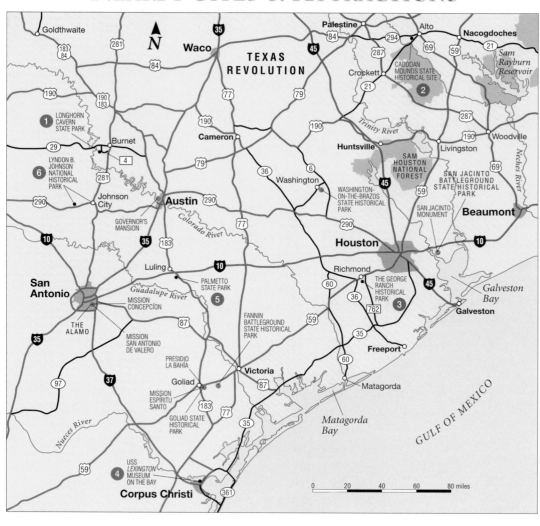

Calcite crystals, below, and other formations found in Longhorn Cavern, such as stalactites, stalagmites, and massive flowstone deposits, were produced by the forces of solution and abrasion.

① LONGHORN CAVERN STATE PARK

The highlight of this 708-acre park in central Texas is a huge cave that contains numerous large chambers. The cave formed on the limestone floor of the tropical sea that covered central Texas more than 450 million years ago. Some of the chambers have nearly flat ceilings, others have developed arched or domed roofs, and many of them contain stalagmites, stalactites, and interesting formations of flowstone and dripstone. Few plants or animals live in the cavern today, although the bones of prehistoric animals have been found here, including elephants, bison, bear, and deer. Archeological evidence suggests that early Native American tribes used the cave for shelter. During the Civil War, Confederate soldiers used bat guano from the cavern to make gunpowder, and in the 1870's the cavern is believed to have been a hideout for the outlaw Sam Bass, who, according to legend, hid a treasure worth $2 million here. The cavern, with temperatures that remain at a constant 64°F, was used by local residents on hot summer evenings during the Depression as a nightclub. The mile-long tour of the cavern takes about an hour and a half to complete. Located 10 miles southwest of Burnet off Park Rd. 4.

② CADDOAN MOUNDS STATE HISTORICAL SITE

The Caddo Indians belonged to the powerful Mound Builder culture of about 1000 B.C. to A.D. 1500, whose territory and trading network stretched across eastern North America. The historical site includes a partially excavated Caddo village, which was the southwesternmost ceremonial center of the Mound Builder peoples. The Caddos moved to the site around A.D. 500 because of its fertile land, abundant wildlife, and access to the nearby Neches River. Visitors can view a reconstructed Caddoan dwelling, a burial mound, two temple mounds, and numerous artifacts, such as ceremonial stone implements, pipe bowls, and copper-covered stone ear spools. The Caddoans were part of an extensive trade network, and some of the artifacts found at the site are from the Gulf Coast and the Great Lakes. A mile-long trail connects the mounds and the village area. Located six miles southwest of Alto on Hwy. 21.

③ THE GEORGE RANCH HISTORICAL PARK

In this 480-acre park, costumed guides help visitors interpret 100 years of Texas history from the early 19th to the early 20th centuries. The living history

72

park, which is located on a 23,000-acre working ranch, includes sites that portray ranch life during three periods. At the 1830's stock farm, with its rustic cabin and barn, visitors can try their hands at grinding corn, spinning cotton, and cooking in a Dutch oven. The Victorian farm includes a furnished mansion, a carriage house, greenhouse, grape arbor, and servants' quarters. The 1930's site has a cookhouse, smokehouse, and a cistern, and visitors can watch cowboys demonstrate their skills at riding, roping, and working cattle. Located five miles southeast of Richmond off Hwy. 762.

4 USS *LEXINGTON* MUSEUM ON THE BAY

The World War II aircraft carrier USS *Lexington* serves as a floating museum dedicated to all ships of the same name. The aircraft carrier is 910 feet long and was commissioned in 1943. It was dubbed the Blue Ghost by the Japanese because on four occasions they reported the *Lexington* had sunk, only to find it hadn't. During World War II the ship saw action in the Pacific theater, including the Battle of Leyte Gulf, and the Gilbert, Marianas, and Marshall operations. It was also the first American carrier to enter Tokyo Harbor in September 1945. On its way to Pensacola, Florida, in 1962 to be used as a training carrier, the ship was put on alert because of the Cuban Missile Crisis. Tours of the ship include the captain's quarters, bridge, sick bay, flight deck, and the hangar deck where several aircraft are on display. Photographs, paintings, and statistics for four other ships with the name *Lexington* recount their histories. These include a ship that was commissioned in 1776 and served in the Revolutionary War; a 127-foot-long sloop that saw action during the Mexican War of 1846–47; a 177-foot-long sidewheel steamer involved in the Civil War battles of Shiloh and Vicksburg; and an aircraft carrier that sank during the Battle of the Coral Sea in 1942. Located at 2914 North Shoreline Blvd. in Corpus Christi.

5 PALMETTO STATE PARK

This state park was established to protect the dwarf palmetto tree, which grows profusely in the Ottine Swamp. Some 550 species of eastern and western plants, including elm, oak, and pecan trees also flourish in the swamp. The San Marcos River, which runs through the park, offers numerous sites for picnicking and camping, and is also popular with swimmers and boaters. The park has an oxbow-shaped lake, which is filled with bass, perch, catfish,

and crappie. Hiking trails wind through the woodlands, which provide a safe haven for more than 240 species of nesting birds, including caracaras, kingfishers, and red-shouldered hawks. Other wildlife includes white-tailed deer, armadillos, squirrels, and raccoons. Located six miles south of Luling off Hwy. 183.

6 LYNDON B. JOHNSON NATIONAL HISTORICAL PARK

This park focuses on the life of the nation's 36th president, Lyndon Baines Johnson, who assumed office in November 1963 after Pres. John F. Kennedy was assassinated. During the five years of his administration, Johnson expanded the nation's social welfare and space programs and spearheaded the push to get the Civil Rights Act of 1964 passed by Congress. The park is divided into two districts: Johnson City and the LBJ Ranch. (The ranch is accessible by tour bus only.) The visitor center at Johnson City presents two films and displays photographs and exhibits on Johnson's life and career. The modest five-room structure where Johnson spent his early years is located across the street from the visitor center, and a two-room log cabin that was the home of Johnson's grandfather, Sam Ealy Johnson Sr., is a short walk away. In 1951 Johnson bought LBJ Ranch, a 2,000-acre Hereford cattle ranch, located 14 miles west of Johnson City. During his presidency Johnson used the ranch, which became known as the Texas White House, to entertain foreign dignitaries and as a retreat from the frantic pace of Washington, D.C. The National Park Service offers tours of the reconstructed home where Johnson was born, the one-room schoolhouse that he attended as a child, and the Johnson family cemetery, where he is buried. Johnson City and the LBJ Ranch are located off Hwy. 290.

Early Caddoan Indians lived in beehive dwellings similar to one that has been reconstructed at the Caddoan Mounds State Historical Site, left.

The refectory in Palmetto State Park, below, which was built by the Civilian Conservation Corps in the 1930's, now serves as a picnic shelter for visitors.

THE WILD WEST

The mixture of history, tall tales, and sheer invention that is Cody embodies the spirit of the West.

Back East, many people just refused to believe the reports they had heard about the faraway West. Some Easterners called the accounts outright lies. How could such a land really exist? Who could imagine a mile-deep canyon, steamy basins of erupting geysers, majestic mountains, endless expanses of waist-high buffalo grass, and sun-baked deserts, or, for that matter, summer snowstorms, buffalo herds that stretched the length of the horizon, and fallen forests of petrified trees? When their stories were greeted by skepticism, adventurers such as Jim Bridger would either clam up or spin their yarns into whoppers. One time Bridger obligingly told his wide-eyed listeners that he had traipsed through a petrified forest where "a petrified bird was sitting on a petrified limb singing a petrified song."

Bridger's lies illustrate a key element of the history of America's Old West: it exists as an irresistible mixture of incredible truth and extravagant fabrication. The Old West was a larger-than-life land, where some of the people, history,

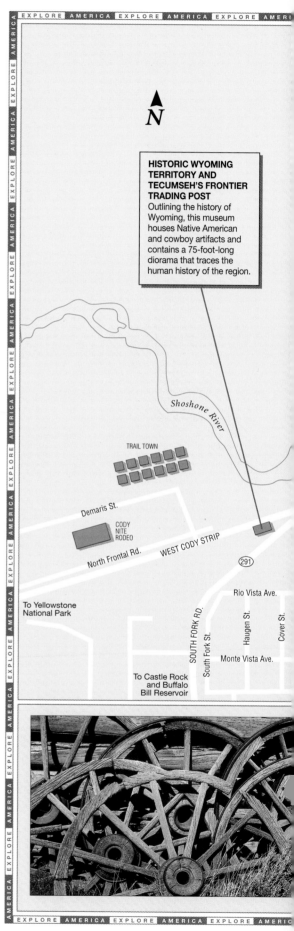

HISTORIC WYOMING TERRITORY AND TECUMSEH'S FRONTIER TRADING POST
Outlining the history of Wyoming, this museum houses Native American and cowboy artifacts and contains a 75-foot-long diorama that traces the human history of the region.

BUFFALO BILL'S PUBLICITY CAMPAIGN
Fanciful posters publicizing Buffalo Bill's Wild West Show romanticized frontier life and whetted the public's appetite for adventure stories. The poster, above, showing Cody, an unidentified Indian, and a scene of Native Americans canoeing up a river, was first issued in the 1880's.

SPECTACULAR SCENERY
Overleaf: Against a background of snow-covered ridges, Beartooth Lake glistens like a diamond. This is just one of the magnificent vistas afforded travelers driving toward Cody on the Beartooth Highway.

and folklore were of similarly grand stature. Perhaps nowhere west of the Mississippi is the irrepressible spirit of the Wild West as vibrant and colorful as it is in Cody, Wyoming.

OLD WEST FLAVOR

Though this Wyoming town has its convenience stores, discount shopping, and fast food places, it retains the flavor of the Old West. Location has helped. Cody country, with its wide-open spaces and dramatic terrain, epitomizes the American West. A 52-mile drive from Cody through Wapiti Valley takes travelers to Yellowstone National Park, making Cody the eastern gateway to the park's spectacular natural wonders. In the north lies the Beartooth Highway, which some tout as the most scenic stretch of road in America. To the southwest, South Fork Road winds along the Shoshone River and, some 40

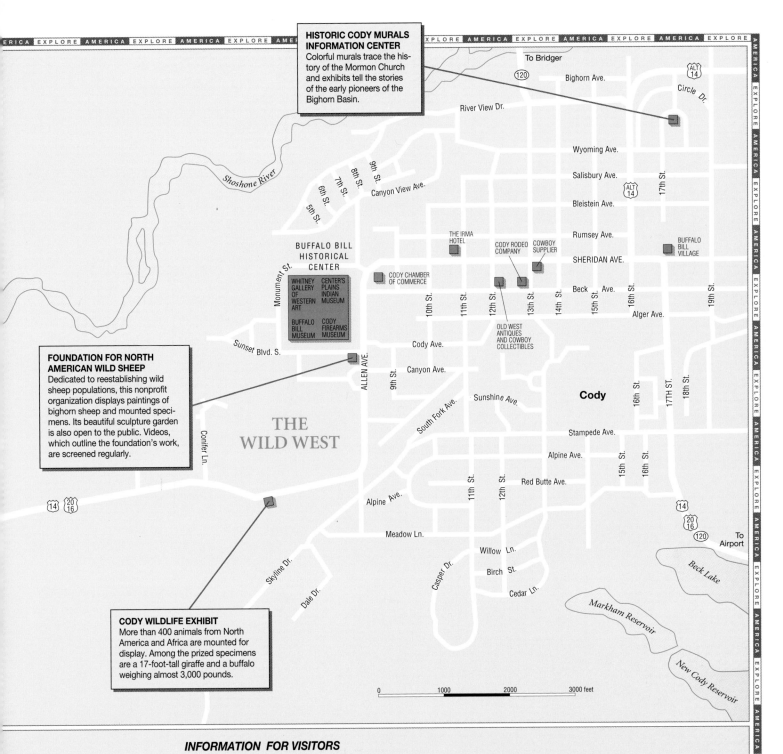

HISTORIC CODY MURALS INFORMATION CENTER
Colorful murals trace the history of the Mormon Church and exhibits tell the stories of the early pioneers of the Bighorn Basin.

To Bridger

(120)

ALT 14

Bighorn Ave.

Circle Dr.

River View Dr.

Wyoming Ave.

Salisbury Ave.

ALT 14

Bleistein Ave.

Canyon View Ave.

9th St.
8th St.
7th St.
6th St.
5th St.

17th St.

Rumsey Ave.

THE IRMA HOTEL

CODY RODEO COMPANY

COWBOY SUPPLIER

BUFFALO BILL VILLAGE

SHERIDAN AVE.

BUFFALO BILL HISTORICAL CENTER

WHITNEY GALLERY OF WESTERN ART

CENTER'S PLAINS INDIAN MUSEUM

BUFFALO BILL MUSEUM

CODY FIREARMS MUSEUM

CODY CHAMBER OF COMMERCE

Beck Ave.

16th St.

19th St.

10th St.
11th St.
12th St.
13th St.
14th St.
15th St.

Alger Ave.

OLD WEST ANTIQUES AND COWBOY COLLECTIBLES

Monument St.

Cody Ave.

FOUNDATION FOR NORTH AMERICAN WILD SHEEP
Dedicated to reestablishing wild sheep populations, this nonprofit organization displays paintings of bighorn sheep and mounted specimens. Its beautiful sculpture garden is also open to the public. Videos, which outline the foundation's work, are screened regularly.

Sunset Blvd. S.

ALLEN AVE.

9th St.

Canyon Ave.

16th St.
17th St.
18th St.

THE WILD WEST

South Fork Ave.

Sunshine Ave.

Cody

Stampede Ave.

Conifer Ln.

Alpine Ave.

15th St.
16th St.

Red Butte Ave.

14 20 16

11th St.
12th St.

Alpine Ave.

14 20 16

Meadow Ln.

Willow Ln.

120

To Airport

Skyline Dr.

Casper Dr.

Birch St.

Cedar Ln.

Beck Lake

CODY WILDLIFE EXHIBIT
More than 400 animals from North America and Africa are mounted for display. Among the prized specimens are a 17-foot-tall giraffe and a buffalo weighing almost 3,000 pounds.

Dale Dr.

Markham Reservoir

New Cody Reservoir

0   1000   2000   3000 feet

Shoshone River

WAGON RELICS

Weathered wagon wheels, left, on display in Trail Town, serve as a reminder of the days when people and goods were transported by horse and wagon.

INFORMATION FOR VISITORS

From Casper, take Hwy. 20 west to Thermopolis then travel north on Hwy. 120 to Cody. To get to Cody from Billings, Montana, take I-90 west to the Laurel exit, then Hwy. 310 to Bridger. From there take Hwy. 72 south into Wyoming where it becomes Hwy. 120. The Buffalo Bill Historical Center is open seven days a week between 7:00 a.m. and 8:00 p.m. in the summer; hours may vary during the rest of the year. As well as hosting changing exhibits of major Western artists and artifacts, the center also holds the Buffalo Bill Celebrity Shootout every August. Located in the northwestern corner of the state, Cody country can experience extremes in weather. In the summer,

mosquitoes can be thick in wet, wooded areas. Summers can be very hot and winters in and around the mountains are subject to plunging temperatures, strong winds, and violent snowstorms that dump heavy snows. Winter sports enthusiasts will find the region ideal for skiing, snowmobiling, and snowshoeing. Overnight camping at Yellowstone National Park requires a permit.
For more information: The Cody Country Chamber of Commerce, P.O. Box 2777, Cody, WY 82414; 307-587-2777.

MERICA EXPLORE AMERICA EXPLORE AMERICA EXPLORE AMERICA EXPLORE AMERICA EXPLORE AMERICA EXPLORE AMERICA EXPLORE AMERICA EXPLORE

THE WILD WEST 77

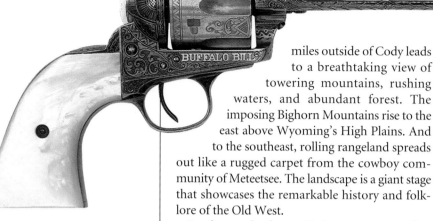

The Colt Flat Top, above, complete with a gold-plated cylinder, pearl grips, and Buffalo Bill's name engraved prominently below the bullet chamber, was presented to Cody by Howell H. Howard in 1895. Cody grew up in LeClaire, Iowa, in the modest clapboard home, right. Built in 1840, the house was moved to Cody in 1933 where it is currently on display at the Buffalo Bill Historical Center.

miles outside of Cody leads to a breathtaking view of towering mountains, rushing waters, and abundant forest. The imposing Bighorn Mountains rise to the east above Wyoming's High Plains. And to the southeast, rolling rangeland spreads out like a rugged carpet from the cowboy community of Meteetsee. The landscape is a giant stage that showcases the remarkable history and folklore of the Old West.

For thousands of years, Cody country was Indian land—a favorite hunting ground for the Crows and Shoshones. When, in the early 19th century, fur trappers and explorers like John Colter first set eyes on the area, they were dazzled by its magnificent peaks, canyons, and geysers. Colter wandered down the South Fork Valley, where he reportedly dubbed an impressive red rock butte with the name Castle Rock, and made his way to the region now known as Yellowstone National Park. Astonished by a sublime terrain that today attracts millions of vacationers annually, Colter proclaimed its wonders to the outside world and was greeted with hoots of disbelief. His descriptions of this land were too much for most people to accept, even from this veteran of the Lewis and Clark expedition.

They called Yellowstone Colter's Hell because the bubbling geysers he told them about reminded them of the devil's kingdom. (Old Faithful, the most reliable of the 200-odd geysers in Yellowstone National Park, continues to eject a 1,000-gallon plume of boiling water and steam about 150 feet into the air every 75 minutes.) Many people who heard Colter talk about the region, however, were intrigued by his description, and before long an endless stream of travelers was headed west: mountain men were followed by explorers, who were succeeded by pioneers, soldiers, ranchers, and settlers—until the marks of civilization could be found all across the landscape.

But Cody country refused to be tamed. And its development—centered around the town of Cody—was spurred by one of the West's true living legends: William F. Cody, popularly known as Buffalo Bill. His presence is still strong in Cody country, and his long-lasting legend has probably done as much to preserve and promote the Old West as Cody did on his own.

MIX OF FACT AND FICTION

Separating reality from legend is no small challenge when dealing with the Old West, especially in the case of a figure like Buffalo Bill. Born in Iowa in 1846, Cody was a boy of 12 when he signed on as a messenger with Russell, Majors & Waddell, the Missouri company that went on to establish the fabled Pony Express. The young Cody, who had earned his stripes on wagon trains and cattle drives, was soon hauling freight across the vast western Plains and experiencing their raw power firsthand. At the age of 15 Cody started riding for the Pony Express—a favorite subject of the day's dime novels. Although the endeavor lasted a mere 18 months, it was long enough for Cody to make a name for himself as a hard-riding mail carrier: in one year the teenager reportedly logged a grueling 322 miles for the Pony Express.

ELEGANT EATERY
With its ornate carving and rich color, the 48-foot-long cherry-wood bar is the main attraction of Cody's Irma Hotel.

Cody joined the Union Army during the Civil War and served in the 7th Kansas Cavalry, eventually becoming a U.S. Army scout on the western Plains. In 1867 he took a job supplying fresh food for construction crews working on the Kansas Pacific Railroad. By his own count the crack marksman shot 4,280 buffalo in eight months, earning himself the nickname of Buffalo Bill.

The following year, the 23-year-old Cody was back scouting for the army during the Indian conflicts that inflamed the West. Such duty usually gave scouts little more than saddle sores, trail dust, and the army pittance, but Cody achieved nationwide fame. In 1869 the well-known New York City dime novelist E. Z. C. Judson, who wrote under the pen name Ned Buntline, caught wind of Cody's exploits and turned his real-life feats into the stuff of melodrama in a novel called *Buffalo Bill, the King of the Border Men.*

A war-weary public eager for diversion seized on the image of the heroic scout tracking across the lonely Plains, and Buffalo Bill Cody became an instant celebrity. Building on their success, New York publishers cranked out some 557 Buffalo Bill dime novels. In 1872 Cody began to capitalize on his new fame, supplementing his scouting income with theatrical performances—playing himself.

In late June 1876, Americans were shocked by the news that Lt. Col. George Armstrong Custer and his immediate command had been massacred by Lakota and Cheyenne warriors at the Battle of the Little Bighorn. At the time, Cody was scouting with the U.S. 5th Cavalry in eastern Wyoming Territory. The sobering news of Custer's last stand reached Cody and the cavalry troopers on July 5, shortly before they were dispatched to intercept a large force of Cheyennes that the army considered hostile. The Cheyennes were discovered near Hat Creek in western Nebraska just as, according to some reports, they were preparing to attack an army wagon train that was lightly armed. The first contact was made by Cody and a small detachment of troops, who surprised an advance party of Cheyenne warriors.

At the head of the war party was a Cheyenne leader named Yellow Hair, so named because he murdered and scalped a blond woman. He and Cody fired at each other simultaneously. Yellow Hair missed, but Cody's bullet went through the chief's leg and killed his horse. Cody's mount stumbled in the excitement and Cody jumped clear. Both men were left on their feet. Yellow Hair got off another shot—and again missed. Cody's second round went true, striking Yellow Hair in the head and killing him instantly.

Yellow Hair's was the only death in what became known as the Battle of Hat Creek. Realizing they were seriously outnumbered by the troops, the

Cheyennes returned to the reservation. After trading fire with Yellow Hair, Cody gathered the chief's long feathered war bonnet, weapons, and horse whip as trophies, and cut off the dead man's long scalp lock. "The first scalp for Custer!" Buffalo Bill reportedly cried as he waved the topknot before the troops. Cody sent the scalp back to Rochester, New York, where he and his wife had settled, and it was put on display in the window of a men's clothing store. This story, called "The first scalp for Custer," was embellished in art, print, and on stage, further enhancing Buffalo Bill's fame.

Three years later, at the age of 33, Cody published his autobiography, flamboyantly titled *The Life of Hon. William F. Cody: An Autobiography; Known as Buffalo Bill, the Famous Hunter, Scout and Guide.* In 1882, riding the crest of his celebrity, Buffalo Bill discovered the means to propel himself—and the image of the Wild West—into international fame. For an Independence Day celebration in North Platte, Nebraska, the con-summate showman organized a unique performance that was part rodeo, part melodrama, and part circus. It was the birth of the Buffalo Bill Wild West Show, which opened officially the next year to enthusiastic crowds in Omaha.

In the three decades that followed, Cody's show traveled throughout America and Europe, packing audiences under circus-style tents. He awed spectators with reenactments of Indian hunts, buffalo stampedes, stirring cavalry charges, stagecoach races, mock battles, trick shooting, and roping demonstrations. Cody had an unerring eye for talent and a flair for promotion. He took an unknown Midwestern woman named Phoebe Anne Moses, a highly skilled marksperson, and made her famous as Annie Oakley. He even lured Hunkpapa Lakota leader Sitting Bull—who was seen by many whites as the villain of Custer's last stand—onto the stage and sent him on a grand tour. (Five years later the chief was shot to death in a confrontation with reservation police in South Dakota.)

REMEMBERING THE ARTIST
The studio of Frederic Remington, which has been reconstructed at the Buffalo Bill Historical Center, is arranged to look as if the artist has just stepped out after completing the painting Radisson and Groseilliers, *below. Although he was renowned for artworks of distinctly Western scenes, Remington worked primarily in New York state.*

Cody proved to be as brilliant a showman as he had been a scout. Audiences loved his Wild West Show, which went on in the 20th century to serve as the inspiration for countless novels, movies, and television shows. Although he earned a fortune, Buffalo Bill was not a good businessman and he was repeatedly beset by financial woes. Cody gave his money away to friends and strangers as quickly as he made it. Sadly, the Wild West Show went bankrupt in 1913, and four years later Cody died suddenly while visiting his sister in Denver.

LASTING LEGACY

The region that became Cody country was one of Buffalo Bill's favorite haunts. During his show business days, he built a getaway ranch in the nearby South Fork Valley. In the 1890's he lent his name to an irrigation project, the Cody Canal, which was designed to attract settlers to the area. After a slow start, the town that Buffalo Bill and his investors envisioned began to take shape, and it was appropriately dubbed Cody, Wyoming. Five years later, the Burlington Railroad chugged into town and blew life into the fledgling settlement.

Despite his recurring financial problems, Cody's name carried clout, and his namesake town attracted a steady influx of settlers. Persuading his friend Pres. Teddy Roosevelt to allocate federal funds for the building of the Shoshone Dam and Reservoir—which was later renamed the Buffalo Bill Dam and Reservoir—Cody was instrumental in promoting early development in the region.

Visitors who wish to better understand the man and the myth that was Buffalo Bill Cody should take the time to explore the Buffalo Bill Historical Center. This comprehensive Western showcase, known as the Smithsonian of the West, encompasses 250,000 square feet of Old West heritage and history, laid out in four first-class museums.

The center's Whitney Gallery of Western Art houses works by most of the great Western artists of the 19th and early 20th centuries. From the plain gritty realism of cowboy scenes by the artist Charlie Russell to the magnificent landscapes of Albert Bierstadt, the Old West almost leaps from the canvas. A number of works by Frederic Remington—who depicted Western life on canvas, in sculptures, and in novels—are also found here. Visitors can also walk through a reconstruction of his studio in New York state, where the man considered by many to be the greatest Western artist actually did most of his work. Some of the contents of his real studio are on view in the museum.

The center's Plains Indian Museum takes a similarly comprehensive approach to that Native American culture. The displays include a full-scale indoor reproduction of a late 19th-century Lakota camp, along with a collection of more than 5,000 historic Plains Indians artifacts.

The Cody Firearms Museum, which traces the history and development of guns from 1540 to the present, is an essential stop for buffs. Firearm aficionados can spend hours looking at the 4,200 weapons in the collection. The museum's one-of-a-kind Winchester Arms Collection is a fascinating reminder that the "shootin' iron" was indispensable equipment on the Western frontier.

The main attraction in this complex is the Buffalo Bill Museum, which interprets the life of the great showman, and presents a range of displays, from a bona fide stagecoach, chuck wagon, and other

The brass buttons, fringes, and embroidered floral patterns on Cody's moose-hide jacket, right, express the flamboyant personality of its owner. The jacket is on display at the Buffalo Bill Historical Center.

icons of the West, to rare motion picture footage of Buffalo Bill's Wild West Show.

Near the museum is one of Cody's most enduring landmarks, the Irma Hotel, a modest inn and restaurant built by Buffalo Bill in 1902 and named for one of his daughters. The hotel's restaurant is a popular eatery among locals and vacationers alike, who come to sample exotic Western fare, such as buffalo burgers and Rocky Mountain oysters. Guests can also savor the authentic Western atmosphere, created in part by a magnificent hand-carved cherrywood bar and mirror that was a present to Cody from England's Queen Victoria. Built in France, the massive, ornate piece was said to have been shipped through the Panama Canal, then hauled overland by rail and freight wagon. For a real step back in time, travelers can reserve the very room that was used by Cody.

When visitors aren't dining at the Irma, they can watch cowpokes ride their steeds every summer evening at the Cody Nite Rodeo, or vacationing greenhorns can outfit themselves in everything from big-bucks cowboy hats to big-buckled belts at a variety of Western-wear shops. Tourists stock up on an array of Western items, ranging from cowboy boots to "rattlesnake eggs"—a toy made from a wound-up rubber band in an envelope that makes a noise similar to that of a rattlesnake when it unwinds. Craft shops abound in Cody, as do Western art galleries selling historical prints and original works by contemporary Western artists.

TRAIL TOWN TOUR

Trail Town, located on the edge of Cody near the rodeo grounds, is another premier attraction. The rustic pioneer town is the life's work of historians Bob and Terry Edgar. Since 1967, the husband and wife team have prowled Wyoming in search of authentic Western structures. Aided by obliging ranchers, they have erected a town of 24 genuine Old West buildings, reassembled one piece at a time. Visitors today can mosey down Old Trail Town's plank sidewalk and sashay into Rivers, a cramped Old West saloon built in 1888 that is still "decorated" with bullet holes. A log cabin that served as the hideout for infamous outlaws Butch Cassidy and the Sundance Kid, and their notorious gang, the Wild Bunch, looks much as it did when they occupied it.

A line up of old wagons along the street leads to the grave of Jeremiah "Liver-Eatin'" Johnson, who waged a one-man war against the Crow Indians. Johnson reportedly made a lasting impression on the Crows by cutting out the livers of his fallen enemies, then rubbing the liver across his face. Countless Western artifacts are on display, including rusted six-shooters and Native American war bonnets and buffalo robes.

Tucked among the peaks, valleys, and forests of Cody country are approximately two dozen dude ranches. At new ranches such as the South Fork Valley's Double Diamond X and at old ones like Bill Cody's Pahaska Tepee, today's tenderfoot can enjoy the West the way many in Wyoming believe it ought to be experienced—from the saddle. Riding along the well-worn trails, riders are entertained by cowpokes and fiddlers and treated to cookouts or home-style meals, nature hikes, raft trips, and lazy hours on the ranch house porch—all amid truly spectacular scenery.

Of course, Cody country's main draw is what Buffalo Bill loved most: the land. Yellowstone National Park is surrounded by a state-sized parcel of national forests and protected wilderness lands. Hunters stalk big game in the winter months, and amateur photographers chase the elusive perfect shot in the summer. Fly fishermen cast for cutthroat, rainbow, and speckled trout in the region's many streams. Paved roads lead sightseers to South Fork Valley, Sunlight Basin, and Wapiti Valley, where scenic overlooks reward them with impressive views of the surrounding terrain.

This is the land of Buffalo Bill, where broad expanses and endless horizons inspired generations of adventurers to break away and blaze new trails westward. The frontier was a place where larger-than-life characters played out tragedies and comedies before a stunning natural backdrop. The heritage of the Old West, part fact, part fable, was celebrated, promoted, and preserved by Buffalo Bill. And while many of the world's wildest places have become civilized, in the small Wyoming town that still bears his name, the swaggering spirit of Buffalo Bill Cody and his cohorts still flourishes in all its undisciplined grandeur.

GLIMPSE INTO THE PIONEER PAST
A gentle morning mist settles on the buildings in Trail Town, below. A saloon, trading post, and trapper's cabin are among the relocated buildings at the site.

Nearby Sites & Attractions

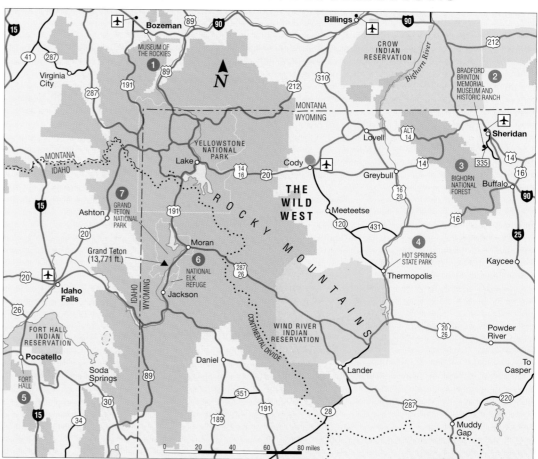

A reclining bull elk, below, seems to pose for the camera at the National Elk Refuge. Elk spend the summer fattening up for the lean months of winter.

A boater is dwarfed by one of the craggy peaks that surround Grand Teton National Park's Jenny Lake, right. The lake is used by visitors for canoeing and fishing.

1 MUSEUM OF THE ROCKIES, MONTANA

This museum's artifacts, fossils, photographs, dioramas, and a planetarium tell the story of the Rocky Mountains. An exhibit titled "One Day 80 Million Years Ago" uses dioramas and fossils to introduce visitors to some of the animals that once roamed the area. The fossilized bones of a *Tyrannosaurus rex* that were unearthed in 1990 are on display, and a group of robotic *Triceratops* root for food in a re-created forest scene. One section of the museum is devoted to the Native Americans who have lived in the region for more than 11,000 years; another focuses on the settlers and fur trappers who immigrated to Montana. The Taylor Planetarium, one of the few planetariums in the world that use computer graphics to simulate three dimensional effects, offers visual tours of the nighttime sky. Located at 600 West Kagy Blvd. in Bozeman.

2 BRADFORD BRINTON MEMORIAL MUSEUM AND HISTORIC RANCH, WYOMING

This 19th-century ranch and homestead, which is decorated with period furnishings and paintings, transports visitors back to the days when Wyoming was the domain of cowboys and ranchers. The 600-acre property is surrounded by the towering peaks of the Bighorn Mountains. The house was built in 1892 by William Moncrieffe. Its second owner, Bradford

Brinton, purchased the ranch in 1923 and enlarged the house to 20 rooms. Brinton was a patron and friend of many famous artists. His art collection includes more than 600 oil paintings, watercolors, and sketches by American artists. Western artist Charles M. Russell's painting titled *The Cowboy and the Lady Artist,* as well as Frederic Remington's *Fight on the Little Bighorn* are just two of the outstanding works on display in the house. Perusing the titles on the living room shelves, visitors will come across numerous rare books, including a first edition of the biography of British writer and critic Samuel Johnson. Plains Indian crafts, turn-of-the-century furniture, and historic documents also are shown. Located 12 miles south of Sheridan off Hwy. 335.

3 BIGHORN NATIONAL FOREST, WYOMING

Located east of the Continental Divide and rising sharply above the Great Plains, Bighorn National Forest stretches from the Montana-Wyoming border into central Wyoming. This dense forest of lodgepole pines and Engelmann spruce is located in the heart of the Bighorn Mountains, whose peaks average 8,000 feet in elevation. The highest point, Cloud Peak, soars to more than 13,000 feet. Hundreds of miles of fishing streams and 256 lakes are stocked with brook, cutthroat, and rainbow trout, and the forest supports deer, elk, and antelope. There are more than 45 campground and picnic sites within the forest, all of which are accessible along an extensive network of roads. The area is popular with mountain climbers, skiers, and snowmobilers. Located 10 miles west of Buffalo on Hwy. 16.

4 HOT SPRINGS STATE PARK, WYOMING

Hot springs, mineral baths and pools, and two resident bison herds are the highlights of this state park. The large concentration of mineral hot springs was opened for public use in 1898 when the local Shoshone and Arapahoe Indians ceded one-quarter of the "healing water" as a stipulation of their treaty with federal officials. Bighorn Hot Spring releases 2.7 million gallons of water daily, making it one of the largest mineral springs in the world. The water temperature of the springs ranges between 127°F and 129°F. The park also has large indoor and outdoor swimming pools, picnic shelters, summer flower gardens, and water slides for children. More than a dozen bison make up the Hot Springs herd. These magnificent animals roam freely through the pasture, providing visitors with opportunities for close-up views of them. Located in Thermopolis.

5 FORT HALL, IDAHO

The artifacts and archival photographs housed in this reconstructed fort illustrate the compelling history of the region's fur trappers and the westward migration of settlers into Idaho. In 1834 New England businessman Nathaniel Jarvis Wyeth oversaw the construction of the fort, which he named after a senior member of the New England Company, the sponsor of his expedition. The fort operated a successful trading post for several years until the

Hudson's Bay Company built Fort Boise nearby. With his prices being undercut by the fur company, Wyeth was forced to sell the fort to his competitor in 1837. From 1843 to 1849 the fort served as a major stop for emigrants traveling west along the Oregon Trail. The Hudson's Bay Company continued to operate the fort until 1855 when it was abandoned and fell into disrepair. Using original documents, a replica of Fort Hall was constructed in 1963 within Upper Ross Park, close to the fort's original location. Elk, deer, antelope, and buffalo can be seen grazing in the field adjacent to the fort. Located in Pocatello.

6 NATIONAL ELK REFUGE, WYOMING

The refuge was established in 1912 largely because the death by starvation of 10,000 elk in 1897 aroused the concern of local citizens. Today the refuge boasts the largest wintering herd in the world, attracting some 10,000 elk from November until March. Sleigh rides alongside the herds allow visitors to observe the elk at close range, including bull elk, which, on average, weigh 700 pounds and support antlers six feet wide. Every year Boy Scouts collect and sell the antlers that the elk shed, with most of the profits going to buy winter food for the elk. Other animals in the refuge include bighorn sheep, moose, antelope, mule deer, coyotes, and badgers. Birds include bald and golden eagles, red-tailed hawks, sandhill cranes, and trumpeter swans—the largest species of waterfowl on the continent. Located one mile east of Jackson on Hwy. 191.

7 GRAND TETON NATIONAL PARK, WYOMING

With the youngest mountains in the Rocky Mountain chain, and 11 peaks that top 11,000 feet in elevation, this park is a climber's dream. The highest of the Tetons is the towering Grand Teton, which soars some 13,771 feet. But this mountain range is not the only spectacular geological formation found within the 485-square-mile park. The terrain also features canyons, glaciers, snowfields, forests, and several isolated peaks with sharp vertical drops. Fragrant stands of spruce, pine, and fir share the landscape with a wide variety of wildflowers, including lupine, balsamroot, wild buckwheat, and scarlet gilia. Spring beauties, yellowbells, and sagebrush buttercups fill in the ground that was scraped bare by the receding snowpack. The park's numerous lakes offer anglers the chance to fish for cutthroat, whitefish, brown, brook, mackinaw, and rainbow trout, and the powerful current of the Snake River promises exciting rides for boaters and rafters. The park features more than 200 miles of hiking and horseback riding trails. Black bears, grizzlies, pronghorns, moose, and coyotes occupy the lower regions of the park, and at higher elevations bighorn sheep graze on sheer mountainsides. A small herd of bison gathers in the Jackson Hole Valley during the summer. Each year an impressive herd of up to 3,000 elk summers in the park. Ponds and small lakes created by beaver dams are shared by Canada geese, great blue herons, and trumpeter swans. The park headquarters are located at the Moose Visitor Center 10 miles north of Jackson on Teton Park Rd.

Green algae coat Tepee Fountain, above, an unusual travertine formation in Hot Springs State Park that is nourished by mineral-rich water left behind by sediment.

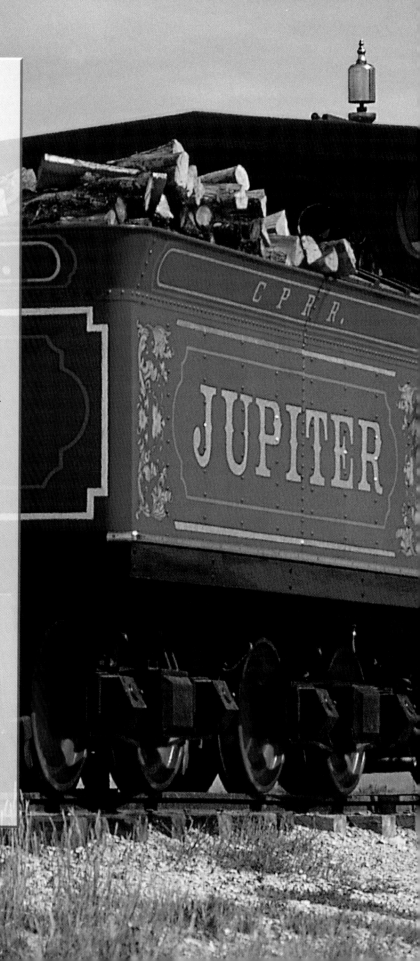

THE GOLDEN SPIKE

The final spike of the nation's first transcontinental railroad was driven home in Promontory, Utah.

In a lilting Irish brogue, Bob Dowty, an engineer at the Golden Spike National Historic Site at Promontory, boasts of the advantages of the first transcontinental railroad to a crowd that has gathered in the high lonesome desert of Utah Territory. "Ladies and gentlemen, today in Baltimore they lined an ordinary boxcar with cork and put oysters from the Chesapeake Bay on ice. They'll be shipped to San Francisco fresh and ready for market—from the Atlantic Ocean to the Pacific. No longer will you have to take your lives in your hands going across the country in wagons. You will travel in plush comfort in Pullman palace cars in less than a week, getting there so fast you don't even have to take a bath."

Dowty is portraying his 19th-century counterpart, Sam Bradford, who operated one of the locomotives during the spike-driving ceremony at the completion of the transcontinental railroad on May 10, 1869. Everyone for miles around turned out to celebrate one of America's greatest achievements. On that momentous day the

LAYING THE LINE
In this historic photograph, a construction crew poses in front of a wood-burning, balloon-stack locomotive at a crossing of the Green River, above. The nation's second transcontinental telegraph system was strung beside the track.

ENGINE TO ENGINE
Overleaf: Replicas of the two locomotives present in 1869—the Union Pacific's No. 119 and the Central Pacific's Jupiter—meet on the tracks in Promontory, Utah. The trains run throughout the summer at the Golden Spike National Historic Site.

rails of the Central Pacific and the Union Pacific—some 1,776 miles of track—met and became one as the last spike was driven. The six-month ordeal of traveling across the country by wagon train was over. Now the trip from New York to California was a pleasurable six-day, 20-hour excursion.

A GREAT ENTERPRISE

The re-creation of the linking of the tracks helps contemporary visitors imagine what the railroad meant to 19th-century Americans. Although there is no record of Bradford making a speech that day, he played no small part in the great enterprise. For many years, Bradford operated the Union Pacific's No. 119, one of the two engines that faced each other on the tracks that historic day. Like so many other young men, Sam had come west, eager to take part in the building of a railway line from the muddy little town of Omaha, on the banks of the Missouri River, all the way to California. His elation, however, was soon tempered when his best friend, also an engineer, was killed in an Indian ambush in Nebraska Territory. Guests at the 1869 Promontory ceremonies placed their hats over their hearts in honor of those who died constructing the railroad. The

rest of the day was filled with stentorian speechmaking and high-spirited merrymaking.

The dream of a railroad that would one day span the continent had hardly seemed imaginable to most people in the 1850's. The U.S. government sent out surveyors to determine the best route for such a line. In California surveyor and engineer Theodore Judah became such an evangelical booster of the railroad that he was called Crazy Judah. Nevertheless, Judah almost single-handedly outlined the route the Central Pacific would take eastward from Sacramento over the daunting obstacle of the Sierra Nevada. In the East, railroad executive "Doctor" Thomas Durant of the Union Pacific dispatched civil engineer Grenville Dodge to discover the path of the rival Central Pacific. In 1859 Dodge met in Council Bluffs, Iowa, with soon-to-be president Abraham Lincoln who questioned Dodge thoroughly on all aspects of the railroad.

Finally, in 1862, President Lincoln signed the Pacific Railroad Act. Three of Central Pacific's head honchos—Mark Hopkins, Leland Stanford, and Charles Crocker—were ready for the challenge. They put symbolic shovels to the ground in Sacramento in January 1863, beating the Union Pacific's ground breaking by nearly a year.

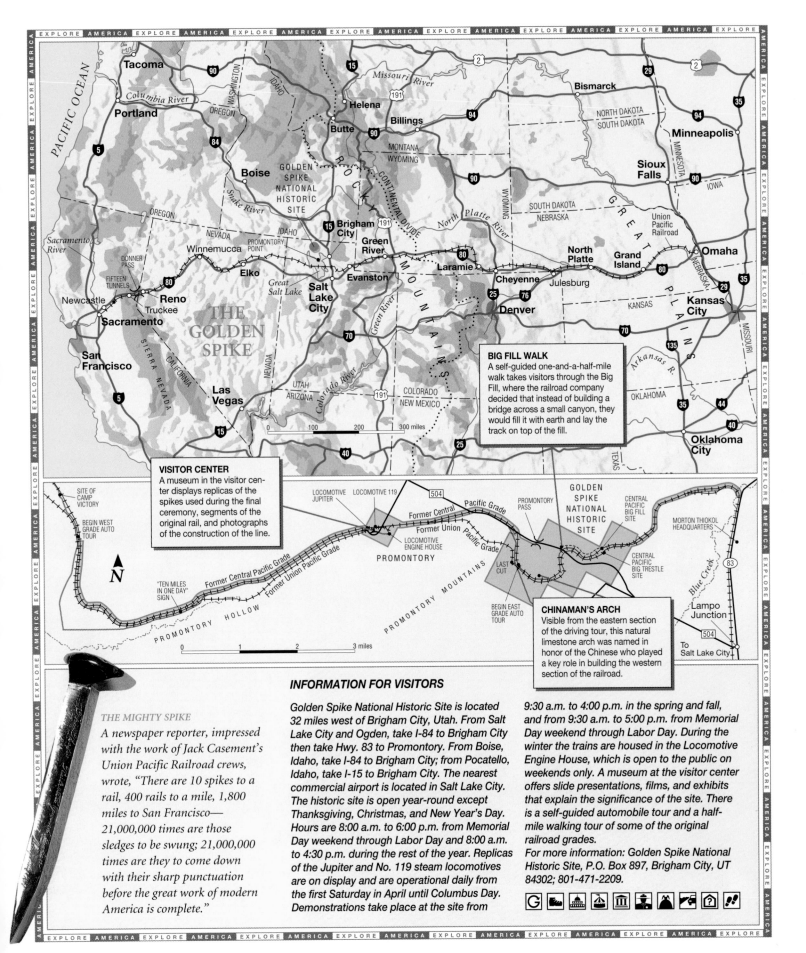

VISITOR CENTER
A museum in the visitor center displays replicas of the spikes used during the final ceremony, segments of the original rail, and photographs of the construction of the line.

BIG FILL WALK
A self-guided one-and-a-half-mile walk takes visitors through the Big Fill, where the railroad company decided that instead of building a bridge across a small canyon, they would fill it with earth and lay the track on top of the fill.

CHINAMAN'S ARCH
Visible from the eastern section of the driving tour, this natural limestone arch was named in honor of the Chinese who played a key role in building the western section of the railroad.

INFORMATION FOR VISITORS

THE MIGHTY SPIKE

A newspaper reporter, impressed with the work of Jack Casement's Union Pacific Railroad crews, wrote, "There are 10 spikes to a rail, 400 rails to a mile, 1,800 miles to San Francisco— 21,000,000 times are those sledges to be swung; 21,000,000 times are they to come down with their sharp punctuation before the great work of modern America is complete."

Golden Spike National Historic Site is located 32 miles west of Brigham City, Utah. From Salt Lake City and Ogden, take I-84 to Brigham City then take Hwy. 83 to Promontory. From Boise, Idaho, take I-84 to Brigham City; from Pocatello, Idaho, take I-15 to Brigham City. The nearest commercial airport is located in Salt Lake City. The historic site is open year-round except Thanksgiving, Christmas, and New Year's Day. Hours are 8:00 a.m. to 6:00 p.m. from Memorial Day weekend through Labor Day and 8:00 a.m. to 4:30 p.m. during the rest of the year. Replicas of the Jupiter and No. 119 steam locomotives are on display and are operational daily from the first Saturday in April until Columbus Day. Demonstrations take place at the site from

9:30 a.m. to 4:00 p.m. in the spring and fall, and from 9:30 a.m. to 5:00 p.m. from Memorial Day weekend through Labor Day. During the winter the trains are housed in the Locomotive Engine House, which is open to the public on weekends only. A museum at the visitor center offers slide presentations, films, and exhibits that explain the significance of the site. There is a self-guided automobile tour and a half-mile walking tour of some of the original railroad grades.

For more information: Golden Spike National Historic Site, P.O. Box 897, Brigham City, UT 84302; 801-471-2209.

EXPLORE AMERICA EXPLORE AMERICA EXPLORE AMERICA EXPLORE AMERICA EXPLORE AMERICA EXPLORE AMERICA EXPLORE AMERICA EXPLORE AMERICA EXPLORE

THE GOLDEN SPIKE 89

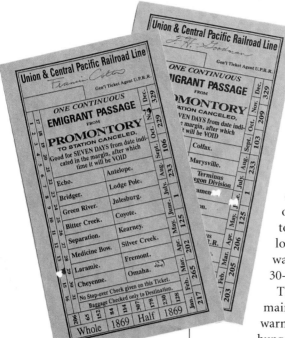

Union & Central Pacific Railroad Line tickets, above, were used by passengers heading east and west out of Promontory. The wooden trestle, below, built in 1889, is the oldest intact bridge at the Golden Spike National Historic Site.

Both companies needed gigantic workforces—and fast. Charles Crocker brought in from 8,000 to 12,000 Chinese laborers for the CP and set them to work opening up a passage through the Sierra Nevada. The work crew blasted its way through the hard granite, progressing in a couple of years by what seemed like only inches. They dug tunnels by torchlight and dangled in baskets lowered by ropes from sheer cliff walls to plant powder blasts in 30-inch-deep drill holes in the rock.

The Chinese toiled 12-hour days, maintaining their pace by drinking warm tea that was delivered in kegs hung from bamboo poles. They endured harrowing Sierra winters, and avalanches buried some of their kinsmen. On Saturday evenings some forgot their homesickness in a sweet blur of opium.

Meanwhile, under the supervision of brothers Dan and Jack Casement, the Union Pacific's brawny Irish graders and track layers sped westward across the flat prairie of the Platte River Valley. The Casements developed the first work trains on the railroad—completely self-contained cars equipped with bunk beds, kitchens, tools, and blacksmith shops. They even had their own herd of cows travel alongside the trains, so their workers were ensured a fresh supply of beef.

As work trains moved down newly laid railway line, end-of-track towns sprang up, which quickly gained notoriety. The temporary communities included Julesburg, on the Colorado-Nebraska border, reputed to be the wickedest city in America during its brief fling. Corinne, Utah, a town of canvas and board shanties 28 miles west of Promontory, appeared in March 1869. According to one report it was "fast becoming civilized, several men having been killed there already." The account added that there were 300 whiskey shops between Promontory Summit and Brigham City.

THE RACE BEGINS

The race between the Union Pacific and Central Pacific to reach the Salt Lake Valley was under way as early as 1866. At first, the UP appeared to be winning, spiking in a month what it took the CP a year to accomplish. But as the Central Pacific hit easier terrain in Nevada, the pace started to even out and the contest heated up. Still, neither company knew where the finish line would be. All the workers knew was as long as they were working, grading the route or laying the rails, they were going to get paid.

In Utah, graders from the two railroad companies met, passed each other, and overlapped for 250 miles. At times, the crew of one company set off blasts without warning the rival crew, working only on the other side of a boulder. In a blinding snowstorm in February 1869 the CP filled a deep gorge on the slope east of Promontory with 10,000 cubic yards of dirt and rock. In the same gorge, paralleling the fill, the UP hastily constructed a shaky 400-foot-long wooden trestle. The site of the Big Fill and the Big Trestle, easily seen by visitors today, was of great interest to observers in the spring of 1869. The tracks finally followed the Big Fill, and the Big Trestle was removed.

To end the absurd duplication of effort, Pres. Ulysses S. Grant ordered both companies to agree upon a meeting place. The principals of the two firms settled the issue in an all-night marathon. Promontory Summit was chosen and Congress made it official on April 10, 1869.

Still, the contest went on. Central Pacific's Crocker wagered $10,000 with UP's Durant that CP crews could beat the UP record of eight and a half miles of track laid in a single day. At the signal at daybreak on April 28, CP spikers, tampers, and track layers set to work, a line of a thousand men advancing one mile per hour. The crew even stopped work to eat lunch at a place called Victory Station, later known as Rozel Station, on the western slope. By dusk they had put down a total of 10 miles and 56 feet of track. A group of eight Irishmen actually laid the track; with each section

of iron rail weighing more than 500 pounds, that meant each man had lifted 132 tons in that day.

By early May, work camps with names like Deadfall, Murder Gulch, and Last Chance climbed up the east and west slopes of Promontory Summit, flanked by the hills of the Promontory Mountains. The waters of Great Salt Lake shimmered to the south. Tents sprouted up in the waterless valley of the last end-of-track town, Promontory, once inhabited only by jackrabbits and sagebrush. The town upheld the shady reputation of its predecessors; shootings and fracases frequently erupted between Chinese gangs and among the ubiquitous whiskey sellers and gamblers.

On May 5 Sam Bradford's engine No. 119 chugged across the Big Trestle, and two days later the CP and UP tracks were within a couple of thousand feet of each other. May 8—the date set for the ceremony—was upon them. But some unforeseen problems got in the way. On that day angry UP workmen were holding Thomas Durant captive in his lavish private car on a siding in Wyoming Territory. The men demanded payment of $500,000 in back wages before they would let his train proceed. In the meantime Leland

ONCE A CANYON
The original track bed can still be seen crossing the Big Fill near Promontory, above. The rails were removed from the area in 1942 and the metal donated to the nation's war effort.

DETAILS COUNT
Sand domes, such as the one on the replica of No. 119, left, were used to store sand that was released when the tracks were wet and slippery. The painting on No. 119's dome is believed to depict Johnny Appleseed. The replicas of No. 119 and Jupiter were built by the O'Connor Engineering Laboratories of California, whose employees worked from old photographs of the original engines.

Stanford's private train hit a downed tree and had to be hitched up to another locomotive. He and other CP dignitaries rolled into Promontory under the power of the Jupiter.

On the morning of May 10, everyone was present and the final ceremony was set to begin. Naturally, the two companies disagreed up to the last minute on the details of the event. But by noon the sun shone down on a crowd of 500 to 1,000, 21 women among them, who lined the tracks. As bands played, Western Union telegrapher W. N. Shilling sat at his table ready to tap the news to the nation. Sam Bradford, in the cab of No. 119, and George Booth, in Jupiter, pulled the gleaming engines nose to nose on the tracks.

THE FINAL SPIKE

Reverend Todd from Pittsfield, Massachusetts, said a prayer, and two gold spikes were dropped into predrilled holes in a polished laurelwood tie. A silver spike from Nevada and an iron-silver-gold spike from Arizona were also presented. Durant, who had retired to his car to nurse a throbbing headache, made only a brief appearance to initiate the spike driving. He and Stanford gently tapped the four ceremonial spikes for show. An iron spike, the final one, was wired to the telegraph for the nationwide broadcast. Stanford and Durant both took swings at the spike,

and missed. Finally, a railway worker picked up the hammer and drove it home. At 12:47 p.m. Shilling sent out the message over the wire: "Dot. Dot. Dot. Done." The crowd cheered, the locomotives proudly blew their steam whistles, and bells chimed throughout the country.

Each company operated its trains only as far east or west as Promontory during the early years. At that point cross-country passengers detrained and

DEDICATED VISIONARY
A monument, right, in Old Sacramento, California, the terminus of the Central Pacific Railroad, is dedicated to railroad engineer Theodore Judah. Judah was one of a group of visionaries who helped conceive and build America's first transcontinental railroad. Today the California Zephyr, seen below near Crescent Junction, Utah, travels along the same route.

switched lines. For 50 cents they could buy a meal at the Golden Spike Hotel before they resumed their journey. One story tells of a stranger who came into a restaurant and sat down at a table with two men. When one of these men took too much gravy, the other shot him dead on the spot. The gunslinger then ordered the stranger to keep his seat. The stranger duly obeyed and finished his meal with the corpse beside him.

In 1904 the railroad completed a mainline cut-off across the Great Salt Lake and Promontory's glory days were over. Freight trains still ran through town twice a week, but in 1942 the track was pulled up and the scrap metal donated to the war effort. Today visitors can drive along six miles of the original transcontinental railroad grade. Interpretative signs describe many of the highlights of the Golden Spike National Historic Site and the great railroad race that culminated in Promontory. In the summer replicas of the original locomotives are on display and costumed interpreters play the roles of the historical figures who participated in the joining of the two railroads. The sky fills with black smoke as locomotives No. 119 and Jupiter rumble their way down a section of original roadbed. Time seems to reverse itself, taking visitors back to the ceremony of long ago.

One of those present at the 1869 ceremony was Mary Epson, who had lived long enough to witness the undriving of the last spike 73 years later. Mary had walked across the country to Utah with her family when she was a little girl. The idea of a six-day transcontinental train trip must have seemed miraculous to her that May day as she watched the last spike being pounded into the gleaming iron road.

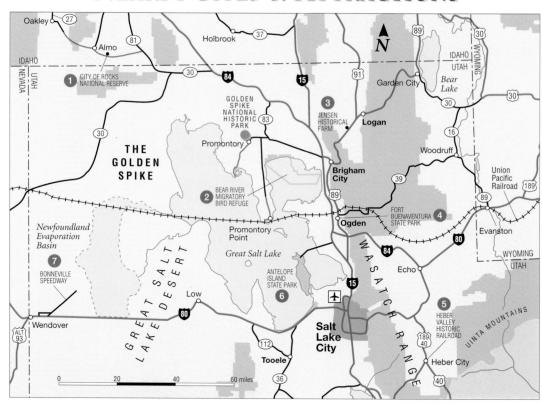

Oakley 27
Almo 81
Holbrook 37
89
30
IDAHO
NEVADA
UTAH
1 CITY OF ROCKS NATIONAL RESERVE
30
84
15
91
IDAHO
UTAH
WYOMING
30
Garden City
Bear Lake
30
GOLDEN SPIKE NATIONAL HISTORIC PARK
83
3
JENSEN HISTORICAL FARM
Logan
89
16
30
Promontory
Woodruff
Union Pacific Railroad
189
THE GOLDEN SPIKE
2 BEAR RIVER MIGRATORY BIRD REFUGE
Brigham City
39
89
89
189
Newfoundland Evaporation Basin
FORT BUENAVENTURA STATE PARK
4
Evanston
Ogden
84
80
WYOMING
UTAH
Promontory Point
Great Salt Lake
Echo
7
BONNEVILLE SPEEDWAY
GREAT SALT LAKE DESERT
ANTELOPE ISLAND STATE PARK
15
WASATCH RANGE
UINTA MOUNTAINS
Low
6
5
HEBER VALLEY HISTORIC RAILROAD
80
Salt Lake City
189 40
Wendover
ALT 93
112
Tooele
36
Heber City
40
N
0   20   40   60 miles

In 1969 a 2,000-acre state park was created on Antelope Island, below, and in 1981 the entire island, which is about 15 miles long and 5 miles wide, became the Antelope Island State Park.

1 CITY OF ROCKS NATIONAL RESERVE, IDAHO

City of Rocks is named for its imposing skyline of 60- to 70-story-high rock pinnacles. Climbers from across the country are eager to test their mettle on the granite formations with such imaginative names as Rabbit Rock, Animal Cracker Dome, and the Boxtop. The area contains some of the oldest rock west of the Mississippi River. Shoshone and Bannock Indians once traveled through this region on hunting and gathering forays. Later the rocks served as landmarks for emigrants traveling the trails west to Oregon, Salt Lake City, and the California goldfields, some of whom left their marks on the rocks in axle

grease; traces of pioneer graffiti are visible today. City of Rocks was designated a national historic landmark in 1964. Stands of lodgepole pine, limber pine, and Douglas fir grow at high elevations here, cottonwood, and quaking aspen thrive at midelevations, and sagebrush, juniper, and piñon pine at lower elevations. Elk, mountain lions, coyotes, and bobcats roam the region, and a section of the Minidoka Bird Refuge provides a habitat for eagles, falcons, hummingbirds, and mountain bluebirds. Located 13 miles south of Oakley off Hwy. 27.

2 BEAR RIVER MIGRATORY BIRD REFUGE, UTAH

Located between the Wasatch Range and the Promontory Mountains, the refuge is visited by millions of birds during their annual migrations. In the fall about 12,000 tundra swans, the largest concentration found anywhere on earth, often stop here. Thousands of golden-tufted eared grebes, some 500,000 swallows, and hundreds of long-billed dowitchers and marbled godwits make regular stopovers. Nesting birds include black-crowned night herons, northern harriers, and avocets. A 12-mile auto tour takes visitors through the refuge. Located 15 miles west of Brigham City off Hwy. 83.

3 JENSEN HISTORICAL FARM, UTAH

This 1917 working farm encompasses 120 acres of animal pastures, crop fields, vegetable gardens, and orchards, re-creating life on a Cache Valley farm. The

5 HEBER VALLEY HISTORIC RAILROAD, UTAH

This train gives passengers a scenic tour of some of Utah's most beautiful landscapes, passing by farmlands, fields, and streams, and through several valleys. A 1907 steam locomotive pulls the restored vintage coaches through Heber Valley, around Deer Creek Lake, and into Provo Canyon. The train stops for 30 minutes at Vivian Park so that passengers can get out and explore or take a closer look at the engine. By the time the train arrives back in Heber, it will have used up about two-and-a-half tons of coal. Located in Heber City.

6 ANTELOPE ISLAND STATE PARK, UTAH

The Gosiute Indians called this 28,000-acre island Pa'ribina, meaning "Elk Place"; the explorer John C. Frémont gave the island its English name after the resident antelope. In the 19th century the Mormon leader Brigham Young bred horses here, and more than 10,000 sheep grazed on the island. Now some 22 mammal species, including mule deer, bobcats, and coyotes, and an estimated 257 bird species, such as sage grouse and chukar partridge, live in the area. American bison were introduced to the island in 1892 and today the herd numbers more than 600. Visitors are welcome to camp, picnic, and hike in the park. The sandy beaches and warm waters of Great Salt Lake invite swimmers to plunge in. Located eight miles northwest of Salt Lake City off Hwy. 15.

7 BONNEVILLE SPEEDWAY, UTAH

The Bonneville Salt Flats are the ancient bed of Lake Bonneville, which evaporated and left potash salt flats behind. The hard surface of the flats makes an ideal track for speed racing. In 1925 a Studebaker driven by Ab Jenkins raced a train across the flats and won. A number of speed records have been set here, including that of Sir Malcolm Campbell in 1935, who topped 300 miles an hour, and one set by John Rhodes Cobb, who exceeded the 400-mile-an-hour barrier in 1947. Located five miles northeast of Wendover off Hwy. 80.

The Jensen Historical Farm, left, an outdoor museum run by Utah State University, gives demonstrations of farmsteading methods in the early 20th century in Utah.

farm buildings, which were relocated here from different locations within the Cache Valley, include an 1875 farmhouse, machine shed, root cellar, summer kitchen, and smokehouse. The farm offers a self-guided walking tour, and the staff, dressed in period clothing, show visitors the techniques of shearing sheep, milking cows, plowing soil, and threshing grain. Cooking, canning, and quilting demonstrations are offered throughout the year. Located six miles south of Logan off Hwy. 89.

4 FORT BUENAVENTURA STATE PARK, UTAH

Built by a fur trapper named Miles Goodyear in 1846, Fort Buenaventura was the first permanent Anglo settlement in the Great Basin. When the demand for beaver pelts waned, Goodyear began to breed horses. In 1847 the Mormons, who had settled 35 miles to the south, purchased Goodyear's property and the horse breeder became a prospector in the California gold mines. This re-created fort was built on the site of the original one in 1980, using 19th-century tools and techniques, such as wooden pegs instead of nails. Guided tours of the fort, cabins, and trading post are offered to travelers. Located on A Ave. in Ogden.

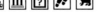

The granite spires of the Twin Sisters, below, in Idaho's City of Rocks National Reserve were actually born millions of years apart. The rock on the left is 2.5 billion years old and was formed by a large mass of molten rock below the earth's surface. The rock on the right is only 25 million years old.

KLONDIKE GOLD RUSH

When gold was discovered in the Klondike, every down-on-his-luck digger packed up and went north.

Gold! The word sounded like a clarion call across North America. Newspapers reported a shipment that was being unloaded at Schwabacher Wharf in Seattle. The year was 1897, the month July, and the steamer *Portland*, fresh from the waters of Alaska, was docked in Seattle. On board were 68 miners and more than two tons of gold. Three days earlier another steamer, the *Excelsior*, had arrived in San Francisco with $750,000 worth of gold. The miners swaggered down the gangplanks, boasting of incredible riches waiting to be plucked from goldfields in the Yukon—a region that came to be called the Klondike because gold was found near the junction of the Klondike and Yukon rivers. Rumors spread quickly that gold nuggets brightened the hills of Alaska, and streams filled with ore glittered like the nighttime sky.

However, the pot of gold at the end of the Alaskan rainbow was cached in some of the most intractable terrain on the continent. Towering mountain ranges, surging rivers, and murderous

HISTORIC TOWN

Overleaf: Perched on the banks of the Skagway River, Skagway retains much of its turn-of-the-century flavor. To reach the goldfields, miners had to pass through the forbidding Coast Mountains, whose snowy peaks ring Skagway.

TAKING THE HIGH TRAIN

A narrow-gauge train on the White Pass & Yukon Route, below, chugs along the Tunnel Mountain trestle on its way through the Coast Mountains. The tracks climb 2,888 feet to White Pass summit. Three-hour round-trip excursions from Skagway to White Pass are available throughout the summer. The railroad also offers excursions to Bennett Lake, where prospectors detrained before continuing to Dawson City by boat.

winter weather locked in the Klondike's gold as securely as if it were kept at Fort Knox. Logic said that only the most experienced miners and mountain men should undertake this risky adventure, but hard economic times and the lure of instant wealth clouded the judgment of many.

"Label your luggage for Klondike," went a popular song of the day, "for there ain't no luck in the town today, there ain't no work down Moodyville way. . . ." Quitting their jobs and leaving their families behind, tens of thousands of men and dozens of women across America traveled north into the great unknown. For many, the Klondike was the last frontier—a land of opportunity, where, by all reports, streams virtually ran with whiskey and dollars grew on trees. "Surging crowds fought for passage at Seattle, Portland, San Francisco," wrote historian William E. Brown in *This Last Treasure*. "Classy ships and condemned rust buckets . . . sailed low in the water, packed from keel to rigging with stampeders who jauntily waved straw hats as they steamed north to the unknown, but surely to glory." For other gold-seekers, such as female prospector Clare Boynton Phillips, leaving home was "a sorrowful departure." Phillips noted in her diary, published as *Klondike Tenderfoot*, "The details are too sad to write about."

Yet once gold fever had struck there was no turning back. Of the many routes to the fields, the most popular was by boat up the straits and sounds of the Inside Passage of British Columbia and southeastern Alaska to the boomtowns of Skagway and Dyea.

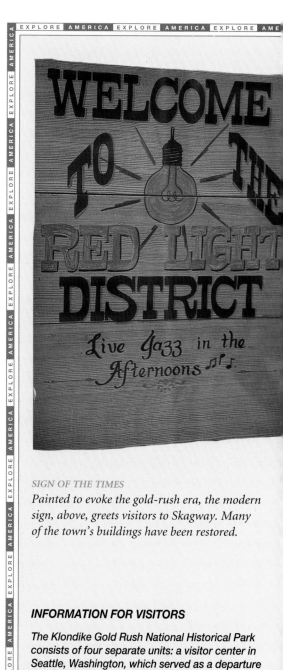

SIGN OF THE TIMES

Painted to evoke the gold-rush era, the modern sign, above, greets visitors to Skagway. Many of the town's buildings have been restored.

INFORMATION FOR VISITORS

The Klondike Gold Rush National Historical Park consists of four separate units: a visitor center in Seattle, Washington, which served as a departure point for miners; the six-block historic district in Skagway; the Chilkoot Unit, including the remains of the town of Dyea and the Chilkoot Trail; and a five-mile segment of the White Pass Trail. Skagway is accessible by car via the South Klondike Highway. The town is also the northern terminus of the Alaska Marine Highway System, and most cruise ships traveling the Inside Passage stop in Skagway. The nearest airports are located in Juneau and Whitehorse, Yukon. A 45-minute commuter flight makes regularly scheduled trips between Juneau and Skagway. The Chilkoot Trail is open year-round. For more information: Superintendent, Klondike Gold Rush National Historical Park, P.O. Box 517, Skagway, AK 99840; 907-983-2921.

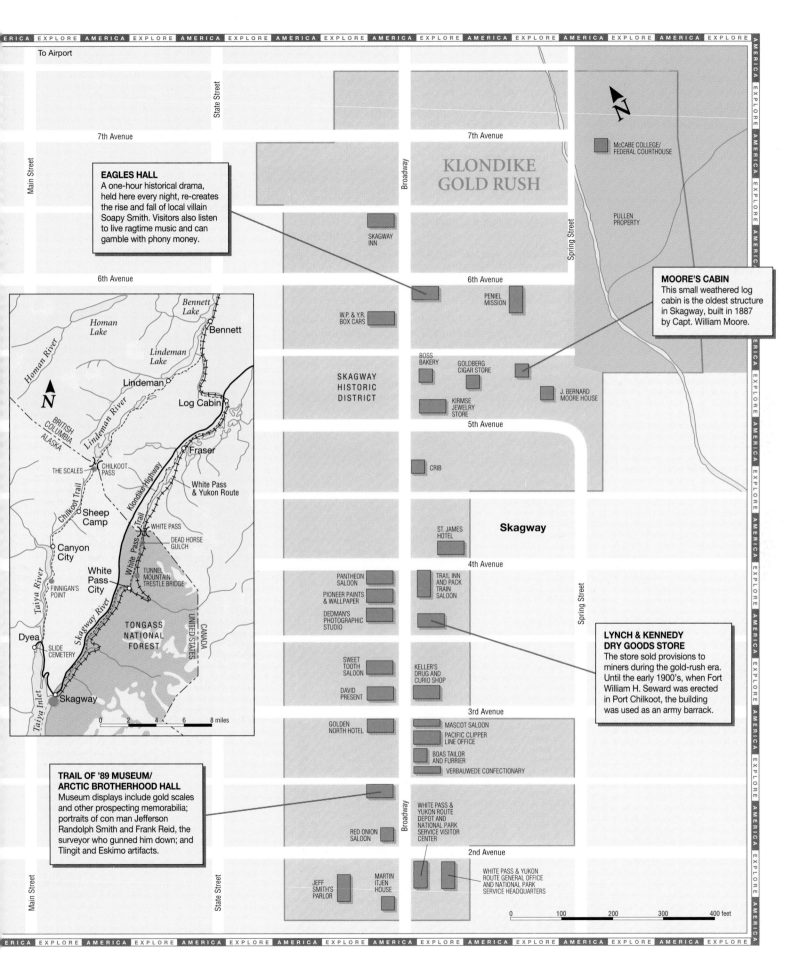

To Airport

State Street

7th Avenue

7th Avenue

Broadway

Main Street

KLONDIKE GOLD RUSH

McCABE COLLEGE/
FEDERAL COURTHOUSE

EAGLES HALL
A one-hour historical drama, held here every night, re-creates the rise and fall of local villain Soapy Smith. Visitors also listen to live ragtime music and can gamble with phony money.

6th Avenue

6th Avenue

Spring Street

PULLEN
PROPERTY

SKAGWAY
INN

PENIEL
MISSION

MOORE'S CABIN
This small weathered log cabin is the oldest structure in Skagway, built in 1887 by Capt. William Moore.

W.P. & Y.R.
BOX CARS

BOSS
BAKERY

GOLDBERG
CIGAR STORE

SKAGWAY
HISTORIC
DISTRICT

KIRMSE
JEWELRY
STORE

J. BERNARD
MOORE HOUSE

5th Avenue

CRIB

Map inset

Bennett
Lake

Homan
Lake

Bennett

Homan River

Lindeman
Lake

Lindeman

Log Cabin

N

BRITISH
COLUMBIA
ALASKA

Lindeman River

Fraser

CHILKOOT
PASS

THE SCALES

White Pass
& Yukon Route

Chilkoot Trail

Klondike Highway

Sheep
Camp

WHITE PASS

Canyon
City

White Pass
Trail

DEAD HORSE
GULCH

Finnigan's
Point

White
Pass
City

TUNNEL
MOUNTAIN
TRESTLE BRIDGE

Taiya River

Skagway River

TONGASS
NATIONAL
FOREST

CANADA
UNITED STATES

Dyea

SLIDE
CEMETERY

Taiya Inlet

Skagway

0 2 4 6 8 miles

St. JAMES
HOTEL

Skagway

4th Avenue

Spring Street

PANTHEON
SALOON

TRAIL INN
AND PACK
TRAIN
SALOON

PIONEER PAINTS
& WALLPAPER

DEDMAN'S
PHOTOGRAPHIC
STUDIO

LYNCH & KENNEDY DRY GOODS STORE
The store sold provisions to miners during the gold-rush era. Until the early 1900's, when Fort William H. Seward was erected in Port Chilkoot, the building was used as an army barrack.

SWEET
TOOTH
SALOON

KELLER'S
DRUG AND
CURIO SHOP

DAVID
PRESENT

3rd Avenue

GOLDEN
NORTH HOTEL

MASCOT SALOON

PACIFIC CLIPPER
LINE OFFICE

BOAS TAILOR
AND FURRIER

VERBAUWEDE CONFECTIONARY

TRAIL OF '89 MUSEUM/ ARCTIC BROTHERHOOD HALL
Museum displays include gold scales and other prospecting memorabilia; portraits of con man Jefferson Randolph Smith and Frank Reid, the surveyor who gunned him down; and Tlingit and Eskimo artifacts.

Broadway

WHITE PASS &
YUKON ROUTE
DEPOT AND
NATIONAL PARK
SERVICE VISITOR
CENTER

RED ONION
SALOON

2nd Avenue

Main Street

State Street

JEFF
SMITH'S
PARLOR

MARTIN
ITJEN
HOUSE

WHITE PASS & YUKON
ROUTE GENERAL OFFICE
AND NATIONAL PARK
SERVICE HEADQUARTERS

0 100 200 300 400 feet

PANNING FOR GOLD

Placer gold glitters in a pan of dirt, right. To separate the gold particles from the dirt, miners submerged the pan and shook it so that the heavier gold ore settled on the bottom. They then tilted the pan back and forth until the dirt was washed away.

MINERS' PORTRAIT

Turn-of-the century miners at Adam Hill, below, pose with the tools of their trade—a pair of gold pans and a sluice box—and some of their hard-won gold.

From there the intrepid prospectors crossed the Chilkoot or White passes into Canada by foot or packhorse. Making it to headwater lakes on the Yukon River, they rafted downriver to Dawson City—the very heart of the Klondike.

Dyea marked the starting point of the 33-mile-long Chilkoot Trail, which led to the goldfields. The trail was too steep for pack animals, so the prospectors hoisted their loads on their backs and climbed up it themselves. Other gold-seekers used the White Pass Trail, which left from Skagway. This equally treacherous route earned the nickname Dead Horse Trail from the bodies of dead animals that littered the bottom of the ravines.

Today Dyea is a ghost town. The foundations of its buildings are the only remnants of the days when thousands of eager prospectors passed through town. Skagway continues to thrive as a tourist destination, especially during summer months when cruise ships dock there. Sometimes as many as five ships a day enter the harbor, disembarking up to 5,000 passengers, who stroll the tidy boardwalks of Broadway Street. They can tour the buildings within the Klondike Gold Rush National Historical Park, each of which has been faithfully restored to its 1890's appearance. A truly unusual structure here is the Arctic Brotherhood Hall, with its facade constructed of 10,000 pieces of driftwood. The visitor center, which is housed in the depot of the 1898 White Pass & Yukon Route Railway, exhibits a collection of gold-rush memorabilia. Park rangers lead daily walks through Skagway's historic district from May through September.

DESPERATELY WICKED TOWN

At the turn of the century the muddy streets of Skagway were thronged with hordes of fortune-seekers jostling for mining supplies. Hucksters kept a sharp lookout for newcomers, sometimes fleecing them the day they stepped off the boat. Clare Boynton Phillips described Skagway in March 1898 as "a most lawless, desperately wicked town. No law and order at all, with shooting day and night." She got out as fast as she could.

Skagway made the perfect base of operations for the likes of Jefferson Randolph "Soapy" Smith, the most notorious outlaw between Washington and the Yukon. Soapy Smith was a wily criminal who ruled a far-reaching underworld of expert con men and bunco artists. His crews would pose as ordinary gold-seekers and fish around for the owners of the fattest wallets in town, reeling them in with offerings of tents, warm fires, hot coffee, and other comforts. After promising to make these men rich through bogus businesses, Smith's men would give them a taste of the good life by inviting them to join a game of poker or find-the-lady. The most gullible victims were left penniless in a matter of hours. No one was off-limits. Soapy even took on Canada's North West Mounted Police.

When Smith's gang learned that Inspector Zachary T. Wood was transporting $150,000 in gold dust and bank notes collected as customs fees over Chilkoot Pass to Victoria, British Columbia, they confronted the officer somewhere between Skagway and Dyea. Unfazed, Wood held Smith

S.T. KINCAID FIRST CLEAN-UP ADAM HILL 1901

100

and his cohorts at gunpoint and made his way to the Skagway dock, where he was supposed to set sail on the steamer *Tartar*. The ship's captain was prepared for trouble, and Smith's men suddenly found themselves outnumbered by a horde of gun-toting crewmen. Inspector Wood was escorted on board, and the customs fees made it safely south.

Smith flouted the law at every turn. In July 1898 he finally stepped over the line one time too many. When two of his henchmen robbed a miner of his gold dust, angry townsfolk gathered on the Juneau Company Wharf in Skagway Harbor to confront him. Smith smelled a lynch mob. He grabbed his rifle and stood his ground. Frank Reid, the soft-spoken town surveyor, spun toward Soapy and gunned him down, but not before taking a mortal wound himself. Both men are buried in Skagway's Gold Rush Cemetery, amid the tombstones of other victims of the violence, hardship, and disease that were the miners' constant companions. Dwarf dogwood trees and a canopy of birches make the cemetery an inviting place to visit during the summer months.

| COLORFUL TALES | Skagway's visitors can ride through town in old-fashioned streetcars and listen as the drivers, dressed in 1890's-era |

garb, talk about Soapy Smith and the hundreds of people who claimed to have witnessed the gun-fight. Harriet "Ma" Pullen is one of them. Ma Pullen always maintained that Soapy Smith was kind to her children, handing out candy to them. Nobody questioned her because she was the upstanding proprietress of Pullen House, famous for its fine dining and lodging. Ma Pullen arrived in Skagway in 1897 and worked from a tent, baking pies in old tin cans she had hammered flat. She saved every cent she made and invested it in a successful packhorse business. This enabled her to buy the old house that she converted into her hotel. In their book *Chilkoot Trail*, historians David Neufeld and Frank Norris wrote that Pullen was an example of someone who rose "quickly and honestly, from poverty to a position of security, fame, and community respect." She died in Skagway in 1947.

Today's adventurers can ride the White Pass & Yukon Route Railway, a narrow-gauge train that follows the contours of Klondike history as it winds along the original route of the White Pass Trail. "It can't be done," announced Sir Thomas Tancrede, a representative for a British consortium, when he went to the region to see if a railway could be built over the mountains. But that was before Tancrede met with Michael "Big Mike" Heney in a Skagway hotel. The Canadian-born son of Irish immigrants, Heney saw things differently:

"Give me enough dynamite and snoose [snuff] and I'll build a road to hell." The two men struck a deal, and from May 1898 to July 1900 a team of hard-scrabble men blasted rock, laid track, and blazed a route over the mountains.

Today the three-hour rail trip traverses wooden trestles as it reaches for the snowy summits. As the train chugs past Dead Horse Gulch, passengers stare silently into the rocky ravine where exhausted miners led their overburdened packhorses in attempts to negotiate boulder fields. Some 3,000

A WALK THROUGH HISTORY
A creek cascades toward the Taiya River, above, on the scenic Chilkoot Trail. The trail's numerous steep climbs tested the endurance of miners, and in the winter, frigid temperatures and frequent avalanches threatened their lives.

Built in 1898 in Skagway, the original Red Onion Saloon, below, was a drinking establishment and bawdy house. The saloon's exterior now sports old-style signs and modern neon types that advertise its offerings today.

horses were killed outright in falls or shot after breaking a leg crossing this treacherous terrain. Maneuvering their horses over the still-warm bodies of dead pack animals, the miners continued on the arduous trek. A monument in Skagway records how the horses met their fate.

"This is one of the most heartrending scenes I witnessed," wrote Clare Phillips. "A man was try-ing to drive up this awful hill with a young spirited horse, with a four foot loaded sled hitched behind. This brute (I cannot call him a man) cursed at and beat this poor horse with an axe handle with all his might for half an hour." Tappan Adney, a veteran correspondent covering the Klondike, wrote, "The cruelty to horses is past belief."

The lure of Klondike gold brought out the worst in some men. It underscored the fundamental struggle between good and evil, the civilized and the brutish. These themes are skillfully treated by Jack London in his novels about the North. *The Call of the Wild* tells the story of Buck, a beloved family dog raised in California that was kidnapped and shipped off to suffer the life of a sled dog for some greedy men in the Klondike. Every good novel has strong elements of truth. London, himself a veteran of the gold rush, had enough raw material in his own mining experiences to fashion stories that, nearly a century later, still ring true for contemporary readers.

UNENDING HARDSHIP

The Klondike offered endless hardships. Not only did miners climb Chilkoot Pass carrying heavy loads on their backs— they did so dozens of times or more. The cargo was inspected by Canadian Mounties, stationed at the top of the pass, who ensured that each man had the 2,000 pounds of supplies needed to survive an entire year in the wilderness.

Some gold-seekers went to great lengths to avoid complying with the rules. The most foolhardy risked their lives by taking an alternate route across the Malaspina Glacier. "Only a few parties," wrote Canadian historian Pierre Berton in *Trails of '98*, "dared to trespass into that tortured land of enormous ice masses, treacherous canyons, and crevasses, unexplored precipices and mountains four miles high." One party of 19 New Yorkers with no prior wilderness experience were "dumped on the shores of Yakutat Bay, their machinery and equipment coated with rust, and all their food, except for their flour and meat, spoiled by salt water."

As soon as they started off across the glacier, the hapless adventurers were buffeted by the elements. Frigid temperatures, snow blindness, avalanches, fatigue, insanity, scurvy, starvation—they suffered all these depredations. Even after half of their party died under horrendous conditions, the surviving members searched for gold in glacial sediments hundreds of miles from the Klondike. Only four of the men stumbled back to Yakutat Bay alive: the glare of the ice had made two of them permanently nearsighted and the other two totally blind. To make matters worse, one newspaper reported that the unfortunate miners had returned with

WHAT'S YOUR PLEASURE?
Authentic furnishings and mannequins dressed in period clothing at the Mascot Saloon, left, evoke the days when the bar did a thriving business.

$500,000 in gold dust, when—like many stampeders—they had returned empty-handed.

In the end, the hardship endured by the goldseekers paled beside the disappointment they felt when they realized that, after chasing their dream across the continent and a frozen wasteland, most of the best claims had already been snapped up. Gold had been discovered in Alaska in August 1896, 11 months before the *Portland* and *Excelsior* arrived in Seattle and San Francisco. Even before the diggers from the lower 48 states had left their homes, miners in the Yukon had staked out the best sites. While some of the late arrivals managed to eke out a living by mining gold in the leftover claims, many of them went home having seen very little of the precious metal.

But pushing ever farther inland, these ambitious prospectors helped pry open Alaska's doors. They tempted others to explore the land to the north, which they advertised through songs, poetry, journals, and stories. Today the legends and myths that were born during the gold-rush era are as much a part of the Alaskan landscape as its churning rivers and sublime mountain peaks.

SOAPY'S GRAVE
One of the most famous graves in Gold Rush Cemetery is that of Jefferson Randolph Smith, left, better known as Soapy. Smith acquired his nickname from one of his cons: He would bury a $50 bill in a bucket of soap and sell it for $5.00 to one of his henchmen posing as an ordinary customer. When his accomplice uncovered the money in the soap, gullible bystanders would greedily purchase buckets themselves—only to find that they contained nothing but soap.

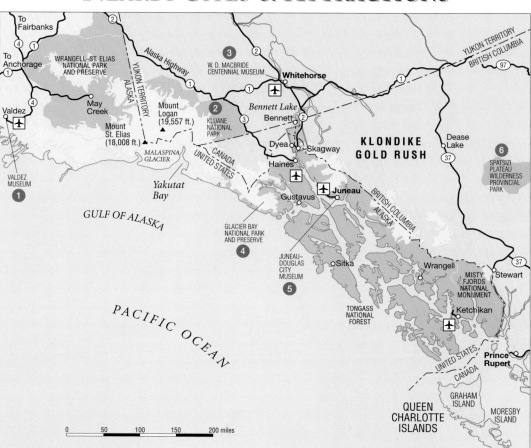

Glacial runoff empties into Glacier Bay, above, after trickling through a massive wall of blue ice.

1 VALDEZ MUSEUM, ALASKA

The artifacts, photographs, and interpretive displays in this museum illustrate the development of Valdez from a gold-rush boomtown in 1898 to a successful oil-producing center in the 1970's. A miner's cabin, complete with a potbellied stove, bearskin rug, and hand-hewn benches, gives visitors an idea of how the town's early settlers lived. An exhibit on Fort Liscum, which was built at the turn of the century, includes a Civil War cannon that helped protect the fort. Also on display in the museum are a mahogany bar built in Chicago in 1880, a Fresnel lens from the lighthouse that once guided ships past nearby Hinchinbrook Island, and a restored 1907 Ahrens steam fire engine decorated with polished chrome and gold-leaf features. The events of March 27, 1964, when a massive earthquake and then gigantic waves devastated much of Valdez, are chronicled in a dramatic photographic exhibit. Another display on the trans-Alaska pipeline includes a barrel of the first oil to flow through the pipeline. Located in Valdez.

2 KLUANE NATIONAL PARK, YUKON

Dominated by towering mountains and expansive ice fields, Kluane National Park is an ideal spot for hiking, fishing, boating, camping, and skiing. In 1942 the region was designated as the Kluane Game Sanctuary; it was made a national park in 1972. Ten peaks in the park's St. Elias range soar to some

15,000 feet or more, including Mount Logan, the highest peak in Canada at 19,557 feet, and 18,008-foot Mount St. Elias. The world's largest nonpolar glacier systems are also found here. Visitors to the region can see sand dunes and dust storms formed of debris left by glaciers as they ground their way across the land. White spruces dominate the thick boreal forest of the river valleys; dwarf birches and lichens are sprinkled across the tundra landscape in the northern part of the park; and hardy Arctic flowers push through the crevices and ledges at higher elevations. Caribou, moose, grizzlies, and wolves inhabit the region. The park's major rivers and lakes, including 184-square-mile Kluane Lake, are renowned among anglers for their kokanee salmon, lake trout, northern pike, and Arctic grayling. Visitors can explore more than 150 miles of hiking trails, old mining roads, and river routes. Located 120 miles west of Whitehorse on Hwy. 1.

3 W. D. MACBRIDE CENTENNIAL MUSEUM, YUKON

This museum's collection ranges from the natural history of the Yukon and its wildlife and geology to the history of its Native American population, Whitehorse and the North West Mounted Police. Also featured are turn-of-the-century transportation and the gold rush. An exhibit titled "Rivers of Gold" celebrates the 100th anniversary of the discovery of gold in the Klondike. The mining era is brought to life with displays of picks, shovels, guns, gold scales, and the single-room cabin of Sam McGee, one of the estimated 30,000 prospectors who flocked here in 1898. Many of the fortune-seekers arrived by train on the White Pass & Yukon Route Railway, which left from Skagway, Alaska. Engine #51, which traveled for 120 miles through spruce forests and mountain passes to the mining camps, is on display. Artifacts and photographs recount the story of how the North West Mounted Police established order in a region that experienced a rapid influx of lawless miners. Other displays include a blacksmith's shop, the original Whitehorse Government Telegraph Office, and a copper specimen that weighs more than a ton. Located on 1st Ave. and Wood St. in Whitehorse.

④ GLACIER BAY NATIONAL PARK AND PRESERVE, ALASKA

This 3.3-million-acre national park is distinguished by its massive glaciers, deep fjords, towering mountains, and majestic forests. It was established as a national monument in 1925 and a national park and preserve in 1980. There are 16 glaciers in the park, including 9 tidewater glaciers, some of which are retreating, that terminate in Glacier Bay. Huge chunks of ice occasionally break off the tidewater glaciers and crash into the water in a display called "White Thunder" by the Tlingit Indians. When Capt. George Vancouver first explored the region in 1794, much of the spectacular landscape was covered by a sheet of ice 20 miles wide and 4,000 feet thick. Since that time, many of the glaciers have retreated, creating the bay and exposing terrain that is being taken over by new plant life. A rain forest of spruce and hemlock trees now thrives at the southern end of the bay, which, just 200 years ago, was hidden under a mantle of ice. Cottonwood, fireweed, willow, moss, mountain avens, and alder have reclaimed land that was revealed as recently as 30 years ago. The vegetation attracts wildlife to the area, and today wolves, and black and grizzly bears prowl in the wilderness areas of the park and preserve. Harbor seals, sea lions, porpoises, and minke, humpback, and orca whales patrol the bay, and salmon, Dolly Varden and cutthroat trout, and halibut slice through the region's many rivers. The Fairweather Range, whose highest peak is 15,320-foot Mount Fairweather, runs along the western boundary

of the park. The best time to visit the park and preserve is from late May to mid-September. The park's visitor center is located at Bartlett Cove.

⑤ JUNEAU–DOUGLAS CITY MUSEUM, ALASKA

In 1880 Richard Harris and Joe Juneau discovered gold in what is now downtown Juneau. News of the find traveled quickly, and fortune-seekers flooded the area. A video of Juneau's mining past and displays of numerous artifacts offer visitors a look at daily life both inside and outside the mines. The museum also focuses on Juneau's Native American heritage. For thousands of years the area served as a fishing, trading, and hunting site for the Tlingit Indians. Artifacts and totem poles help show the Tlingits' early influence on the area. Located at 155 South Seward St. in Juneau.

⑥ SPATSIZI PLATEAU WILDERNESS PROVINCIAL PARK, BRITISH COLUMBIA

The approximately 2,600 square miles of this park in northern British Columbia offer evidence of the glaciers that carved its valleys, lakes, and steep-walled canyons eons ago. Snowfields and small glaciers are still found in the park. The Spatsizi Plateau, which stretches across the park's southeastern section, is marked by rolling upland and wide valleys where elevations range from 5,000 to 6,500 feet. Dominating the park's northwestern region are the Skeena Mountains, highlighted by 8,205-foot-high Mount Will. Dwarf birch, lodgepole pine, and trembling aspen thrive at mid-range elevations, whereas boggy areas and boreal forests of white and black spruce are found at lower elevations. American golden plovers and Smith's longspurs are among the 140 species of birds sighted here, along with beavers, wolves, caribou, moose, Arctic ground squirrels, wolverines, black bears, and grizzlies. Visitors may also spot mountain goats whose fur is colored red from rolling in exposed iron-oxide dust. Two major canoe routes take visitors along the Stikine and Spatsizi rivers. Located 122 miles southeast of Dease Lake off Hwy. 37.

Dwarf fireweed blooms along the rocky shore of Quill Creek, above, in Kluane National Park.

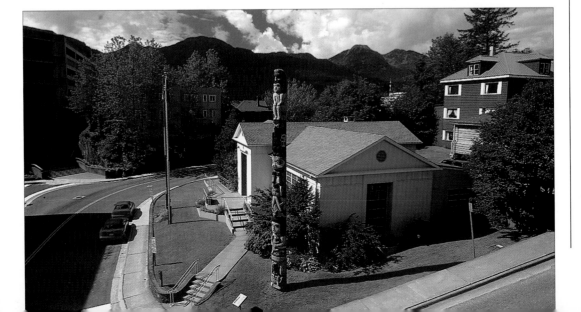

Visitors to the Juneau–Douglas City Museum are greeted by a colorful Haida totem pole, left. The museum provides an annotated map and a walking tour that takes in the totem poles and historic sites.

LAND OF FIRE

The hot-tempered goddess Pele continues to fuel the fiery explosions of Hawaii's volcanoes.

Alone among the ancient Hawaiian deities, Pele, goddess of volcanoes, is said to live to this day. She is still perceived, diaphanous, in the sulfurous mists of Kilauea and Mauna Loa, two of the world's most active volcanoes, both of which stand within Hawaii Volcanoes National Park on Hawaii, also known as the Big Island. Believers discern her form in the twisted contortions of pahoehoe lava that glisten jet black in the Pacific sun. They see her rise, a wraith in the fiery fountains that burst from the earth. At Volcano House Hotel, a lodge within the park, guests sometimes claim to see her form dancing in the flames of the hearth. Her presence haunts the Kilauea Iki Trail traversing Kilauea, which is warm underfoot from smoldering underground fires. Steam curls in ghostly vapors from crevices, and the smell of sulfur fills the air.

Before every major eruption there are sightings of Pele throughout the islands. To some people she appears as a lovely young maiden with a complexion like bright moonlight. Her hair is alternately as dark as the shade of night and as light as the intense point of a flame. Her robes

are divided into *kaao*, or fictional tales, and *moole-lo*, narratives based on actual events or people. The exploits of the gods are considered to be *moolelo*.

The most common version of the birth of Pele says she emerged as a tongue of flame from the mouth of Haumea, mother of all living creatures. She came from Kauihelani, a mystical land in the region of Kahiki, far beyond the western sea. One of Hawaii's oldest *oli*, or chants, begins:

The woman Pele comes from Kahiki,
From the land of Polapola,
From the ascending mist of Kane, from
     the clouds that move in the sky,
From the pointed clouds born at Kahiki.
The woman Pele was restless for Hawaii.

Some say she was born in Bora Bora, in Tahiti, or in Java, long, long ago. David Kalakaua, Hawaii's last king and a statesman, scholar, and world traveler, wrote in his 1888 book, *The Legends and Myths of Hawaii*, that Pele and her family were driven from Samoa in the 12th century and came to Hawaii. In his respected 1880's work, *An Account of the Polynesian Race*, Abraham Fornander noted similarities between Samoan goddess Fee and Pele.

Pele was a wanderer, and no land would hold her for long. She is said to have arrived in Hawaii by canoe with her brothers, sisters, and a retinue of other deities, and tried to establish a home on each of the Hawaiian Islands. Beginning with Niihau in the north, she would open a crater in the earth with her magic digging stick, releasing volcanic flames and rivers of molten lava. She stayed for a while on Maui, excavating the vast Haleakala Volcano, now the highlight of Haleakala National Park. Although the crater is dormant, its immense proportions—2,720 feet deep and 19 square miles in area—attract visitors to the park. Haleakala means "House of the Sun" in the Hawaiian dialect. The name comes from the story of the demigod Maui who captured the sun and placed it in the gigantic crater, promising to release the ball of fire only after it agreed to move slowly across the sky. A road through a section of the park leads to the Leieiwi and Kaalahaku overlooks, where visitors can get a view of the crater. More than 30 miles of hiking paths cut across the region, including the Halemaumau Trail, which begins at an elevation of 8,000 feet and descends to the crater floor. Daily horseback rides also go to the lunaresque crater.

Interestingly, even the conclusions of modern geologists do not contradict the ancient tale of the formation of the Hawaiian Islands. According to the plate tectonics theory, the Hawaiian Islands were created when the Pacific Plate moved northward across a hot spot in the submarine crust of

HISTORY THROUGH MOTION
Dancers, above, adorned with leis, prepare to tell their history through the hula. Once a dance performed only by men, the hula began as a form of worship practiced at religious ceremonies. The dance almost vanished in the 19th century when missionaries came to the islands and persuaded converts that the hula was heathen.

TEMPER TANTRUM
Overleaf: Erupting in one of its periodic outbursts, Kilauea volcano proves to believers that Pele continues to reside in its pit. Each year thousands of visitors brave sulfurous fumes and uneven terrain to approach the fiery giant, whose peak soars to 4,000 feet above sea level.

are the incandescent colors of the setting sun, her eyes sear the soul. There are Hawaiian families who trace their lineage to the tempestuous goddess, and others who claim her as *aumakua*, their guardian spirit. She is also affectionately called Madame Pele and Tutu Pele—Grandmother Pele.

PASSION AND POWER

The moment visitors see the Big Island from the air, they encounter the awesome power of Pele. The landing strips at the Keahole Airport on the Kona Coast are hacked out of lava, which stretches in bleak obsidian fields toward the volcanoes of Kohala, Hualalai, Mauna Kea, Mauna Loa, and Kilauea.

The stories of the goddess Pele, her romances and her exploits, form the body of Hawaii's vast store of unwritten literature—a mythology as rich, dramatic, and populated with deities as the Greek myths. Like their Hellenic counterparts, the Hawaiian gods are passionate, powerful, and full of cunning and malice. Their lives are entwined with those of the mortals, whom they rule with equal measures of compassion and callousness.

Because the Polynesians had no written language, the epic adventures of the gods and goddesses, the genealogies of kings and nobility, and tales of the great voyages of exploration and the settlement of the Pacific have been passed down through the generations in a rich tradition of poetic chants and dance. The stories, recounted by hula dancers bedecked with fragrant flowers, ferns, and vines,

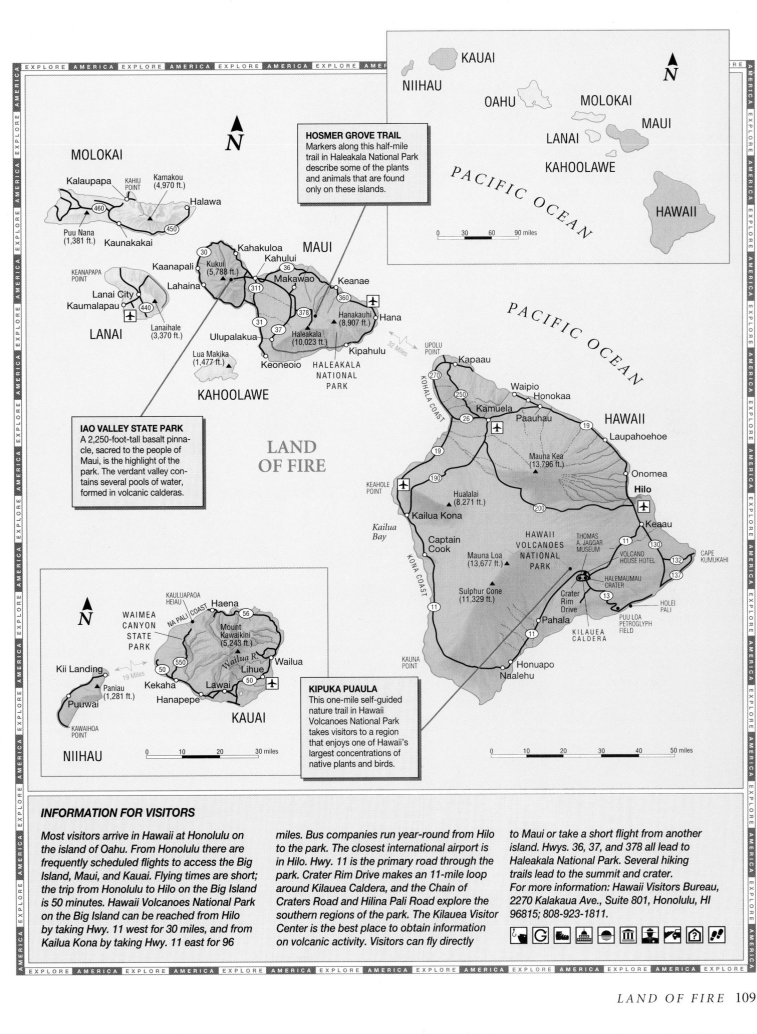

MOLOKAI

Kalaupapa
KAHIU POINT
Kamakou (4,970 ft.)
Halawa
460
450
Puu Nana (1,381 ft.)
Kaunakakai

HOSMER GROVE TRAIL
Markers along this half-mile trail in Haleakala National Park describe some of the plants and animals that are found only on these islands.

KEANAPAPA POINT
Lanai City
Kaumalapau
440
LANAI
Lanaihale (3,370 ft.)

MAUI

30
Kahakuloa
Kahului
Kaanapali
Kukui (5,788 ft.)
36
Makawao
311
Keanae
360
Lahaina
31
378
Hanakauhi (8,907 ft.)
Hana
37
Haleakala (10,023 ft.)
Ulupalakua
Kipahulu
Lua Makika (1,477 ft.)
Keoneoio
HALEAKALA NATIONAL PARK

KAHOOLAWE

IAO VALLEY STATE PARK
A 2,250-foot-tall basalt pinnacle, sacred to the people of Maui, is the highlight of the park. The verdant valley contains several pools of water, formed in volcanic calderas.

LAND OF FIRE

KAUAI
NIIHAU
OAHU
MOLOKAI
MAUI
LANAI
KAHOOLAWE

PACIFIC OCEAN

0   30   60   90 miles

HAWAII

PACIFIC OCEAN

32 Miles
UPOLU POINT
Kapaau
270
Waipio
Honokaa
250
KOHALA COAST
Kamuela
26
Paauhau
19
HAWAII
Laupahoehoe
Mauna Kea (13,796 ft.)
Onomea
Hilo
KEAHOLE POINT
190
19
Hualalai (8,271 ft.)
200
Kailua Kona
Keaau
Captain Cook
HAWAII VOLCANOES NATIONAL PARK
THOMAS A. JAGGAR MUSEUM
11
130
Mauna Loa (13,677 ft.)
VOLCANO HOUSE HOTEL
132
CAPE KUMUKAHI
Kailua Bay
Sulphur Cone (11,329 ft.)
HALEMAUMAU CRATER
137
KONA COAST
Crater Rim Drive
13
Pahala
KILAUEA CALDERA
HOLEI PALI
11
PUU LOA PETROGLYPH FIELD
KAUNA POINT
Honuapo
Naalehu

WAIMEA CANYON STATE PARK

KAULUAPAOA HEIAU
Haena
56
NA PALI COAST
Mount Kawaikini (5,243 ft.)
550
Wailua R.
Wailua
Kii Landing
50
Lihue
19 Miles
Kekaha
Lawai
50
Paniau (1,281 ft.)
Hanapepe
Puuwai
KAUAI
KAWAIHOA POINT

NIIHAU

KIPUKA PUAULA
This one-mile self-guided nature trail in Hawaii Volcanoes National Park takes visitors to a region that enjoys one of Hawaii's largest concentrations of native plants and birds.

0   10   20   30 miles

0   10   20   30   40   50 miles

INFORMATION FOR VISITORS

Most visitors arrive in Hawaii at Honolulu on the island of Oahu. From Honolulu there are frequently scheduled flights to access the Big Island, Maui, and Kauai. Flying times are short; the trip from Honolulu to Hilo on the Big Island is 50 minutes. Hawaii Volcanoes National Park on the Big Island can be reached from Hilo by taking Hwy. 11 west for 30 miles, and from Kailua Kona by taking Hwy. 11 east for 96

miles. Bus companies run year-round from Hilo to the park. The closest international airport is in Hilo. Hwy. 11 is the primary road through the park. Crater Rim Drive makes an 11-mile loop around Kilauea Caldera, and the Chain of Craters Road and Hilina Pali Road explore the southern regions of the park. The Kilauea Visitor Center is the best place to obtain information on volcanic activity. Visitors can fly directly

to Maui or take a short flight from another island. Hwys. 36, 37, and 378 all lead to Haleakala National Park. Several hiking trails lead to the summit and crater.
For more information: Hawaii Visitors Bureau, 2270 Kalakaua Ave., Suite 801, Honolulu, HI 96815; 808-923-1811.

Mauna Kea volcano, above, which has been dormant for 3,500 years, is home to Poliahu, one of Pele's arch rivals. Today skiers flock here in winter when the volcano's slopes are completely covered with snow.

DELICATE DETAIL

The colors of pahoehoe lava, right, paint the Hawaiian landscape in iridescent blue, gold, and pink. Scientists believe that the color is determined by the level of gas in the lava prior to eruption.

the earth, forming one tropical island after another. The Big Island, which is a million or so years old, is the youngest of the Hawaiian Islands.

A spate of eruptions since 1960 has added more than 1,300 new acres to the Big Island. Residents express sharply contrasting views of the whims of the volcanoes. When the lava flows force *malihini*, or newcomers, to flee their homes, they are often devastated by the loss. Old-time Hawaiians, however, display a surprising lack of bitterness, saying they are living here by Pele's grace, and that naturally she will try to take back what is hers.

Visitors to Hawaii Volcanoes National Park will often see flowers and other offerings wrapped in the leaves of the ti plant near recent lava flows and on the lip of Halemaumau Crater. Any Hawaiian who picks the red ohelo berries, a cranberrylike fruit, will offer the first fruit to Pele. The crimson ohia lehua blossom is also sacred to her. In a modern twist on the offerings, it is said that Pele has cultivated a taste for gin; this, too, is tossed into the crater—by the bottleful.

Even the National Park Service pays homage to Pele. Rangers who are thoroughly conversant with scientific terms and theories about volcanoes speak of the goddess without a trace of skepticism. Visitors to the Thomas A. Jaggar Museum, perched on the brink of the main caldera, are greeted by massive murals showing Pele and her various exploits, painted by the artist and historian Herb Kawainui Kane. Also on display are samples of the goddess' tears and hair: The teardrops are small globules and pendants of opalescent glass formed by the volcano, and the fine "hair," blond in color, is glass that has been ejected through vents in the volcano and spun by the air. Adjacent to the museum is the Hawaii Volcano Observatory, whose VAX computers can pinpoint the location of an earthquake anywhere on the island of Hawaii within 20 seconds of the first tremor.

IN SEARCH OF CREATIVE FIRE

At the park's visitor center a case displays chunks of lava that tourists took as souvenirs. Accompanying letters describe how misfortune, mayhem, and just plain bad luck pursued the visitors until they mailed the lava back. The nearby Volcano Village boasts a thriving colony of artists, potters, and glassmakers, whose works are on exhibit within the park. At Kilauea, hula dancers can sometimes be seen swaying to ancient rhythms as they recount stories about the gods.

A favorite tale among islanders speaks of Pele's marriage. She took as her husband the demigod Kamapuaa of Nahum who was a *kupua*, meaning he could change from a man into an animal. As a man he was handsome and young, bristling with power and energy. In his usual animal form, a pig, he was brutal and greedy for supremacy; while in his fish form he wielded power over the ocean. Pele detested Kamapuaa's swinish nature and taunted him for displaying the traits of a pig. He, in turn, had no patience for Pele's frequent outbursts. The marriage was tempestuous, and every islander was aware of the couple's titanic battles.

The violence escalated when Kamapuaa poured all the water he could gather from the rains and the sea into the pit of Pele. Horrible explosions rent the walls of the crater. Floods poured into the depths of the pit, so that Pele herself almost drowned. She was saved only by a spark of flame that was safeguarded in the breast of her mentor, Lonomakua, who had taught her the care of fire. After this close call, Pele's entire family rallied against Kamapuaa, fanning their fires into massive rivers of molten lava that surged toward him. As Kamapuaa fled to the sea, Pele hurled lava toward him, churning the waters to a full rolling boil. Her husband escaped by assuming the form of a fish that had a pig's snout and skin thick enough to endure the heat of the cauldron. The *humuhumunukunukuapuaa*, or trigger fish, with its piglike snout is Hawaii's state fish. Some people claim that this strange finned creature even grunts.

Pele had another romance—which also ended in disaster. In a dream state she traveled from her home to Ka Uluapaoa Heiau on the Na Pali Coast of Kauai, drawn there by hula drums and the beat of hundreds of dancing feet. She took the form of a beautiful woman and fell in love with the handsome chief, Lohiau. He was enchanted by her, and the two married. Later, wrongly believing that her sister, Hiiaka-i-ka-poli-o-Pele, and Lohiau were lovers, Pele incinerated the chief in lava. Lohiau was later revived and lived on Kauai with the gentle Hiiaka-i-ka-poli-o-Pele until he died of old age.

According to some stories, Pele's predominance was challenged by three dragon women of Kauai,

APPEASING THE GODDESS
A dancer dressed in traditional garb, below, performs a hula in honor of Pele. His lei will be offered in homage to the goddess.

Pele's eyes blaze with fire in a mural depiction of her, right, by local artist Herb Kawainui Kāne. The extensive mural is housed in the Thomas A. Jaggar Museum at Hawaii Volcanoes National Park. The cranberrylike ohelo berries, below, Pele's favorite food, are often left at the rim of the crater.

who did not recognize her. Angered, the fiery goddess danced a hula of the winds. She called the breezes that blow through drafty houses, then she summoned the winds that carry the rain and toss the waves into white-haired surf. Unleashing the great storms that scour the land and tear away the trees and houses, Pele reasserted her power.

Pele's arch enemy has always been Poliahu, the snow goddess of Mauna Kea, or the White Mountain, on the Big Island. Poliahu is known for her beauty and wit. Sometimes she puts aside her pristine mantle of snow and appears robed in sunlight to melt the ice into life-bearing streams that flow down the mountainsides, watering the valleys and plains where mortals reside.

Both Pele and Poliahu were fond of the Hawaiian sport of *holua*, riding wooden sleds with polished runners down mountain slopes packed with slippery grass. The two goddesses once met on a *holua* run south of Hamakua, although Pele at first concealed her identity. When Pele thought Poliahu was besting her in the sport, she fumed. The ground grew warm and Poliahu identified her rival. The enraged Pele called for fire fountains and lava rivers to flow over the cliffs, forcing Poliahu to retreat to the summit of Mauna Kea. Poliahu marshaled her forces, summoning wintry war clouds to snow on the lava, and freezing it into strange twisted shapes such as those seen on the slopes today. Powerful

Petroglyphs, right, found in the Puu Loa Petroglyph Field on the coast in Hawaii Volcanoes National Park, were carved between 500 and 700 years ago. Amid the petroglyphs are numerous small holes in the surface of the lava field, in which generations of fathers have placed pieces of their newborns' umbilical cords as offerings to the gods to ensure a long life for their offspring.

earthquakes shook the island during the battle between hot and cold, fire and ice.

Out of the tumult, the lava arch at Onomea—which collapsed in 1958—and the rugged apron of Laupahoehoe were created, along with the entire jagged lava coastline of the Big Island. Finally, weary of battle, Pele retreated to Kilauea, while Poliahu continued to abide in the snow swirls at the top of Mauna Kea. Today skiers crisscross the white slopes of the extinct volcano, and sailors guide their ships by its glistening dome. At 13,796 feet above sea level, Mauna Kea is the tallest peak in the Pacific. It enjoys such a pure, clear atmosphere that a complex of telescopes has been mounted up there, providing detailed astronomical information to scientists around the world.

Travelers with a four-wheel-drive vehicle can access a road outside of Hilo that leads to the summit of this volcanic peak. After passing through ferns and stunted trees in the lowlands, drivers climb at a steep grade—more than 8,000 feet in 15 miles. On the way up to the snow-covered peak, modern explorers traverse an eerie land where the earth is tinged red, and cinder cones instead of trees and plants jut upward. When the cloud that often shrouds Mauna Kea lifts, visitors are offered stunning vistas of the Big Island sprawled at its base. To the south, the rugged peak of Mauna Loa seems to float on a tranquil sea of cloud.

FROM MYTH TO HISTORY

Hawaii's volcanoes shaped the mythology and human history of this area—beginning with the early years of the ancient Polynesian settlements, the period of royal rule, and the myths that survive to this day. Indeed the volcanoes' presence is woven into the very fabric of life throughout the Hawaiian Islands.

In 1790, during King Kamehameha's campaign to unite the Hawaiian Islands into one nation, his

SIMMERING CAULDRON
Ferns soften the edges of the Halemaumau Crater, above, within the rim of Kilauea Caldera in Hawaii Volcanoes National Park. The craters fume regularly, and on Kilauea's east flank an eruption has been spewing lava since 1983. The latest volcanic information is posted every day in the visitor center.

cousin Keoua set out to make war on him. Keoua divided his army into three companies and allowed his soldiers to take their wives and children with them as they crossed the Big Island. As they passed close to Kilauea, it erupted, shooting out towering clouds of ash and steam and flashing red and blue light. Some people in Keoua's first company were killed instantly by burning cinders. Survivors, who reported difficulty breathing, fled as fast as they could. Those in the rear, closest to the volcano, escaped with minor injuries, probably because they were protected by prevailing winds. They ran ahead only to come upon the entire middle company of 80 men, women, and children—stock still. Some of them were locked in an embrace or clutched children, others stood nose to nose in the act of leave-taking. All were dead—perfectly mummified. Their bodies were never buried and their bones served as a warning to trespassers for many years. The groups' ghostly footprints can still be seen in the hardened ash along the Mauna Iki Trail within Hawaii Volcanoes National Park.

Scientists attributed the sudden deaths to a burst of sulfurous gas or a shower of embers. But the people of that time regarded the disaster as a sign that Pele had bestowed her blessing on King Kamehameha and favored his rule.

THE POWER OF FAITH

In the 19th century, the powerful hold that tradition and myth had on the people of the Hawaiian Islands was weakened through the unflinching efforts of one woman, Kapiolani, the daughter of the high chief of Hilo and wife of the high chief of Kona. An early convert and zealous proponent of Christianity, Kapiolani was determined to challenge Pele's ascendancy in Hawaiian religious life.

In December 1824, Kapiolani walked more than 100 miles from her home, crossing a landscape of hardened lava to the very lip of the summit caldera. At that time, the pit was surrounded by a surging lava lake, five miles in circumference and shot with fire fountains. It was a wild and fearsome spectacle. Onto this stage stepped the lone figure of Kapiolani. Having heard about Kapiolani's intentions, a huge throng of onlookers had assembled to prepare to mourn her almost certain death. She spoke: "If I

THE STEAMING SEA
As molten lava enters the sea on the Puna Coast of the island of Hawaii, below, it sends up steam clouds. Lava flows harden when they hit the sea, adding acres to the island every year.

Long as the lava light
Glares from the lava-lake,
Dazing the starlight;
Long as the silvery vapor in daylight
Over the mountain
Floats, will the glory of Kapiolani be
mingled with either on Hawa-i-ee.

PELE'S WORK GOES ON

Although there have been few major eruptions in recent years, some people say Pele is only biding her time. Even now, she is busy constructing a new site, the Hawaiian island called Loihi. The active underwater volcano, lying 20 miles southeast of Pahala on Hawaii, continuously pumps out lava—so hot that the flames, unquenched by water, light up the cold, dark depths of the ocean, 3,000 feet below the surface. The goddess' underwater furnace generates thousands of earthquakes a week. Her outpourings of lava are mounded in pillows and great black submarine hills. Scientists predict that in another 10,000 years Loihi will break through the waves into daylight. The people of Hawaii expect Pele will be around to see it happen.

SOLITARY LEI

A newly woven lei has been placed on the edge of Halemaumau Crater, left, in the hope that Pele will remain peaceful for another day.

GOLDEN GLINTS

Hardened pahoehoe lava, below, shows its distinctive ropy formation at Holei Pali, inside Hawaii Volcanoes National Park. In the fields of lava lie strands of golden volcanic glass that have been ejected through vents.

am destroyed then you may all believe in Pele, but if I am not, you must all turn to the true writings," by which she meant the Holy Scriptures.

According to witnesses, Kapiolani descended several hundred feet into the pit, to the black ledge over the lake of fire. Waves of magma assaulted the outcropping where she stood, and explosions of gas roared like cannons around her. The people trembled, but Kapiolani, without fear, stood at the edge of the inferno and prayed to Jehovah as steam billowed around her. Flames licked at her feet, strands of Pele's golden hair swirled wildly about her head. She defiantly ate Pele's sacred berries and threw stones into the lake of flames— but she was unharmed. Alfred, Lord Tennyson, wrote a long poem for Kapiolani. It reads in part:

NEARBY SITES & ATTRACTIONS

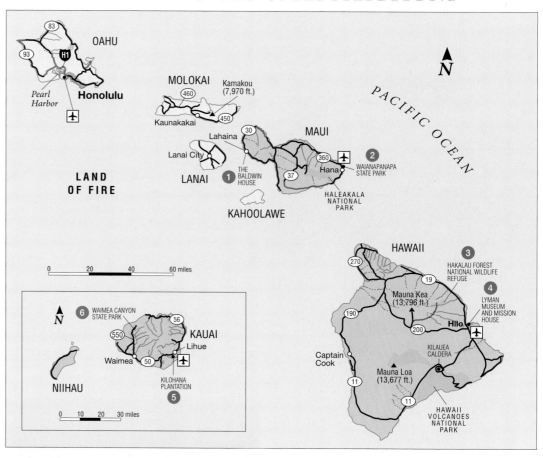

A red iiwi, right, hangs upside down from an ohia blossom in the Hakalau Forest. The iiwi's resplendent feathers were prized as ornamentation for the capes and helmets of the Hawaiian royal family.

① THE BALDWIN HOUSE, MAUI

The 19th-century home of missionary-physician Dwight Baldwin, his wife, Charlotte, and their eight children has been faithfully restored by the Lahaina Restoration Foundation. The two-story house where the Baldwins lived from 1835 to 1868 contains exhibits illustrating the important role Baldwin played in the history of the region. Originally from Durham, Connecticut, Baldwin is credited with being the

first doctor in Hawaii. He gained the Hawaiians' respect by treating the people of the islands of Molokai, Maui, and Lanai during the great smallpox epidemic of 1853. The two-foot-thick walls of his house are made of blocks of lava held together with a mortar of crushed coral. The inside doors are called Christian doors because the upper panels form a cross and the lower panels are carved in the shape of an open Bible. Of special interest inside the house are a wooden commode and an 1859 Steinway piano. Located in Lahaina.

② WAIANAPANAPA STATE PARK, MAUI

A nature trail circles two small lava tube caves that are ideal for amateur spelunkers to explore. According to Hawaiian legend, a princess, fleeing from her jealous husband, took refuge in the caves. There the princess hid until her husband discovered her hiding place and murdered her. Every spring opae shrimp overrun the water-filled caves, turning the water red, which, as the story goes, is a tribute to the princess. Another trail winds through a forest of pandanus trees and leads to a bay, fringed by a beach of black volcanic sand and stark lava arches. The bay is an excellent site for swimming and snorkeling, although caution should be exercised when the surf is heavy. Located three miles north of Hana off Hwy. 360.

pestles, and stone lamps. Also on display is a bust of Mark Twain that was carved from a piece of the monkeypod tree planted by the author himself in the tiny town of Waiohinu in 1866. The second floor of the museum houses exhibits on mineralogy and the geology and volcanology of the Hawaiian Islands. Located at 276 Haili St. in Hilo.

5 KILOHANA PLANTATION, KAUAI

This manor house-turned-museum was once the center of a 26,000-acre sugar plantation belonging to Gaylord Wilcox. In 1935 Wilcox had the lavish 16,000-square-foot Tudor-style mansion built for his wife, Ethel. The home has been faithfully restored with the help of family photographs and architectural records. Trails wind through a farm area of plantation cottages and gardens. Located two miles west of Lihue off Hwy. 50.

Hardened black lava formations contrast with clear blue water along the coast of Waianapanapa State Park, left.

3 HAKALAU FOREST NATIONAL WILDLIFE REFUGE, HAWAII

Hakalau, which means "many perches" in Hawaiian, is a dense forest that is home to many species of plants, insects, and birds that are found nowhere else on earth. The refuge's elevation ranges from 2,500 to 6,600 feet, and lower elevations receive some 300 inches of rain a year. A forest of koa trees, some of which have trunks six feet in diameter, is believed to be between 300 and 500 years old. Endangered bird species such as tiny akiapolaaus live in the refuge. Tall stands of ohia trees flower year-round and attract many species of insects that, in turn, serve as an important staple for native birds. The colorful species include scarlet iiwis, yellow-green amakihis, crimson apapanes, the endangered orange akepa and green Hawaiian creeper. Located 45 miles northwest of Hilo off Hwy. 200.

4 LYMAN MUSEUM AND MISSION HOUSE, HAWAII

Built in 1839, this New England–style building is the oldest remaining frame house on Hawaii, and was once the home of missionaries David and Sarah Lyman and their seven children. The house is listed on the National and State Registers of Historic Places. Floors, mantels, and doors are all made from native koa wood, and the furnishings date from the 1850's. Displays include Mrs. Lyman's diary, containing records of the region's earthquakes, volcanic eruptions, and tsunamis, which have become of great interest to geologists over the years. A three-floor museum, adjacent to the home, focuses on the cultural heritage and the natural history of the Hawaiian Islands. The third floor has exhibits of ancient tools, including fishhooks, mortars and

6 WAIMEA CANYON STATE PARK, KAUAI

Sculpted over time by the Waimea River, the Waimea Canyon gained the nickname Grand Canyon of the Pacific because of its yawning chasm painted in striking desert hues. The gorge's 2,857-foot-deep walls are colored in rich tones of red, orange, and brown, and draped with blue and mossy green vegetation. Hiking trails lead to the bottom of the canyon. Twenty species of native plants grow along the Iliau Trail, many of which are found only on Kauai. These include lobelias, mokihana, and iliaus—the green-leafed cousin of Haleakala's silversword plant. Waimea Canyon Lookout, at an elevation of 3,400 feet, and Kalalau Lookout, a 4,000-foot-high vantage point, offer sensational panoramic views of the canyon and the surrounding region. Located eight miles north of Waimea on Hwy. 550.

The Pacific sun illuminates the porch of the Baldwin House, above. During the mid-19th century, Dr. Baldwin's fees ranged from $3 for a simple diagnosis to $50 for treatment of a major illness.

Schoolhouse near Leadville, Colorado.

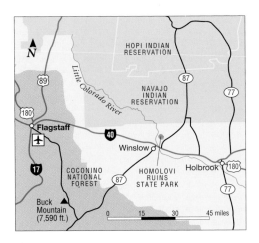

According to Hopi oral tradition, their ancestors emerged from the underworld through an opening in the Grand Canyon. Traveling northward, the *hisatsinom,* or "long ago people," stayed for a time at Homolovi before migrating in stages to the current Hopi settlements in present-day Arizona on what are called the First, Second, and Third mesas. Designated in 1986, Homolovi Ruins State Park preserves the remains of four Ancestral Pueblo villages, Homolovi I, II, III, and IV.

Homolovi, which means "place of little hills," is sacred to the Hopis, who continue to leave prayer feathers there for spirits of the windswept country. The half-dozen 14th-century pueblos within the 10,000-acre park provide visitors and archeologists with a unique opportunity to examine the rich Hopi heritage.

Researchers became aware of Homolovi in the early 1890's when Jesse Walter Fewkes of the Smithsonian Institution's Bureau of American Ethnology visited the Hopis and listened to the story of their origins. Fewkes returned to the area in 1896 and unearthed a portion of the legendary settlement, which he said was found to be exactly where the Hopi stories had placed it. Subsequent excavations at Homolovi have uncovered pit houses and pueblos dating from A.D. 600 to 1380.

The first inhabitants built pit houses in the gravel terraces overlooking the river. Rabbit, deer, and wild sheep bones excavated near the pits indicate that these early farmers supplemented their diet of corn, beans, and squash with fresh meats. An interpretive trail near the visitor center leads to a pit house open to the public.

Around A.D. 1260 Native American settlers constructed masonry pueblos of stone and mud, the first one being a 200-room pueblo called Homolovi IV. A series of pueblos sprang up about 20 years later within 15 miles of the town of Winslow.

The largest pueblo in the park is Homolovi II. Occupied from 1250 to 1380, the pueblo once boasted a population of 2,000. The community enclosed three plazas, and included two- to three-story buildings, with at least 1,200 rooms, some of which have been excavated and are open to the public.

UNIFIED COMMUNITY

Archeologists believe the clans that settled along the Little Colorado River were unified by a belief in kachinas—the ancestral spirits who visited the people during rain-making and other ceremonies. Today some Hopi and Zuni Pueblo people still practice the kachina religion, a form of ancestor worship that promotes harmony with nature and with each other.

Cotton was a valuable crop for the Homolovi people, who traded it for yellowware pottery and obsidian—a black volcanic glass used in making arrows. Cotton fibers also provided the material for ceremonial kilts, sashes, and burial shrouds.

The garments were woven in underground rooms called kivas, which were usually found in the plaza areas. Some of the kivas were painted with religious symbols and served as places for meetings and rituals. Homolovi II includes a reconstructed kiva, hearth, and ventilation tunnel.

The ancestors of the Hopi people etched pictures in stone such as the one above, which resembles an elk. Visitors can see examples of Hopi artwork near Homolovi IV in Homolovi Ruins State Park.

Among the numerous artifacts found at Homolovi are projectile points of chert, a rock similar to flint, and sandstone tools used for grinding corn. Since ritual objects were often made of petrified wood, archeologists believe that these people recognized petrified wood as a fossil of a living thing. More than 100 stone hoes were uncovered in an area east of the river, confirming that the people who lived here farmed the land from A.D. 300 to 1380.

While archeologists debate the reason that the Hopis had deserted the pueblos by 1380, numerous legends tell of the departure from Homolovi. One tale describes a night when a brilliant display of lights flashed across the northern sky. Following the event, the clan elders gathered in the kiva to discuss its meaning and concluded that it was a signal for them to continue the migrations that had brought them to the settlement many years before. Abandoning their homes, the Hopis began a journey north from their magnificent settlements at Homolovi to new homes on the mesas about 60 miles away.

FOR MORE INFORMATION:
Homolovi Ruins State Park, HCR 63, Box 5, Winslow, AZ 86047; 520-289-4106.

The low Arizona sun illuminates the ruins of Homolovi II, above. This village once served as a major trading center for the region.

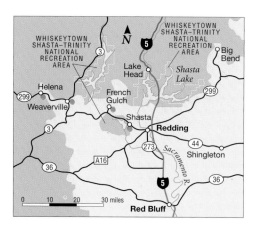

When whisperings of untold riches found in the highlands above the Sacramento Valley filtered down to the Sierra Nevada, prospectors swarmed to the northern mining district, setting up camps in every canyon, wash, and river basin from Cottonwood Creek to the Oregon border. Busy shantytowns mushroomed almost overnight and then withered just as quickly when deposits were mined out and the fortune seekers moved onward to the next claim.

A cluster of ghost towns in the Whiskeytown Shasta–Trinity National Recreation Area bespeaks the frenzied days of 1849. Tucked away in the mountainous backcountry, dusty roads and abandoned buildings whisper tales of deprivation, depravity, and riches.

According to Walter Colton, a chaplain in the area, prospectors were "a mixed and motley crowd—a restless, roving, rummaging, ragged multitude never before reared in the rookeries of man." They worked long hours under the worst conditions, lived in slapdash shelters, and subsisted almost exclusively on pork.

The miners' makeshift towns bore names such as Jackass Flat, Whiskey Creek, One-Horse Town, Muletown, and Bald Hills. But the gem of the northern mines was Shasta. It was here in 1848 that Pierson B. Reading sparked the northern gold rush. After he visited the James Marshall diggings in Coloma, Reading surmised that northern California might be just as rich in gold deposits. His hunch paid off, and by 1852 nearly $2.5 million worth of gold was being shipped out of Shasta County.

Joss House, above, a Taoist temple in Joss House State Historic Park recalls the days when Weaverville had a thriving Chinese community.

The city's runaway prosperity is scarcely evident today. After a fire destroyed the town in 1853, brick-walled, iron-shuttered buildings were put up to replace the wooden structures on Main Street. Vines have overtaken the ghostly ruins, and rusty iron shutters swing on paneless windows.

Visitors can also tour three historic graveyards, a restored jail, and a courthouse offering historical exhibits and period artworks. Although Shasta was the county seat, its decline began in 1857 when a wagon road bypassed the city in favor of the growing settlement at Weaverville.

Weaverville, which is not a ghost town, features brick buildings in its historic district, some with exterior spiral staircases, dating from the 1850's. Its showpieces include the Joss House, the oldest continuously used Chinese temple in California, and the J. J. Jackson Memorial Museum with its rich displays of antique firearms, historic photographs, and pioneer items. On the museum grounds, visitors can examine a steam-powered gold ore stamp mill and step inside a cabin used by a ditch tender for the nearby La Grange Mine.

LUCKY MINERS

Although some of the Trinity County mines operated into the second half of the 20th century, early prospectors thought there was too little gold to go around. Driven off a claim near Rich Bar by American miners, a group of French prospectors had the last laugh when their new settlement at French Gulch yielded the richest diggings in the area. Today visitors can stroll French Gulch's quaint streets and visit its well-preserved church and wooden and brick buildings.

While French Gulch is only part ghost town, tiny Helena is all but deserted. Listed on the National Register of Historic Places, the town's two stone edifices and handful of antique wooden structures are maintained by one family. The downstairs of one building served as a brewery, and the upstairs as a school by day and a brothel by night—an embodiment of the contradictions of the mining era.

FOR MORE INFORMATION:
California State Parks, P.O. Box 2430, Shasta, CA 96087; 916-225-2065.

The hulks of buildings from the mid-1800's, left, have been preserved in a state of arrested decay within Shasta State Historic Park.

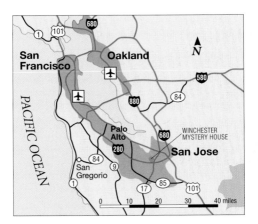

The Winchester Mystery House, above, displays the ornate and bizarre architectural and decorative whimsies of a woman who believed she was controlled by the spirits.

Nestled in the high-tech heart of Silicon Valley, a resplendent Victorian mansion in San Jose stands as a monument to age-old superstitions. Doors in the sprawling house open onto solid walls, passageways lead to nowhere, stairs head straight to the ceiling, and some of the skylights never open to the sky. Winchester Mystery House is the bizarre legacy of a woman whose life was governed by her belief in spirits.

In 1862 New England socialite Sarah Pardee married William Wirt Winchester, heir to the Winchester rifle fortune. Sara's life was touched by tragedy in 1866 when her infant daughter died weeks after her birth. In 1881 William died of tuberculosis. Devastated by her losses, Sarah consulted a Boston psychic who said that her troubles were inflicted by the souls of those who had been killed by Winchester guns. According to the medium, salvation rested in building a luxurious home for kindly spirits, who would protect Sarah from vengeful ones for as long as she kept adding to the house.

Shortly after she received this news, Mrs. Winchester left Connecticut and moved to California, where she bought a 161-acre farm in the Santa Clara Valley. In the hands of Sarah and her army of carpenters, the eight-room farmhouse grew into a rambling rabbit warren of oddly shaped rooms and twisting passageways.

The carpenters worked around the clock for 38 years, putting up walls and tearing them down again, according to Sarah's whims. At the time of her death in 1922, the mansion boasted 160 rooms, 10,000 windows, 2,000 doors, 47 fireplaces, and 6 kitchens. It had only three mirrors—because ghosts do not favor reflections.

Sarah spared no expense in her effort to placate the spirits, purchasing rare French, English, and Oriental tapestries, custom-made Lincresta wall coverings, hand-carved staircases, solid silver candlelight fixtures, and the finest glassware. A single Tiffany window cost her more than $1,500. In all, Sarah spent a total of $40 million renovating her house of the spirits.

The exotic mansion retains its strange beauty. Capped with scarlet-tiled roofs, the exterior features turrets and trellises, cupolas and cornices, porches, balconies, and jigsaw ornamentation.

To confuse the evil spirits, Sarah had sections of her mansion built in unusual proportions. In some places five-foot-high doorways lead to hallways only two feet wide. Cupboard doors open onto half-inch-deep spaces, doors open to walls, and some fireplaces have no chimneys. One staircase with 7 switchbacks and 44 steps climbs up a mere 9 feet.

A DIFFERENT ROOM EVERY NIGHT

Sarah's servants learned to accommodate her many eccentricities. Only her butler was allowed to see her face, and she fired two workers who accidentally saw her without a veil. Although the wealthy widow avoided company, she often entertained 12 invisible guests, serving them gourmet delicacies on solid gold plates.

At midnight Sarah would steal away to the Blue Room to commune with the spirits and devise a blueprint for the next day's construction project. Then she would play the organ for a couple of hours and retire to one of 40 bedrooms, choosing a different one each night to elude malevolent ghosts.

Despite her efforts to find eternal life, Mrs. Winchester died a recluse at the age of 82. In her will—with 13 parts and 13 signatures—she divided her remaining $4 million between a niece and a tuberculosis foundation. Local residents purchased the incredible house and opened it to the public the following year.

Visitors can tour 110 rooms in this fascinating museum. On display are Sarah's Tiffany glass collection and an assemblage of muskets, pistols, and early rifles made by arms manufacturers, including Colt, Remington, and Winchester.

Sarah believed in the mystical power of the number 13. Visitors will count 13 lights in the chandeliers, 13 panes in the windows, 13 cupolas in the greenhouse, and 13 drain holes in the sinks. Psychics claim the mansion is haunted, so guests should not be surprised if, when they wander off, they encounter the petite widow herself.

FOR MORE INFORMATION:
Winchester Mystery House, 525 South Winchester Blvd., San Jose, CA 95128-2588; 408-247-2000.

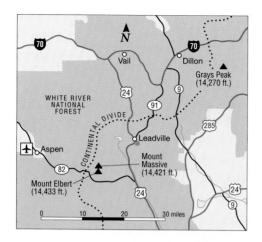

C rowded with hard-bitten, rowdy miners, gamblers, and entertainers, Leadville epitomized the legend of many Western mining towns in the late 1800's. Red-light districts beckoned wayfarers, seedy saloons did a swift business, and the scandalous affairs of mining magnates made national headlines. A host of colorful visitors added to the town's infamy, among them Kit Carson, Buffalo Bill Cody, and the notorious outlaw brothers, Frank and Jesse James. Wyatt Earp and his gunfighting partner Doc Holliday shot two men during their stay in Leadville.

Situated at an elevation of 10,430 feet, Leadville is the nation's highest incorporated city. The town is nestled in a valley at the bases of Mt. Elbert and Mt. Massive, Colorado's two tallest peaks. Early fortune hunters in Leadville, then called Cloud City, dismissed the heavy black sands they found there as worthless. In fact, the bustling town was lined with silver. Massive veins of the precious metal were discovered inside carbonate of lead during the late 1870's.

Established in 1878, Leadville soon became one of Colorado's richest cities, with mines yielding $82 million worth of silver between 1879 and 1889. Many Leadville natives became success stories, including the Unsinkable Molly Brown, a heroine of the *Titanic* disaster, and millionaire philanthropists Meyer Guggenheim and Charles Boettcher. The boomtown numbered nearly 30,000 citizens by 1880 and drew such famous figures as John Philip Sousa and early feminist Susan B. Anthony, who gave a speech on women's suffrage in a local saloon.

Although the town declined with the fall of silver prices in the 1890's, Leadville mines continued to produce lead, zinc, manganese, and molybdenum until the 1980's. During Prohibition entrepreneurs stepped up production of another valuable commodity: Leadville Moon was distilled in the old mine shafts and touted as one of the best whiskeys in the West.

WILDE SPREE

Flamboyant Irish author Oscar Wilde once came to speak to the miners, urging them to value gold as the raw material of fine art rather than as a source of wealth. The miners responded by leading him on a wild gambling spree through town, followed by a liquid dinner at the bottom of the Matchless Mine. Of the meal, the witty poet recounted, "Having got into the heart of the mountain, I had supper, the first course being whisky, the second whisky and the third whisky." Legend has it that Wilde scuttled the miners' plans to get him drunk by out-imbibing his hardscrabble hosts. The prospectors were so impressed by Wilde's joie de vivre that they made him an honorary member of the mining fraternity.

Wilde delivered his speech at Leadville's erstwhile hub of culture, the Tabor Opera House, which hosted a variety of performers ranging from the escape artist Harry Houdini to New York Metropolitan Opera singers. Built in 1879, the hall's elaborate foyer, huge stage, and velvet furnishings are still impressive in their faded elegance.

The opera house was erected by Horace A. W. Tabor, hero of Leadville's most dramatic rags-to-riches story. The onetime postmaster got his start in the mining business when he financially backed two German prospectors. In 1878 the pair hit a 30-foot-thick vein of silver. Two more good strikes and Tabor was a silver baron. His affair with the beautiful divorcée Elizabeth "Baby Doe" McCourt scandalized the nation. He divorced his wife, Augusta, in 1881 and eventually married his mistress.

In 1893 a crash in silver prices left Tabor penniless, and he died in 1899. Baby Doe, now poverty-stricken, lived in a little cabin at Tabor's Matchless Mine for 36 years, until she was found frozen to death in 1935.

Vestiges of the Tabor saga are seen throughout Leadville's historic district. Tabor House, where Horace and Augusta lived before he struck it rich, features small rooms crammed with Victorian furnishings, photo albums, dolls, and lamps. Tabor Grand Hotel and Tabor Opera House are monuments to the couple's fortune, while Baby Doe's shack north of town bears witness to her pitiful end. Inside the one-room cabin are Baby Doe's meager furnishings and the last known photographs of her.

Housed in a renovated Victorian schoolhouse, the National Mining Hall of Fame and Museum is a tribute to the industry that transformed Leadville into a mining mecca. Visitors can follow the evolution of mining techniques from gold panning and hand-drilling, to blasting and modern mining equipment. Items on display include a 23-ounce gold nugget retrieved from a mine near Leadville, artifacts from each of the 17 states that experienced significant gold rushes, and a life-size replica of an underground mine, complete with a mine-gauge track, ore cars, and chutes.

Every August Leadville celebrates the region's mining heritage by hosting Boom Days. Miners participate in a variety of events, ranging from drilling contests, using traditional and modern-day techniques, to the International Pack Burro Race. This unique contest pits teams of men against mules in a 28-mile race up and down 13,186-foot Mosquito Pass.

FOR MORE INFORMATION:
Greater Leadville Area Chamber of Commerce, P.O. Box 861, Leadville, CO 80461; 719-486-3900 or 800-933-3901.

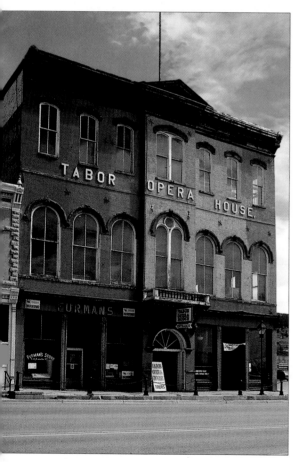

Except for its faded red-brick facade, the Tabor Opera House, above, looks much the same today as it did in the late 1800's.

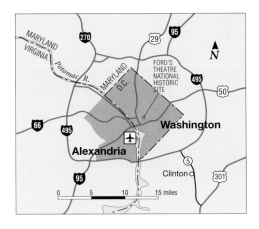

The presidential box where Abraham Lincoln was assassinated, right, is marked by several flags and a portrait of George Washington.

O n April 10, 1865, the day following Gen. Robert E. Lee's surrender, the streets of Washington bustled with crowds celebrating the end of the Civil War. Just five days later, the capital would mourn the tragic death of Pres. Abraham Lincoln, who was assassinated by acclaimed Shakespearean actor and supporter of the Confederacy John Wilkes Booth.

At about 8:30 p.m. on April 14, the Lincolns and their guests, Clara Harris and Maj. Henry Reed Rathbone, settled into their balcony seats to watch a performance of the comedy *Our American Cousin.* Partway through the third act, Booth entered the theater and climbed the stairway to the unguarded presidential box. At around 10:15 p.m. Booth shot the unsuspecting president in the head, and stabbed Major Rathbone in the arm.

Booth swiftly made his way to the stage and escaped. One unauthenticated story describes Booth dropping the 12 feet from the box to the stage and injuring his left leg. Some say he shouted out, "*Sic semper tyrannis!*" (Thus always to tyrants) as he landed. After the assassination witnesses told investigators that Booth headed out to the back alley where he mounted a horse and rode from the city.

Mortally wounded, the unconscious president was carried to a boardinghouse across the street from the theater. There he was tended throughout the night by doctors but to no avail. He drew his last breath at 7:22 the next morning.

FORD'S THEATRE TODAY

The house in which Lincoln died and the reconstructed state box where he was shot belong to Ford's Theatre National Historic Site. The theater, which had just been rebuilt in 1863, was gutted shortly after the assassination. Initial efforts to reopen it were met with such a public outcry that the government purchased the building and converted it into offices and storage space. In the 1930's the first floor became a museum and in the late 1960's the theater was returned to its 1865 appearance.

Red carpets and period decorations re-create the scene of Lincoln's assassination. Visitors can retrace Booth's route to the presidential box, furnished as it was in 1865, and peer down at the stage and gauge the distance Booth may have leapt.

Directly across the street, a cramped bedroom in Petersen House is furnished with period articles and a bed similar to the one Lincoln died in. Also preserved are the front parlor, in which Mary Lincoln and her son kept vigil, and the back parlor, where Secretary of War Edwin Stanton questioned eyewitnesses and issued the orders for Booth's arrest.

The threshold to the site of one of the most tragic episodes in American history, left, was used by both President Lincoln and his murderer, John Wilkes Booth.

Booth's small single-shot derringer is on display at the Lincoln Museum downstairs from the theater, along with his knife, his diary, and the suit worn by Mr. Lincoln that night. Visitors can read sections of Booth's diary describing his motives for committing the heinous crime. The actor was an outspoken advocate of slavery. "Because our cause, being almost lost," he wrote, "something decisive and great must be done."

A woman named Mary Surratt was also involved in the plot, along with her son John, and David Herold, George Atzerodt, and Lewis Powell; all were hanged on July 7, 1865. Booth was shot on April 26, 1865, either by a soldier or by his own hand, when Federal troops raided the farm in Virginia where Booth and Herold were hiding in a drying shed.

FOR MORE INFORMATION:

Ford's Theatre National Historic Site, 511 10th St. NW, Washington, DC 20004; 202-426-6924.

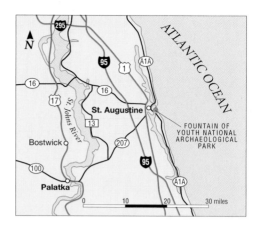

Hearing rumors of an island in the Bahamas where a miraculous fountain flowed that promised eternal youth for anyone who drank its waters, Juan Ponce de León set off in March 1513 for the island of Bimini. Leading a privately outfitted expedition from Puerto Rico, the Spanish explorer never found a fountain of youth, but his quest changed the face of the area he named Florida.

A month after setting out on his voyage of discovery, Ponce de León landed on the coast of North America. The earth was covered in spring blooms and so he named the new territory La Florida, or Land of Flowers. Going ashore to take possession, the explorer came upon an Indian village near a glistening spring. Believing he had discovered the mythical fountain of youth, Ponce de León drank from the spring and filled the ship's casks with the water. Next he laid out a large cross near the fountain to signify Spanish possession of the territory.

The Spanish crown eventually sent the country's most celebrated adventurer, Don Pedro Menéndez de Avilés, to explore and colonize the territory. Menéndez first sighted the coast on the Feast Day of St. Augustine on August 28, 1565. Eleven days later, with banners flying and trumpets blaring, he and his 600 soldiers captured the ancient Timucuan Indian village of Seloy and renamed it St. Augustine, America's first permanent European settlement.

Vestiges of the ancient Spanish colony still survive in St. Augustine. Visitors can tour an authentic 17th-century Spanish fort and take a sip of water from the fountain that Ponce de León believed to be the spring of eternal youth.

A cross made of coquina stones, a native shell-stone formation, was uncovered in 1868 near the fountain and is now protected within the park grounds of the Fountain of Youth. Measuring 14-by-9½ feet, the Latin cross lies along the ground with its staff in an east–west line. It has 15 stones studding the staff and 13 in the cross beam, signifying the year 1513 in which it was planted by Ponce de León.

Ancient Native American burial grounds, discovered by orange tree planters in 1934, are located nearby. Excavations have uncovered more than 100 skeletons from both prehistoric and Christian graves. Skeletons and pottery fragments reveal human occupation in the area from as far back as 1000 B.C., suggesting that the spring had been used for thousands of years.

Just south of the park on the grounds of Mission de Nombre de Dios, visitors can tread on the spot where Menéndez landed. Franciscans established a mission there in 1572 to convert Native Americans to Christianity. A 208-foot-high cross, erected in 1965, marks the place where the first mass was held in the New World 400 years earlier. Every September 8 cassocked priests and costumed settlers reenact the historic event.

Once established, the fledgling colonial outpost was garrisoned to protect Spanish treasure vessels bound for Europe. As English colonies expanded to the north, assaults on St. Augustine increased in violence and in number. After the pirate Capt. John Davis pillaged St. Augustine in 1669 and killed 60 inhabitants, the colony received Spain's permission to build a stone fortress to defend the town.

STANDING GUARD

The Castillo de San Marcos, which took 23 years to build, was a formidable deterrent to would-be attackers. In 1740 the massive fort withstood a 27-day British siege. The fort still looms over Matanzas Bay today. Complete with 10-foot-thick walls, jutting bastions, and a moat, the limestone fort reverberates with the sound of explosions on weekends, when costumed interpreters don period military garb and fire the ancient cannons.

Visitors to St. Augustine can take in the sights from aboard open-air trolleys or a horse-drawn carriage along the cobbled streets of the historic district. The Gonzalez-Alvárez House, built in the 1720's, is St. Augustine's oldest residence. A museum housed within its elegant colonial walls displays furnishings from the Spanish, British, and American periods of this colorful city's history.

In the restored Old Spanish Quarter, flowering hibiscus and bougainvilleas spill over the coquina walls of restored Spanish Colonial houses. Interpreters dressed in period costumes demonstrate 18th-century colonial trades in a general store, and in blacksmith, weaver, spinner, and carpenter

The sign beside the arched entrance to the Fountain of Youth, above, a national archeological park, welcomes visitors to "the first chapter [of] our U.S. history." Among the park's many attractions are life-size moving models that recreate Ponce de León's historic landing.

shops. Houses and workshops painted in shades of alabaster, beige, pastel pink, and blue crowd the narrow streets.

A statue of Ponce de León, across from the Old Market, honors the explorer whose quest for eternal youth led to the planting of a new Spanish colony. Ponce de León failed to discover the elixir of life but his journeys have earned him immortality in the annals of history. Furthermore he did live longer than many of his contemporaries: he was 61 years old when he was mortally wounded by a poison arrow during a battle with Seminole Indians near Charlotte Harbor in Florida.

FOR MORE INFORMATION:
St. Johns County Visitor and Convention Bureau, 88 Riberia St., Suite 250, St. Augustine, FL 32084; 904-829-1711 or 800-OLDCITY.

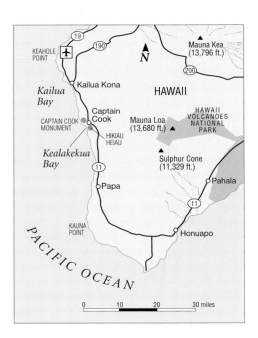

Travelers to Kealakekua Bay can see the ruins of the Hikiau Heiau temple site, above.

W hen he first glimpsed the black volcanic shores of Kealakekua Bay from the deck of the *Resolution* on January 17, 1779, Capt. James Cook had no inkling that he would die on this pebbled beach. A seasoned traveler, Cook had explored enough Pacific islands to recognize that the Polynesians canoeing toward him were genuinely friendly. Singing and waving, they rushed to the bay by the thousands, greeting Cook and his men with gifts of breadfruit, coconuts, and hogs. But five weeks later the *Resolution* would set sail without its captain.

What Cook did not know was that his arrival coincided with the celebration of the annual *makahiki* festival in honor of Lono, a benevolent god. Hawaiian legends prophesied that one day Lono would reveal himself from a floating island covered in trees. The ragged sails and timber masts of Cook's ships, the *Discovery* and the *Resolution,* fitted this description and Cook was mistaken for the long-awaited deity. Ushered ashore by a chief and four officials, Cook was escorted to a platform made of flat stones atop high wooden scaffolding. The temple, dedicated to Lono, was decorated with the skulls of sacrificial victims.

CELEBRATION FIT FOR A GOD
Cook and his men were honored with a feast of baked pig, breadfruit, vegetables, and *awa,* a mild narcotic made from the root of a pepper plant. Following the meal, the islanders prostrated themselves before

The Captain Cook Monument, right, stands on the site of Cook's landfall in Hawaii.

the 180-member crew, shared the bounty of their table, and even allowed parts of the temple to be dismantled and used for firewood. The crew basked in the adulation for more than a fortnight and tolerated their hosts' frequent pilfering of metal scraps and iron tools from their ships.

The two ships left Kealakekua Bay on February 4 and set sail to the north. Several days later, the winds rose to gale force and damaged the *Resolution*'s foremast. Because it was impossible to repair the ship while at sea, Cook made the decision to head back to Kealakekua Bay.

But Cook's second coming was ill timed. By February 11 the *makahiki* season had waned and Lono's reign had all but ended; furthermore, the Polynesians were weary of feting the men who had eaten most of their pigs and sweet potatoes. The tensions between the Hawaiians and the sailors came to a head when a small boat was stolen from the *Discovery*.

Cook led an armed party ashore to seize a Hawaiian chief as ransom for the vessel. To protect Cook as his party dragged the chief to the water's edge the crew fired their muskets, but the gunfire only provoked the islanders to anger. Cook realized that they would not be able to take the chief hostage without killing some people, and tried to leave. But the crowd surrounded and began to throw rocks at him. When Cook turned his back to signal a cease-fire, he was stabbed in the neck, then clubbed to death in the shallows. Four sailors were also killed during the fight.

Cook's body was placed on an altar as a gift to the gods, then cut into pieces—one of which was wrapped in a cloth and given to the horrified English crewmen. On February 22 the two ships hoisted anchor and sailed to the open sea.

"Thus left we Kealakekua Bay," wrote Lt. James King, "a place become too remarkably famous, for the very unfortunate, & Tragical death of one of the greatest Navigators our nation ever had."

A modest plaque, visible at low tide, marks the place where the 50-year-old captain fell on February 14, 1779. A grander monument to the navigator was erected by his countrymen in 1874 at the northern end of the bay. The 27-foot white obelisk can be seen from the tour boats that travel down the coast from Kailua.

At the southern end of the bay, visitors can walk up a stone path to Hikiau Heiau, the sun-baked temple platform where Cook was honored by his hosts. Napoopoo Beach Park's transparent waters are a haven for swimmers and an abundance of sea life thrives in the ocean water and cool springs.

Although Captain Cook never ventured beyond the bay, modern-day travelers can explore the countryside, where they will see glossy-leafed coffee trees, little box houses perched on the edges of hillsides, and townsfolk vending leis and shell jewelry.

At the Sunset Coffee Cooperative Mill, north of the bay, coffee lovers can sample Kona beans. The Pu'uhonua o Honaunau National Historical Park, situated south of Napoopoo, encompasses the reconstructed Hale-o-Keawe temple, where 23 ruling Kona chiefs were interred and deified between 1650 and 1818. Wooden figures of gods still face menacingly out to sea.

FOR MORE INFORMATION:
Hawaii Visitors Bureau, 250 Keawe St., Hilo, HI 96720; 808-961-5797.

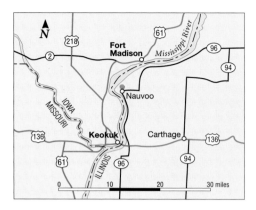

O n February 9, 1846, one of the longest and largest migrations in American history began in Nauvoo, Illinois, and crossed a 1,400-mile route to Salt Lake City, Utah. Over the next 20 years some 80,000 people undertook this arduous journey, called the Mormon Trail, in wagon trains. The voyage westward was especially painful for them because they had to leave behind their homes in Nauvoo, the treasured Zion that they had worked so hard to build on the banks of the Mississippi River.

The Mormons had arrived in Nauvoo six and a half years before, after fleeing religious persecution in Ohio and Missouri. Under the leadership of Joseph Smith, founder of the Church of Jesus Christ of

The 1844 Stoddard Home and Tin Shop, above, which belonged to the tinsmith Sylvester Stoddard, is one of two dozen restored buildings in Nauvoo's historic district.

Latter-Day Saints, the settlers built a thriving community on the site of the town of Commerce. Smith named it Nauvoo, after the Hebrew word for beautiful place.

Between 1839 and 1846 Nauvoo's population swelled to more than 12,000, rivaling Chicago as the largest city in Illinois. As the Mormons' fortunes grew so did their political power. In 1844 Smith announced his candidacy for the U.S. presidency. This act, along with rumors that he practiced polygamy (Smith's support for polygamy was not made public until 1852), created tensions both among Mormons and non-Mormons. When an anti-Mormon newspaper press in Nauvoo was destroyed, Smith and several other Mormons were jailed in nearby Carthage City. On June 27, 1844, an angry mob attacked the jail and murdered Smith and his brother Hyrum.

It had become clear to the Mormons that it was time to move on. Brigham Young took up the reins of leadership and organized a mass exodus of followers to Utah to find freedom from persecution.

NAUVOO HISTORIC SITE
Many of the buildings in Nauvoo, which date back to the 1840's, have been faithfully restored or reconstructed. The Joseph

Smith Historic Center offers tours of the 1803 log house where Smith lived with his wife, Emma Hale, and the gravesite where Emma, Joseph, and Hyrum are buried. The Joseph Smith Mansion, which was built in 1843 as the leader's permanent residence, is situated across the street from the log house. The Brigham Young Home has also been restored. After he led the Mormons west to Great Salt Lake, Young served as governor of the territory of Utah.

The glory of Nauvoo was its majestic Mormon temple fashioned from gray limestone, once the largest structure west of Cincinnati. A small replica sits at the Temple Site in Nauvoo. All that is left of the original are three hand-carved sunstones, from the tops of the columns, and two moonstones, which sat at the column bases. One of the capitals is in Nauvoo State Park; the other is on exhibit at the Smithsonian Institution's Museum of American History, in Washington, D.C.

FOR MORE INFORMATION:
Nauvoo Chamber of Commerce, State Hwy. 96, Box 41, Nauvoo, IL 62354; 217-453-6648.

The statue of Joseph and Emma Smith, above, stands in Nauvoo. Though it is thought that Smith wed several times, Emma was the only woman he acknowledged publicly as his wife.

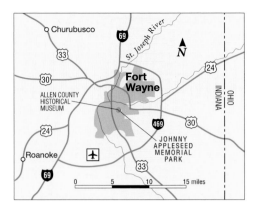

He appeared out of nowhere in northern Pennsylvania in the 1790's, preaching an obscure theology called Swedenborgianism and planting apple seeds all along the frontier from the Alleghenies to central Ohio and beyond. This passionate planter, whose real name was John Chapman but who was called Johnny Appleseed, was regarded with wary admiration by the settlers in the wild forested region northwest of the Ohio River. Today almost every community in America claims at least one apple tree believed to have descended from the seeds planted by this folk hero. But the community of Fort Wayne has a particular claim on Johnny Appleseed: he died here in 1845 at the age of 71. His grave is located in Archer Cemetery within the confines of the Johnny Appleseed Memorial Park.

A HERO'S LIFE STORY

John Chapman was born in Leominster, Massachusetts, on September 26, 1774. The details of his early life are unknown, but he is believed to have embarked on his nomadic life after a failed love affair with a woman named Dorothy Durand. Durand's parents disapproved of the match, and their daughter died of a broken heart after being cruelly separated from her lover. Legend has it that Chapman planted apple blossoms on the grave of his young lover. An apparently well-educated man, Chapman is said to have attended Harvard as a theological student. It may have been there that he first learned about the teachings of Emanuel Swedenborg, an 18th-century scientist and philosopher. Swedenborg's tenets asserted the divine nature of man and the belief that an optimistic view of life was essential to a person's well-being.

Legend has it that Chapman would arrive in a town dressed in an old coffee sack with holes cut out for his arms and legs, a tin pan on his head, and garlanded with dog fennel, which he believed warded off malaria. He was said to have always carried a large bag of apple seeds in a leather sack. Some contemporaries remembered him paddling up and down the Allegheny and Wabash rivers in two canoes lashed together, his bags of apple seeds beside him.

Often Chapman would barter his seeds for food before he began to preach a message that came "right fresh from heaven." Although his meaning was lost on many frontiersmen who were more concerned with their day-to-day existence, Chapman's sincerity earned their respect and they accepted his apple seeds, obtained from cider presses in western Pennsylvania.

Chapman planted seeds instead of making grafts because he believed grafts harmed the trees. His planting technique was efficient: he would clear a 30-square-foot area, girdle the surrounding trees, and build a protective brush fence before planting the seeds in the middle of the enclosure.

Chapman's sympathy for living things was legendary. Often settlers would tell how they heard him talking to animals and birds as he approached their settlement. Legend says that he once accidentally killed a snake with a scythe while clearing a plot of land and, years later, he would break down and cry whenever he recounted the tale. At one point, Chapman even had a pet wolf, which he had rescued from a trap, that followed him like a dog.

A simple gravestone, above, in Johnny Appleseed Memorial Park in Fort Wayne, marks the burial place of one of America's most beloved heroes, Johnny Appleseed.

After Chapman's death due to exposure in 1845, a controversy arose concerning the location of his grave, as two local groups looking to establish a memorial site in his name claimed he was buried in different cemeteries. After years of debate, those who advocated the Archer Cemetery in Fort Wayne as John Chapman's final resting place won out, and in 1949 the Johnny Appleseed Memorial Park was dedicated there in an elaborate ceremony.

Visitors to the 42-acre park, which stretches from Coliseum Boulevard to Parnell Avenue, can read about Chapman's life on a marker and visit his grave. The park's rolling green knolls offer an oasis to travelers who picnic among the trees, fish in the river, and enjoy its campgrounds. Walkers and bicyclists take advantage of the picturesque greenway that extends for three miles along the riverbank. The park is the site of a yearly festival, held in September, which celebrates the legend of Johnny Appleseed. The fair features cooking and handicrafts of the 19th century. Craft demonstrations and authentic reenactments of pioneer activities transport visitors back to the early days of Fort Wayne.

The pioneer days are also remembered at Fort Wayne's Allen County Historical Museum, located on East Berry Street. Some of the exhibits focus on the region's Native American heritage and the three forts that were built around present-day Fort Wayne when Europeans explored, traded, and then settled the Indiana frontier. A special exhibit looks at the Wabash and Erie Canal and the booming railroad industry around Fort Wayne.

A detailed model of a Miami Indian village is on display in the museum. The Miamis descended from the first Americans who came to the region following the retreat of the glaciers about 10,000 years ago. They were known to make raids on enemies as far away as New England and the Carolinas. Their removal by the U.S. government to reservations in the early 1800's was negotiated by Chief Jean Baptiste Richardville, a French-Miami businessman who was one of the wealthiest men in Fort Wayne in the early 1800's. His home is preserved by the Allen County/Fort Wayne Historical Society. The house is located near the corner of Old Trail and Bluffton Road.

FOR MORE INFORMATION:
Fort Wayne Convention and Visitors Bureau, 1021 South Calhoun St., Fort Wayne, IN 46802; 219-424-3700.

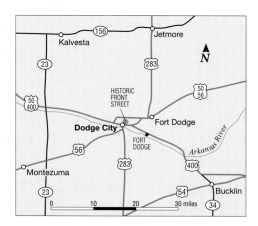

The landmark 1880 Home of Stone, above, constructed of limestone quarried north of Dodge City, once belonged to boot maker and rancher John Mueller.

When the profit-minded merchants of Dodge City prepared for the arrival of spring cattle drives in 1877, they slashed the prices of whiskey and cigars and let it be known that they advocated a policy of live and let live. Their hands-off attitude drew a stampede of cattlemen, and the small cow town quickly turned into an explosive place where rabble-rousers settled vendettas on the streets and the six-shooter stood in for the law. It was up to two-gun marshals such as the Masterson brothers and Wyatt Earp to rein in the rowdy cowboys in the wickedest city in America.

The Santa Fe Railroad, which followed the general route of the old Santa Fe Trail from Missouri to New Mexico, gave birth to Dodge City. Just outside of town, a 143-acre tract of land preserves the largest continuous stretch of Santa Fe Trail ruts. These deep swales, gouged into the hard earth by countless wagon trains that passed this way between 1821 and 1880, are still visible more than 100 years later.

The first building to be constructed in what was to become Dodge City was a three-room sod house belonging to a rancher by the name of Henry L. Sitler. A year later the tracks of the Santa Fe Railroad were laid nearby, and the town consisted of tents and hastily thrown together wooden buildings that included two general stores, a restaurant, blacksmith's shop, dance hall, and—the hot spot in many frontier towns—a saloon, which was set up right next door to Sitler's house.

The town served as a supply center for buffalo hunters and soldiers at nearby Fort Dodge, which had been built in 1865 to protect wagon trains and the U.S. mail from attacks by Native American tribes in the region. Dodge City grew rapidly with the thriving buffalo trade; hunters earned up to $100 a day, and the hide yards along the railroad tracks were piled high with stacks of buffalo skins. Mass slaughter decimated herds that, only a few years before, had been so large they held up trains for five or six hours as they crossed the tracks. By 1876 Texas longhorn cattle became the mainstay of the town's economy. During the next 10 years, more than 5 million head of cattle were driven into Dodge City, where many of them were loaded onto trains and shipped East to slaughterhouses.

RED LIGHT DISTRICT

At the end of a day's hard work, tuckered-out cowboys washed away the trail dust with wine, women, and song in what has been referred to as the beautiful bibulous Babylon of the Western frontier. Card-sharps vied for hefty poker pots at the local saloons, which featured musical shows from solo piano players to singers and a five-piece orchestra. When trainmasters took to carrying their red caboose lamps on visits to the ladies of the night, the area of town where the brothels were located was dubbed the Red Light District.

In the early days, the town had two Front Streets, one on either side of the railroad tracks. The law prohibiting the carrying of firearms in the city was enforced on the north side of the rails; the south side, however, was fair game. Cowboys were not keen to relinquish their weapons on either side of the tracks. The town marshal Ed Masterson was shot to death while trying to disarm a pair of drunken cowboys in 1878. Later that year, a cowboy who opened fire outside the Lady Gay Saloon, was gunned down by two Dodge City lawmen, Wyatt Earp and Ed's brother Jim Masterson.

The most famous Masterson, William Barclay, or Bat, was in and out of Dodge City from 1872 and became county sheriff in 1877. The dapper lawman wore a tailor-made suit, smart bowler hat, and two big silver-mounted, ivory-handled pistols. He was nicknamed Bat for his habit of striking troublemakers on the head with a cane.

As the leader of a clan of lawmen, Bat was kept busy restoring a semblance of law and order to Dodge City. In 1878 alone, Bat captured the elusive Kinsley train robbers, chased horse thieves, warded off Indian attacks, and brought in the killer of the beautiful singer Dora Hand.

One of Dodge City's most infamous residents was John "Doc" Holliday, a well-born dentist and gunfighter from Georgia who lent the law a hand when needed. Doc's friend Wyatt Earp called him "the most dangerous man alive"—and no one had reason to contradict him.

As Assistant City Marshall from 1876 to 1879, Wyatt Earp was regarded as one of the most efficient lawmen Dodge City had ever seen. Recruited by Mayor George Hoover to tidy up the town, the veteran gunslinger sent only one unfortunate criminal to Boot Hill, the town cemetery where outlaws were buried with their boots on.

Old Dodge City is located at the foot of Boot Hill. It brings back Front Street's exciting past with a mixture of authentic and replica houses, storefronts, and saloons. A reconstructed sod house, similar to the one owned by Sitler, demonstrates how early residents lived, and the original Hardesty House displays the elegant Victorian interiors favored by the Dodge City gentry of the 1880's.

Visitors can tour a one-room schoolhouse, examine a Santa Fe Railroad engine, and visit the original 1865 Fort Dodge jail. Dodge City is open year-round, and summer reenactments of shoot-outs, nightly variety shows at the Long Branch Saloon, stagecoach rides, and chuck wagon dinners bring the frontier days to life.

FOR MORE INFORMATION:
Dodge City Convention and Visitors Bureau, P.O. Box 1474, Dodge City, KS 67801; 316-225-8186.

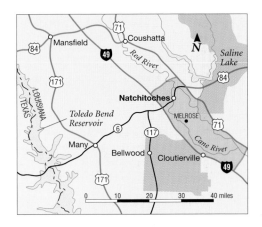

Marie-Thérèse Coin Coin was by any measure a very remarkable woman. But in Cane River country—the thin 35-mile-long valley that runs between Natchitoches and Cloutierville in central Louisiana—she has achieved near mythic stature. She was the matriarch of a Creole dynasty that nurtured the vibrant community centered in Isle Brevelle.

In 17th- and 18th-century Louisiana, the term *Creole* was used to describe New World slaves and free people of color who were known as *les gens de couleur libre.* Some of these people came from Haiti, the Caribbean, and South America. Others were slave children set free by their European fathers. Still others were slaves who bought their own freedom or were given it by their masters in return for some service. Many were skilled craftsmen, artists, businesspeople, educators, property owners, and even slave-owning planters such as Marie-Thérèse Coin Coin.

CREOLE DYNASTY
Coin Coin was born a slave in 1742 in the household of Louis Juchereau de St. Denis, founder of Natchitoches (Nak-i-tish), the first European settlement in Louisiana in 1714. After St. Denis and his wife died, Coin Coin, who was now the mother of four children, was sold to Claude Thomas Pierre Metoyer. Four years later she was freed by him and, while she never married Metoyer, she bore him 10 children. Metoyer deeded Coin Coin a small parcel of land along the Cane River and later she was granted more land on nearby Old River, in the name of the Spanish king. In time, this tenacious woman bought the freedom of all her mulatto (mixed race) children, as well as two of her four black children.

This vibrant painting, right, by the American Creole artist Clementine Hunter, depicts life on a cotton plantation in Louisiana.

Intricate wrought-iron balconies, above, grace the French Creole–style buildings in historic Natchitoches.

Coin Coin and her offspring, along with their slaves, cleared the land, planted tobacco and indigo, raised cattle, and became one of the richest black families in America. Their Cane River property, called the Yucca Plantation (later named Melrose), is now a National Historic Landmark. Visitors to the nine-building complex can often see artisans at work spinning, weaving, and making lye soap. Paintings by Clementine Hunter, the celebrated 20th-century Creole artist who was a maid at Melrose, are on view in African House, a Congo-style building that once served as a jail.

Coin Coin's son, Nicolas Augustin Metoyer, became the leader of the Creole community that grew up around Isle Brevelle. His birthday, January 22, is recognized by the federal government as Creole Heritage Day. St. Augustine Church, which Augustin commissioned his brother Louis to build in 1803, is the first, and possibly the only, Catholic church in the country founded and financed by people of color.

The unique Creole architectural style is reflected in many of the plantation homes that overlook the winding Cane River and the buildings in Natchitoches' 33-block Historic District. The Museum of Historic Natchitoches on Washington Street houses a fascinating display on Creole architecture. At the museum visitors can learn more about Natchitoches' founder St. Denis, who founded and commanded nearby Fort St. Jean Baptiste. A full-scale replica of the fort has been built on its original site in the city, and the staff dresses in period costume.

Beau Fort Plantation, a classic Creole-style home built in the 1790's, is located just south of Natchitoches. It features an 84-foot gallery and a covered courtyard. Farther downriver is Oakland Plantation, the site where cotton was first planted in the state of Louisiana. Many of the Cane River plantations are open to the public.

FOR MORE INFORMATION:
Louisiana Office of Tourism, 1051 North 3rd St., Baton Rouge, LA 70802; 504-342-8100.

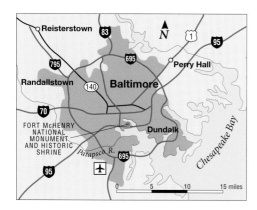

On September 13, 1814, during the latter stages of the War of 1812, 20 British warships weighed anchor about two miles below Fort McHenry. The boats began a shelling that continued all day long and into the night. The limited-range American guns were unable to defend the fort against the British ships, and for 25 hours the bombardment went on, expending some 1,800 bombs, rockets, and shells. Despite the spectacular pyrotechnics and the terrifying shrieks emitted by the Congreve rockets, the new British weapons of war were wildly inaccurate. Then, shortly after midnight on September 14, British seamen and marines attempted a landing behind Fort McHenry but were driven back by accurate artillery fire. The fort, valiantly defended by 1,000 men, sustained minor damage and only a few casualties.

On the night of the bombardment, a young lawyer by the name of Francis Scott Key was aboard a British ship negotiating the release of his friend, William Beanes, who had been taken prisoner after the American defeat at Bladensburg, Maryland. Although negotiations had been completed successfully, the British detained Key on the grounds that he knew too much about the planned attack on Baltimore. Key spent an anxious night watching the shelling of Fort McHenry from an American truce ship on the Patapsco River.

A replica of the flag sewn by Mary Pickersgill flies at Fort McHenry, left. The original can be seen at the Smithsonian Institution's Museum of American History in Washington, D.C.

BY DAWN'S EARLY LIGHT

Finally at daybreak the British withdrew, realizing that further bombardment was futile. As they sailed out of the harbor, the Americans fired the morning salute and hoisted a magnificent 30-by-42-foot flag, sewn by seamstress Mary Pickersgill, which was large enough for the British to see even from a great distance. Key was so moved by the sight of the flag unfurling in the wind that he wrote a poem about it called *The Star-Spangled Banner.*

Key's poem was published anonymously under the title *Defence of Fort M'Henry* and was later printed in the *Baltimore Patriot.* The poem was set to the tune of an English drinking song and became so popular throughout the country that it was adopted unofficially by the army and navy as the American national anthem. Congress formalized the option in 1931.

Fort McHenry never again had to defend itself against attack. During the Civil War it was used as a prison for Confederate soldiers and to sequester political prisoners from Maryland who opposed abolition. It served as a coastal fort until 1912, when it became the second busiest immigration station after Ellis Island. In World War I the 53 acres surrounding the fort were the site of a vast hospital complex used to treat injured service personnel returning from the battlefields of Europe. In 1923 the hospital was dismantled, and two years later Pres. Calvin Coolidge signed legislation creating Fort McHenry National Park. In 1939 it was redesignated as a national monument and historic shrine.

Today the fort looks much as it did during the Civil War. Its bastions, barricades, and officers' quarters contain extensive exhibits on American military history. And flying proudly over the fort is an exact replica of the 15-starred spangled banner that inspired a nation's anthem many years ago.

FOR MORE INFORMATION:

Fort McHenry National Monument and Historic Shrine, End of East Fort Ave., Baltimore, MD 21230-5393; 410-962-4290.

Smooth-bore Rodman cannons defend the thick walls of Fort McHenry, left.

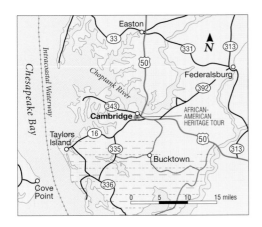

Bazzel's Methodist Episcopal Church, above, sits nestled in a stand of trees. The small wooden church is located on Bestpitch Ferry Road, in Bucktown.

While cruelty and greed ruled the slave trade in America, the Underground Railroad was fueled by courage and compassion. Among its bravest conductors was Harriet Tubman, a runaway slave who was raised in the tobacco fields of Maryland. After she escaped from bondage in 1849, Tubman risked her life countless times to guide more than 300 slaves over the Pennsylvania state line. Landmarks near Cambridge, Maryland, commemorate her heroism.

Established during the decades preceding the Civil War, the Underground Railroad was a network of hiding places and escape routes for fugitive slaves. Boats, ships, trains, and wagons carried bondsmen along invisible rails, and through woods, fields, rivers, and lakes to neutral territories in the north such as Pennsylvania, Massachusetts, Ohio, Indiana, and Canada.

But no matter how far they ran, runaways were never entirely safe, for slave hunters lurked everywhere. Under the Fugitive Slave Law of 1850 the authorities throughout the United States were obliged to help slaveholders recapture escapees. Since slaves were regarded as private property, those who assisted runaway slaves faced fines and the prospect of spending months in jail.

HUMBLE ROOTS

The threat of reenslavement never stopped Harriet Tubman from trying to liberate slaves. She continued to make forays even after plantation owners posted a $40,000 reward for her capture. Stealing through the night, the woman many called Moses sang spirituals such as "Go Down, Moses" that were coded to let slaves know when they were to make their break. It is said that Tubman inspired the lyrics of *Swing Low, Sweet Chariot*, a signal to slaves that she was on her way to collect another caravan.

Harriet Tubman was born in 1820 at the Brodess Plantation in the Bucktown district of Cambridge in Dorchester County. At the age of seven, she was separated from her parents and ordered to care for the plantation owner's baby. Ill-suited to work as a nanny, she suffered frequent beatings and was eventually sent to work as a laborer in the fields.

While still a teenager, Tubman stepped into the path of an overseer to block his pursuit of an escaping slave. The man flung a two-pound weight at her forehead, a blow that left her with a deep scar and recurring seizures, which in turn brought on strange dreams and voices that urged her to flee.

Fourteen years after being hurt, Tubman left her husband of five years and planned her escape. She learned the secrets of the Underground Railroad from a Quaker woman who lived in Dorchester County. With the North Star as her guide and aided by a network of abolitionists, she survived the perilous trek to Philadelphia. Once free, Tubman set about helping other runaways.

As an agent of the railroad, she carried a pistol and threatened to use it on frightened slaves who refused to travel onward. She drove her charges relentlessly, sometimes quieting wounded fugitives and crying babies with tinctures of opium. She was so successful that other conductors boasted that Tubman's train never ran off track and she never lost a passenger.

Tubman's sharp wits made her invaluable to the North during the Civil War. Using her knowledge of the countryside and its escape routes, she served as a spy and scout in South Carolina, and as a liaison between the Union Army and freed slaves.

After the war Tubman worked tirelessly on behalf of schools for black children and for the women's suffrage and temperance movements. She survived on a small government pension and used the farm she purchased in Auburn, New York, as a hospice for the poor and sick. It was here that Harriet died in 1913 at the age of 93.

While hardly a trace of the slave era remains in Dorchester County, several places in Bucktown are associated with Harriet Tubman and the Underground Railroad. Visitors can go on an African-American Heritage Tour, which departs from the Underground Railroad Gift Shop in Cambridge. The tour visits Little Blackwater River, a onetime hideout for runaways, and the Stanley Institute, a one-room schoolhouse that was moved to its present site in 1867. A historical plaque at the site of the Brodess Plantation is all that remains of Harriet Tubman's birthplace.

Each June, Bazzel's Methodist Episcopal Church holds a special service in memory of Harriet Tubman. Rarely open nowadays, the tiny church was Tubman's place of worship in the mid-1800's. A devout woman, Tubman once explained her fearlessness to a fellow conductor by saying that she "ventured only where God sent."

FOR MORE INFORMATION:
Harriet Tubman Coalition, Inc., P.O. Box 1164, Cambridge, MD 21613; 410-228-0401.

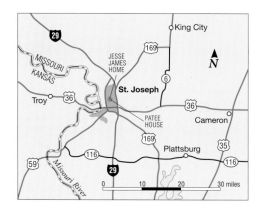

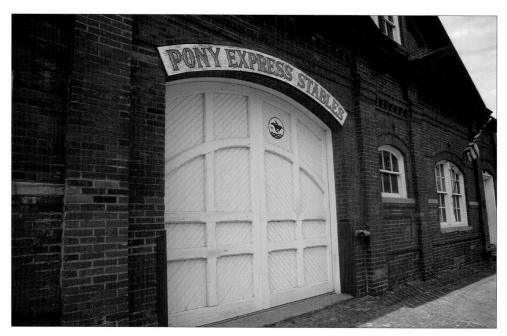

On April 3, 1860, the first westbound rider for the Pony Express headed out of the company's stables in St. Joseph. A reconstruction of the stables, above, houses the Pony Express Museum.

In the spring of 1860, the freighting firm of Russell, Majors & Waddell set up the headquarters of the Pony Express in a luxurious 140-room hotel called the Patee House in St. Joseph, Missouri. The company's ambitious goal was to deliver mail to the almost half-million Americans who lived west of the Rocky Mountains. It would offer a 10-day service to California via a central route that crossed the often dangerous terrain of what today is Kansas, Nebraska, Wyoming, Utah, and Nevada. The system was based on horsemen riding in relays. Soon the Pony Express operated 157 relay stations, located 5 to 20 miles apart, and counted 400 horses and some 80 teenage jockey-weight riders, plus station keepers, stock tenders, route supervisors, and shuttling supply wagons.

The legends surrounding these daring riders, which have been growing rapidly for over a century, include a phony ad, supposedly issued at the time, but really written in the 20th century: "WANTED—young skinny wiry fellows, not over eighteen. Must be expert riders willing to risk death daily. Orphans preferred. Wages $25 per week." The dangers, however, were very real—Indian attacks, outlaws, and the not insignificant perils of weather.

The Pony Express lasted only a little over 18 months. Man and beast could not compete with a recent innovation—the telegraph. Even as the Pony Express was getting under way, line crews were setting up poles for the first transcontinental telegraph along the same route used by the Pony Express riders. On October 18, 1861, the telegraph finally reached Salt Lake City. The first message, sent east to assure President Lincoln of California's loyalty, crossed the miles in minutes, compared with the days it took horse and rider. Within a week the Pony Express had become history, victim to the embryonic electronic age.

FAMOUS OUTLAWS

Pony Express riders weren't the only characters to become legends in St. Joseph. Jesse James and his gang soon blasted their way into the history books.

After a 15-year career of more than 26 train and bank robberies in 11 states and territories, the Jesse James gang, which included Jesse's brother Frank and the Younger brothers, had dispersed. Jesse James hoped to stop running—but he

had a $10,000 bounty on his head, set by Missouri governor Tom Crittenden.

On April 3, 1882, at the age of 34, Jesse James was shot by a friend who couldn't resist the offer of a reward. James had taken off his holster and stepped up on a chair to straighten a picture. James' back was turned to his trusted accomplice, 20-year-old Robert Ford, who felled him—one of America's most notorious outlaws— with a single shot behind the right ear.

The murder took place in a small cottage in St. Joseph, where James had been living for three months under the alias Tom Howard. The cottage, originally located about two blocks north of its present location, was moved in 1977 to a lot next to the Patee House Museum.

Robert Ford and his brother Charles had been living in the James home in the weeks leading up to the murder and were allegedly planning a bank robbery. Two years after James' death Charles committed suicide. Robert gained notoriety as the "dirty little coward who shot Mister Howard, and laid poor Jesse in his grave." He was killed in a barroom brawl in Creed, Colorado, in 1892.

FOR MORE INFORMATION:
Patee House Museum and the Jesse James Home, 12th and Penn Streets, Box 1022, St. Joseph, MO 64502; 816-232-8206.

The Jesse James Home in St. Joseph, left, contains artifacts such as the coffin handles from James' casket and the tie pin he was wearing when he was killed. Visitors can see the hole left in the wall by the bullet that hit him.

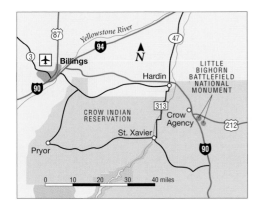

On a hot day in early July 1876, a telegraph from Bismarck, Dakota Territory, began tapping out the message: "General Custer attacked the Indians June 25, and he, with every officer and man in five companies were killed." With these terrible words the massacre of the 7th Cavalry at the Battle of the Little Bighorn was confirmed. The news stunned an America in the midst of celebrating its centennial. It also sealed the fate of the Plains Indians and immortalized, for better or worse, one man, Lt. Col. George Armstrong Custer.

In June 1876 George Custer was in command of one column of what was to be a three-pronged attack to drive the Plains Indians onto reservations. Their targets were the Lakotas and Cheyennes encamped in southern Montana by a stream the Plains Indians called Greasy Grass Creek, and known to the U.S. Army as Little Bighorn.

Since not a single man of the more than 200 under Custer's immediate command survived the bloody confrontation, no one is exactly sure what happened leading up to the massacre. Some historians believe that Custer couldn't wait to force an engagement. Leading his men, he charged ahead of the main expeditionary force. His commander, Gen. Alfred Terry, shouted to him: "Now, Custer, don't be greedy, but wait for us." "No, I won't," came the cheerful reply. Off galloped Custer, driving his men day and night over 115 miles of Montana hill country. By the time the 7th Cavalry came upon the rolling terrain that was to become a battlefield, the soldiers were parched with thirst and bleary-eyed for lack of sleep.

Custer divided his column of more than 600 men into three groups. He ordered the first detachment under Capt. Frederick Benteen to lead the pack mule train across the plain and wait for a possible retreat southward. Advancing farther, Custer ordered a second group under Maj. Marcus Reno to stir up panic among the Indians by charging through the southern end of their village. Meanwhile Custer led his 210 men northward to ford the Little Bighorn River with the intention of capturing women and children as they fled from the village, a tactic he had used successfully six years earlier in the Battle of Washita. These hostages, Custer may have reasoned, would force the warriors to sue for peace.

The Lakotas were waiting for them. Not only had their scouts been alerted to Custer's advance but their leader, Chief Sitting Bull, had experienced visions of a glorious victory. He cut his arms in a hundred places during a blood ritual as part of the holy Sun Dance and declared there would be a victory over the bluecoats.

Reno was the first to face heavy resistance and his detachment was forced to retreat to bluffs, now designated as the Reno-Benteen Battlefield and located within Little Bighorn Battlefield National Monument. Custer took longer to reach the river valley than expected and he then stretched his line too thin. Since his exact route is not known, it is unclear why he took so long. Facing swarms of enemy warriors, Custer and his men were overwhelmed and slaughtered on the exposed slope of Last Stand Hill. The pack train under Benteen was pinned down and couldn't mount a rescue.

In Little Bighorn Battlefield National Monument, stone markers were set down in 1890 to indicate where Custer's troops fell. Most of the soldiers were buried in a common grave on Last Stand Hill, where 50 markers have been placed. Custer is also buried here. Some people believe that he had been mortally wounded and carried up the hill. The grave markers are scattered throughout the deep ravines, raising more questions about what took place. Did the men retreat or fight to the last man? The bodies of Lakota and Cheyenne warriors—numbering some 60 to 100—were removed after the battle by their relatives.

NEW EVIDENCE
A brushfire in 1983 revealed some tantalizing new evidence on the battle's outcome. The cleared landscape exposed skulls, bones, and cartridges. Archeologists were able to examine over 2,000 artifacts and, with the help of forensic scientists, piece together a better picture of the battle.

It appears that Custer may have seriously misjudged the size of the Indian encampment and, therefore, divided the men under his command into three groups. Expecting a force of perhaps 800, Custer and his group of 210 men faced nearly 2,000 Cheyenne and Lakota warriors, under the combined leadership of the Teton Lakotas Crazy Horse and Chief Gall. When Custer's men failed to capture Indians from the camp, they doubled back only to face the warriors that Reno's detachment had been unable to contain. Left without any protected positions, the soldiers crouched behind their dead horses and fired. The Indians, hidden in the tallgrass, picked them off from a safe distance with their arrows and rifles. In little over an hour, Custer and the men with him lay dead.

At Little Bighorn Battlefield National Monument, open year-round, visitors can walk the paved path of the Custer and Reno-Benteen battlefields. Rangers give accounts of the battle during the summer. The visitor center features two documentary films, photographs, and memorabilia, including Custer's buckskin jacket.

FOR MORE INFORMATION:
Little Bighorn Battlefield National Monument, P.O. Box 39, Crow Agency, MT 59022-0039; 406-638-2621.

Custer National Cemetery, below, is the final resting place for more than 5,000 American soldiers and their families.

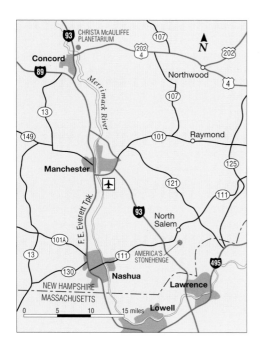

This imposing collection of stone walls, monoliths, chambers, and tunnels is believed to be one of the oldest megalithic sites on the North American continent. The complex, which was formerly known as Mystery Hill Caves, is now called America's Stonehenge because of the similarity it bears to the ancient stone circle of the same name in England. The 30 acres of constructions were built by people who were skilled stonemasons and well versed in astronomy.

The precise date of the monument's construction is unknown, but charcoal samples uncovered during excavations in 1969 and 1971, and subjected to radiocarbon dating, indicate it is 3,000 to 4,000 years old.

Stones found within the site display various markings, including a Celtic sun symbol and a running deer or ibex. Epigraphers have interpreted the carvings as Old World scripts with origins in Phoenician, Arabic, and Celtic languages. Other artifacts excavated at the site date from the 18th and 19th centuries. These include stone tools, pottery, and housewares, which suggest that successive cultures occupied the area. A number of these items are on display at the visitor center, where visitors can obtain maps and view an orientation video that tells the history of the site.

Eerie chambers, scattered across the granite hilltops, are capped with stones ranging in weight from 4 to 11 tons. The site's largest chamber, called the Oracle, has T-shaped passages, a drainage channel, a roof opening, and a tube that tunnels through five feet of stone. Words spoken into the tube at one end can be heard at the other end which opens under a four-and-a-half-ton table located outside the chamber. Similar "talking tables" have been discovered in Europe and are believed to have been used as ceremonial sacrificial tables; their ability to "talk" enhancing the mystery and power of the presiding priest. The table, which is propped on stone legs, has channels etched into it that may have conveyed blood into stone receptacles.

Little is known about the builders who hoisted the stone slabs into place, although the evidence points to a migrant European population. Those who discount the evidence of the inscriptions believe that Native Americans were the architects. Whoever erected the monoliths arranged them according to celestial events recorded in ancient calendars, including lunar phases, the midwinter sunrise, and the summer solstice sunset. These alignments suggest that the site served as a vast outdoor facility to chart the stars and the changing seasons.

Following the Astronomical Trail, visitors come across standing and fallen stones that were originally positioned according to yearly astronomical events. One lineup of a boulder, a wall, a fallen monolith, and a fallen stone determines when both spring and fall equinox will occur. Other monoliths are positioned to predict the timing of the summer and winter solstices.

The earliest recorded references to the site were published in Edgar Gilbert's *History of Salem, N.H.,* which was published in 1907. According to the book, abolitionist Jonathan Pattee and his family lived in the area between 1826 and 1855. The Pattee area of the site includes a small chamber that may have been used as a root cellar; other rooms housed a liquor-distilling operation and served as a station for runaway slaves on the Underground Railroad.

MODERN ASTRONOMERS
At the Christa McAuliffe Planetarium in nearby Concord, amateur astronomers can gaze at the heavens using state-of-the-art equipment. The complex, which was opened in 1990, is equipped with a Digistar planetarium projection system, which stores and retrieves graphic information in a massive computer database. The system uses projected images to simulate space travel in three dimensions, reaching 600 light years from Earth and 1 million years into the past or the future. Visitors can race a comet through space, witness a supernova, the swirling cloud of Jupiter, or a glowing spiral galaxy.

A theater features seats equipped with control panels that enable aspiring astronauts to blaze their way across the cosmos.

A stone wall, above, is one of the many ancient constructions on view at what is possibly the oldest site unearthed in North America.

Visitors can retrieve images of 9,094 stars and 88 constellations, including nebulae and galaxies such as the Milky Way, M31, M42, and Magellanic Clouds. Space fans can determine the perspective of their journeys, watch a simulated meteor shower, and view planets and their moons.

The facility commemorates the life of the only civilian claimed by the 1986 *Challenger* shuttle disaster. Christa McAuliffe was a social studies teacher at Concord High School when she was selected from among 45,000 applicants nationwide to become the first private citizen to be sent into space.

When the craft exploded just 73 seconds after liftoff, McAuliffe, age 38, lost her life; but her mission to advance the pursuit of knowledge continues at the planetarium, which offers interactive methods of learning about space. The center remains true to McAuliffe's motto to "reach for the stars."

FOR MORE INFORMATION:
America's Stonehenge, P.O. Box 84, North Salem, NH 03073; 603-893-8300.
Christa McAuliffe Planetarium, 3 Institute Dr., Concord, NH 03301; 603-271-7827.

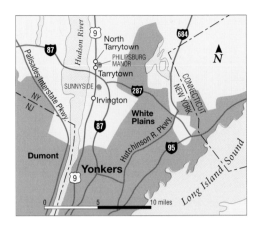

Philipsburg Manor in North Tarrytown, above, is one of six Historic Hudson Valley sites. It is an old mill that was originally owned by the Dutch-born Philipse family.

Tucked away on the east bank of the Hudson River, Sleepy Hollow country is a unique mix of natural beauty, history, and whimsical flights of the imagination. Washington Irving, America's first internationally acclaimed author, immortalized the bucolic glen in his 1820 short story *The Legend of Sleepy Hollow*. Using Sleepy Hollow as the setting for Ichabod Crane's terrifying confrontation with the Headless Horseman, Irving wrote, "If ever I should wish for a retreat, whither I might steal from the world and its distractions, and dream quietly away the remnant of a troubled life, I know of none more promising than this little valley."

Born in New York City in 1783, Irving made a name for himself as an author while living in Europe. Upon his return to the United States during the 1830's, the writer bought a cottage in Tarrytown, where he lived until his death in 1859. In his charming abode Irving entertained the likes of American poet and essayist Oliver Wendell Holmes and English novelist William Makepeace Thackeray.

Sunnyside, the home of Washington Irving, above, features a felicitous blend of European architectural styles.

Travelers seeking an intimate view of Irving should visit his estate called Sunnyside, one of six Historic Hudson Valley sites that are open to the public. Irving expanded a simple two-room stone cottage employing an eclectic mixture of architectural styles that he had become familiar with during his travels in Europe. Arched doorways, Dutch-style gables, antique weather vanes, and a tower modeled after a Spanish monastery combine to give Sunnyside a fanciful feel that no doubt delighted the author of such humorous yarns as *Rip Van Winkle*.

Visitors can walk around the rooms in the main house, many of which include Irving's original furniture and accessories. Of particular interest is the first-floor study, in which he wrote a biography of his namesake, George Washington, whom the six-year-old Irving met in New York in 1789.

Sunnyside's gracious and beautifully tended grounds invite exploration. Winding paths wander through wooded enclaves and picnic areas, offering visitors beautiful vistas of the river and the gently rolling hills in the distance. Tired hikers can rest on the Gothic Revival benches at the entrance to the writer's riverside retreat under lush wisteria planted by Irving in the 1840's. Costumed interpreters, including one dressed as Irving himself, lead visitors on tours of the cottage and grounds.

Special events include storytelling around a bonfire at dusk and nighttime walks through the woods. Sunnyside's annual storytelling festival attracts hundreds of visitors eager to watch puppet shows, dramatic readings, ballads, and plays put on by children. Sunnyside celebrates Halloween in suitable style: master storytellers entertain their guests with the tale of the Headless Horseman and other spine-chillers, followed by a candlelit tour of the cottage.

TARRYING AT THE TAVERN

Visitors to the region should also stop in Sleepy Hollow's historic Tarrytowns, which Irving suggested, with mock seriousness, got their name from impatient wives tired of waiting for their husbands as they tarried at the local tavern.

Picturesque Tarrytown village was established by Dutch settlers in the 17th century. During the Revolutionary War, papers found in the boot of a captured British spy, Maj. John André, revealed Benedict Arnold to be a traitor. Artifacts from this notorious chapter in American history are on display at the Historical Society of the Tarrytowns, which is located on Grove Street. The modest-looking Old Dutch Church in North Tarrytown was built in the 1680's and continues to hold Sunday services in the summer. Adjacent to the church in the Sleepy Hollow Cemetery lies the grave of Washington Irving who vowed to return to his beloved cottage as a "good spirit."

FOR MORE INFORMATION:
Historic Hudson Valley, 150 White Plains Rd., Tarrytown, NY, 10591; 914-631-8200.

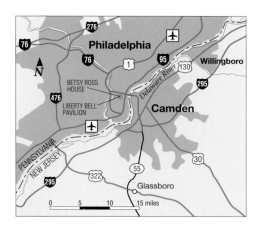

Founded in 1652 by the Quaker William Penn, Philadelphia well deserves its nickname as the Cradle of Liberty. It was here, in 1775, that George Washington was appointed Commander in Chief of the American Army; the First Continental Congress met in Carpenters Hall the same year; and the Declaration of Independence was adopted the following year. The city is also home to America's most beloved symbols: the Stars and Stripes and the Liberty Bell.

On the outskirts of Philadelphia's historic district, a modest house at 239 Arch Street celebrates a legendary seamstress who played a vital role in the history of the United States.

The folklore surrounding Betsy Ross and the American flag has inspired Americans ever since her grandson first publicized the story in 1870. According to William Canby, his grandmother was visited in June 1776 by George Ross, her uncle-in-law, Robert Morris, and George Washington, who worshiped in the pew next to her in church.

The committee of the Continental Congress asked Ross to fashion a flag for the new nation that would be used to declare its independence the following month. When he made a preliminary sketch, Washington reportedly said, "Let the 13 stars in a circle stand as a new constellation in the heavens." The stars were placed in that arrangement so that no colony would have precedence over another. According to legend, Betsy Ross suggested modifications to the design—such as the substitution of five-pointed stars for Washington's six-pointed ones—and then stitched together the famous symbol of American unity in a small back parlor of her house on Arch Street.

In 1777 Congress officially adopted the flag bearing 13 stars against a blue field and 13 red and white stripes. The colors of the flag were selected by the Congress of the Confederation: white symbolized purity and innocence; red stood for valor and hardiness; and blue represented vigilance, perseverance, and justice.

Whether the historic Stars and Stripes was patterned after Betsy's design is unknown, since there is no official mention of Ross' role in the creation of the flag. Nevertheless, the story of Betsy Ross captivated the nation, and more than 2 million people contributed to the preservation of her house, which was designated American Flag House. The Betsy Ross Memorial Association began selling certificates in 1898 as receipts for each contribution; the association ceased operation in 1936. In the meantime, the inspiring image of Ross' patriotic act overshadowed any concerns about historical accuracy.

Elizabeth Griscom was born in Philadelphia in 1752 and married upholsterer John Ross in 1773. He died three years later, leaving his 24-year-old widow to run the upholstery shop on her own. Betsy supplied navy flags during the Revolutionary War, and continued making flags years after the signing of the Declaration of Independence. Ross outlived two more husbands, lost two children in their infancy, and single-handedly raised five daughters and two nieces.

She died in 1836 and is buried next to her third husband, John Claypoole, in the garden adjoining the Betsy Ross House. Restored to its 1770's appearance, the small brick house features a gabled roof (sporting an early version of Old Glory), paneled shutters, winding stairs, and a basement kitchen. Its nine rooms are furnished with period pieces, including several of Ross' belongings. On the first floor, visitors can examine the restored back parlor, the workshop where Betsy is said to have made the first American flag.

LET FREEDOM RING
An equally cherished symbol of national identity is housed in a pavilion a few blocks away. The Liberty Bell was commissioned to commemorate the 1701 Pennsylvania Charter of Privileges, which foreshadowed the liberties obtained for all citizens 75 years later with the signing of the Declaration of Independence. Arriving from the Whitechapel Foundry of London in 1752, the massive bell is inscribed with a passage from the Old Testament that reads, "Proclaim Liberty throughout all the land unto all the inhabitants thereof."

The bell was installed in the Pennsylvania State House, now called Independence Hall, where it pealed to call citizens to town meetings, to signal fires, celebrate victories, and mourn the deaths of great men. In 1776 the Liberty Bell proclaimed the nation's freedom after the signing of the Declaration of Independence on July 4.

During its first year in the New World the bell was recast twice: once because of a crack in the rim and the second time because its tone was considered poor, due to too much copper in the casting. Another crack appeared in the bell later, apparently when it was rung during the funeral of Chief Justice John Marshall in 1835. The cleft that zigzags from the rim to the inscription serves as a tangible reminder of liberty's fragility.

FOR MORE INFORMATION:
Betsy Ross House, 239 Arch St., Philadelphia, PA 19106; 215-627-5343.

Superintendent, Independence National Historical Park, 313 Walnut St., Philadelphia, PA 19106; 215-597-8974.

An example of the first design for Old Glory is prominently displayed outside the Betsy Ross House, above.

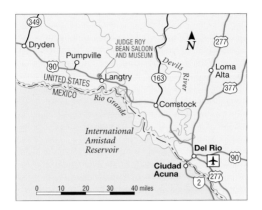

The Judge Roy Bean Visitor Center in Langtry, above, maintains the restored Jersey Lilly Saloon, which stands out back, and a two-acre cactus garden planted with about 100 species of cacti.

I n the rowdy railroad town of Langtry, where Texas borders Mexico near the meeting of the Peco River and the Rio Grande, a convicted felon was fined $45 in 1883 and ordered to buy the jury a round of drinks. The decision was final and not subject to appeal. Such was the rough-and-ready justice dispensed by Judge Roy Bean in his courthouse, which also served as a saloon and billiard parlor. He called his establishment the Jersey Lilly, a misspelled tribute to Lillie Langtry, the English actress with whom he was infatuated.

The American West was opened up in the late 1800's by the railroad, and the towns and tent camps that soon sprang up along the rails were the hangouts of card-sharps, crooks, and women of ill repute. The crime rate in the Trans-Pecos area was so high that the railroad sought help from the Texas Rangers, who, given that the nearest legal authority was some 200 miles

away, urged the appointment of a local justice of the peace. The closest approximation to a responsible citizen was Roy Bean, a 56-year-old saloonkeeper in the tent camp of Vinegaroon. He was appointed in 1883 and set up in Langtry the following year.

Armed with a copy of the 1879 *Revised Statutes of Texas*, a notary seal, handcuffs, and a pair of six-shooters, Bean embarked on a 21-year career as the self-styled "law west of the Pecos." He tried cases between rounds of poker and regularly interrupted legal proceedings to sell liquid refreshment.

JUSTICE WILD-WEST STYLE
Bean's decision in the murder trial of a white railroad worker accused of killing a Chinese laborer best conveys his judicial style: the day of judgment had arrived and with it a surly crowd of the accused's supporters. Judge Roy Bean declared that while the law prohibited homicide, it was silent on the matter of killing a Chinese man. And he acquitted the accused.

In a case where the body of a worker had been found on the railroad tracks with a gun and $40 in his pocket, Roy Bean played both judge and coroner. In his capacity as coroner, he exonerated the railroad; as justice of the peace, he held that the deceased

Langtry was such a dangerous place to live during the days that Roy Bean ruled from the Jersey Lilly Saloon, left, that when Lillie Langtry visited in 1904 she is reported to have said, "Of all the folks buried in the Langtry cemetery, only 15 citizens died of natural causes."

had violated the law by carrying a concealed weapon and thus the court had "the disagreeable necessity of imposing on the deceased a fine of $40." Judge Bean himself pocketed the fine.

There was no jail in Langtry, and Judge Roy Bean's sentences were inevitably pecuniary. When asked to provide a financial accounting, he responded that his court was self-sustaining. In 1896 he staged a boxing match on a sandbar in the Rio Grande between the Mexico and Texas borders, close enough to his saloon to sell beer to fans who got thirsty.

Opinions on Bean's character vary. A Langtry citizen was reported to have said with a straight face, "Roy Bean might have been a murderer and a robber, but he was a good man in his way." A federal judge commented that "he was both law and equity, right and justice. He filled a place that could not have been filled by any other man. He was distinctly a creation of circumstance."

After his death in 1903, the Jersey Lilly Saloon fell into disrepair. Then in 1939 the building was restored and opened to the public. In 1968 the Texas Department of Transportation opened the Judge Roy Bean Visitor Center. Six dioramas recount Judge Bean's colorful career and his singular style of dispensing frontier justice.

FOR MORE INFORMATION:
Judge Roy Bean Visitor Center, P.O. Box 160, Langtry, TX 78871-0160; 915-291-3340.

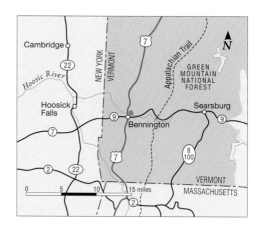

A massive 306-foot-high obelisk of dolomite serves as a dramatic reminder of Bennington's historical importance. It was near this site that on August 16, 1777, Revolutionary patriots aided by the Green Mountain Boys halted the British army's attempt to take over the colonies. The Bennington Battle Monument commemorates this crucial victory, which many historians view as the turning point of the Revolution. The triumph helped boost the morale of a young republic and set it on the course to nationhood.

From the very beginning, Bennington's history has been marked by confrontation and the will of independent New Englanders. In 1750, Gov. Benning Wentworth of New Hampshire took a six-square-mile area from territory that New York claimed as its own and named it Bennington. He granted most of the land to cronies and then took more. By 1764 he had granted 138 towns in the disputed area. Unfortunately many of the new settlers discovered that their so-called Hampshire Grants overlapped those sold to New York settlers by New York. They were harassed by New York surveyors, and occasionally violence broke out.

Sometime during the 1760's an enterprising New Englander named Ethan Allen decided to take matters into his own hands. Newly wealthy from the sale of his ironworks in Salisbury, Connecticut, Allen used to meet with like-minded men at Bennington's Catamount Tavern, where he was often seen tossing back Stonewall, a concoction of 152-proof rum cut with Vermont apple cider. At one of these meetings, so the story goes, the men decided to challenge the New York sheriff and his surveyors. In the resulting confrontation, they whipped the New Yorkers with birch rods and sent them scurrying back home. Today a bronze statue of a catamount, or eastern panther, and a plaque mark the site of the tavern, which was destroyed by fire in 1871.

Emboldened by their victory, the Green Mountain Boys, who took their name from the Green Mountains of their home, formed into companies and, under the leadership of Ethan Allen, joined forces with Benedict Arnold to attack a more formidable target—the British fortress situated at Ticonderoga.

On the night of May 9, 1775, about 350 men under the joint command of Arnold and Allen met on the eastern side of Lake Champlain across from Fort Ticonderoga. Because the Green Mountain Boys did not have enough boats to transport all their men across the lake, only 83 men were able to rush the fort before the break of dawn. Ticonderoga had fallen into disrepair and was held by a small garrison of British soldiers. Allen and his three ranks of armed men were easily able to penetrate the walls. Allen summoned the commander, and demanded that the fort be handed over "in the name of the Great Jehovah, and the Continental Congress." On May 10, 1775, Ethan Allen and his Green Mountain Boys had committed the first act of colonial aggression in the War of Independence.

Bennington, Vermont—just 42 miles east of Albany— is a treasure trove of Revolutionary and pre-Revolutionary monuments. Old Bennington contains many finely preserved Georgian and Federal buildings. The tall Bennington Battle Monument serves as an observation tower, and every August the town sponsors a re-enactment of the Bennington Battle. The Walloomsac Inn, now a private residence, served food to captured prisoners after the Battle of Bennington. Many of those who were killed in this and other Revolutionary conflicts were buried in the Old Burial Ground across the street. They were later joined by Vermont governors and the poet Robert Frost. The Old First Church, built in 1805, replaced a previous structure that was the site of the First Meeting House. The Bennington Museum displays early Vermont furniture, military records and relics, and the largest public collection of paintings by Anna "Grandma" Moses, who lived in the area. The museum houses one of the oldest American flags, once believed to have been carried into the Battle of Bennington but now known to date from around the War of 1812.

FOR MORE INFORMATION:
Bennington Chamber of Commerce, Veteran's Memorial Dr., Bennington, VT 05201; 802-447-3311.

The Walloomsac Inn in Old Bennington, above, was built by Capt. Elijah Dewey, son of the town's first minister, who fought at Ticonderoga, Bennington, and Saratoga during the Revolutionary War.

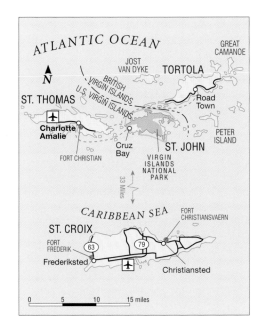

In the late 17th and early 18th centuries, the Virgin Islands became a base for Denmark's trade in slaves, sugar, and Cruzan rum. Legends abound of the pirates who roamed the sea, attacking and pillaging ships as they headed for home. The blackguards and cutthroats terrorized the high seas preying on the Danish merchants.

Bartholomew Roberts was one of the most menacing and successful of these pirates in the Caribbean, where lore claims he captured more than 400 ships in his lifetime. A man of unpredictable disposition, he banned his crew from gambling and always wore his finest clothes into battle. Another pirate, Edward Teach, otherwise known as Blackbeard, is said to have settled on St. Thomas for a spell. Notorious far and wide for his viciousness, Teach was rumored to have captured slave ships, killed

the crews, then auctioned off the slaves and kept the profits for himself. During raids he would terrify his victims by appearing with fuses braided into his long black beard and hair, and lighting them. This scare tactic, while earning him his ominous nickname, enhanced his reputation enormously. According to island folklore, Teach resided in a handsome dwelling on St. Thomas' Main Street before moving into a dilapidated tower that afforded him a view of his heavily armed ships. The tower, which is known as Blackbeard's Castle, still stands on the island.

FORTS OF THE ISLANDS

History tells a different story. Apparently, Blackbeard never lived on St. Thomas at all and his tower, far from being a pirate's lookout, was built by the Danes to supplement the defense of the harbor protected by Fort Christian. While there was a brief period in the 1680's when St. Thomas served as a haven for pirates, by the early 1700's these outlaws began to look elsewhere for plunder. Fort Christian and the other four forts on what were the Danish Islands in the Americas, were constructed not for defense against pirates, but to protect the colony from civil unrest—slave revolts were an ever-present fear—and from invasion by other European nations jealous of Denmark's foothold in the Caribbean. Three of these forts survive today.

Fort Christian is the oldest standing structure in the U.S. Virgin Islands. Built more than 300 years ago, this small yellow brick fort was the center of the early Danish colony. During the course of its turbulent history, the fort has survived hurricanes and fires and has served as a courthouse, church, police station, and jail. It was transformed in the 1970's into the Fort Christian Museum. Fully restored Danish warehouses flank a mile-long promenade, which overlooks St. Thomas' natural harbor.

Fort Christiansvaern, the best-maintained fortification in the Virgin Islands, was built in 1749, some 30 years after Bartholomew Roberts' death. Not one shot was ever fired from the fort, located on the island of St. Croix. The largest of the U.S. Virgin Islands, the island was discovered by Columbus in 1493. In later years, the island was claimed and fought over by the Spanish, Dutch, English, French, and the Knights of Malta before being sold to the Danish, who, in turn, sold it to the

Erected in 1672, Fort Christian, above, is the oldest structure in Charlotte Amalie on the island of St. Thomas. It is now a museum of natural and local history.

United States in 1917. Its Danish heritage is still evident in the pastel-colored buildings. Yellow brick, used as ballast on incoming ships, became the most common building material. Guided tours of Fort Christiansvaern are available by reservation. Visitors can explore the dungeons where privateers were imprisoned, and see the debtors' cell, slave quarters, and the powder stores.

The last of the protective barriers erected by the Danish was Fort Frederik, built between 1752 and 1760 to guard the west coast of St. Croix. It was here on July 3, 1848, that Gov. Gen. Peter Von Scholten declared the end of slavery in the Danish West Indies with the proclamation: "all unfree . . . are now freed."

FOR MORE INFORMATION:

U.S. Virgin Islands Division of Tourism, P.O. Box 6400, Charlotte Amalie, St. Thomas, U.S. VI 00804; 809-774-8784.

Fort Christiansvaern, left, was completed in 1749 to protect the town of Christiansted against raids by pirates and privateers.

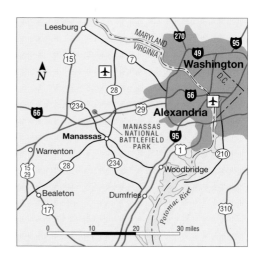

The first major battle of the Civil War is known to Northerners as Bull Run after the placid stream that runs through the area; Southerners know it as First Manassas. The clash at Bull Run attests to the fury of two great armies—and to their inexperience. It is also the battle that earned Gen. Thomas J. Jackson his famous nickname, Stonewall. Jackson's actions on the field are best understood by a visit to the site of what is today the Manassas National Battlefield Park.

Born in 1824, Jackson was educated at West Point and served with distinction during the Mexican War. Later he taught natural philosophy and artillery tactics at the Virginia Military Institute, where his deeply religious nature earned him the nickname Deacon Jackson. At the outbreak of the Civil War, Jackson offered his services to the state of Virginia. He was a stern disciplinarian, trusted and obeyed by his men, who marched with such speed they became known as Jackson's Foot Cavalry.

THE BATTLE BEGINS

On the morning of July 21, 1861, Gen. Irvin McDowell and his army of 35,000 volunteers launched an attack against 20,000 Confederate troops under Gen. P. G. T. Beauregard at Manassas. Making a feint at the Stone Bridge, McDowell's main column maneuvered around Beauregard's line along Bull Run. A small brigade of Southerners managed to delay McDowell's flanking column on Matthews Hill. The arrival of Gen. Bernard Bee's brigade, the first of some 10,000 Confederate reinforcements, was still not enough to stop the Union advance. By noon the Southerners had fallen back in disorder to Henry Hill. Attempting to rally his troops, Bee pointed to the line formed by General Jackson's brigade and shouted out, "There Jackson stands like a stone wall!"

Bee's remark may be taken either as a sign of his admiration for Jackson for steadfastly holding the line, or else as a criticism of Jackson and his men for standing still and not joining the fight. Regardless of Bee's real opinion of Jackson's tactic, the refusal to budge halted the Union advance up Henry Hill and gave the Confederates a chance to reform their lines and launch fresh brigades against the Union front.

As Jackson urged his men to attack the Union batteries on Henry Hill he cried: "Yell like furies when you charge!" Later that afternoon, in the face of more fresh Confederate reinforcements, the exhausted Northerners fled in panic.

A row of cannons and a statue of Jackson astride his horse commemorate Stonewall's famous line on Henry Hill in Manassas National Battlefield Park. At the visitor center, military buffs can view Civil War memorabilia and watch an audiovisual presentation of the battle. Hiking trails and driving routes weave through the 4,500-acre battlefield, which is dotted with interpretative signs that explain the military maneuvers of the armies at Bull Run.

Noteworthy sites include Stone Bridge, where the first shots of the battle were fired; Matthews Hill, where General Bee's brigade was driven back; the grave of Mrs. Judith Carter Henry, the only civilian killed in the battle; the 1848 Stone House, which served as a Union army field hospital; and Chinn

Ridge, where the revitalized Confederate troops shattered the Union right and proceeded to stampede the line.

A humiliating loss for Union forces, Bull Run was a clear sign that the South would not be defeated easily. A second campaign at Manassas a year later ended in another Confederate victory. As Gen. Robert E. Lee's right-hand man in subsequent battles, Stonewall Jackson proved to be one of the war's most skillful tacticians.

While Jackson's brigades won several major battles in the Shenandoah Valley, his greatest achievement was at the battle of Chancellorsville, Virginia, in May 1863. In the moment of victory, however, the 39-year-old Jackson was shot accidentally by his own troops as he rode back to his lines at dusk. The general had to have his left arm amputated and, although he was expected to recover, pneumonia set in and eight days later he died. When the mighty Stonewall Jackson fell, the South lost a mainstay of the Confederacy. At the end, he uttered the words, "Let us cross over the river, and rest under the shade of the trees."

FOR MORE INFORMATION:
Superintendent, Manassas National Battlefield Park, 12521 Lee Hwy., Manassas, VA 20109; 703-361-1339.

A graceful stone bridge, below, crosses over the meandering Bull Run. Two major battles of the Civil War took place near the stream.

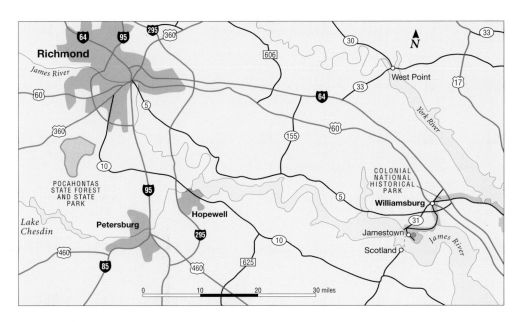

A bronze statue of Pocahontas, above, sculpted by William Ordway Partridge, welcomes visitors to the Jamestown Settlement.

A statue of Capt. John Smith overlooks the James River, above. Archeologists have recently discovered that the statue stands directly on the site of the original fort.

In his *A Generall Historie of Virginia,* published in 1624, John Smith describes an incident that occurred when he was captured by Powhatan Indians in 1607. According to the account, Smith, then 27, was brought before Wahunsonacock, the mighty chief of the Powhatan Nation, who ordered his people to prepare a great feast—and an execution. As the chief's orders were carried out, his comely 11-year-old daughter, Pocahontas, cast her eye upon the intriguing stranger. After the ritual meal was served, the Indians forced Smith's head down on two stones and raised their weapons. But just before they could kill him, the smitten Indian princess clasped the Englishman's head in her arms and laid her own upon it, saving him from certain death.

Smith's romanticized account of the story contains many inconsistencies, casting doubt on its authenticity. But regardless of the true nature of their relationship, Pocahontas' bravery and generosity toward the Europeans have become legendary.

A beautiful child, whose name means "playful one," Pocahontas was curious about the white settlers who arrived in the New World in 1607, and she befriended them after Wahunsonacock freed Smith. She took food to the English settlers at Jamestown and intervened during several potentially violent conflicts between the Europeans and her own people.

John Smith served a term as governor of the colony, then returned to England in 1609 after he was wounded by a gunpowder explosion. Four years later, Pocahontas was kidnapped by the English and held as ransom for the release of seven English prisoners and some stolen guns. Wahunsonacock returned the men after a three-month impasse, then agreed to Pocahontas' marriage to a colonist named John Rolfe—an alliance that forged almost a decade of peace between the cultures.

Visitors to Colonial National Historical Park are greeted by a statue of the young girl who transcended cultural differences. Although a church tower from the 1640's is the only structure of the period still standing, visitors can see traces of the streets of the original settlement and tour the remains of the 17th-century townsite. Excavations have uncovered thousands of artifacts dating from the early 17th century, many of which are on display at the visitor center museum. Near the ruins of a 1608 glassworks factory (Jamestown's first industry), costumed artisans demonstrate the glassmaking techniques of the era.

Baptized and given the European name Rebecca, Pocahontas lived with her husband on his farm beside the James River where they raised tobacco, the product that was destined to become the cash crop of the Virginia settlement.

In 1616 the couple traveled to England with their son, Thomas. The court of King James I regarded the Indian princess, who spoke and dressed like an Englishwoman, as a curiosity. One account by a witness noted that "Master Rolfe's wife did not only accustome herself to civilitie but carried herself as a Daughter of a King, and was accordingly respected." During her visit, Pocahontas also met briefly with John Smith, whom she had presumed dead. She became ill with either tuberculosis or pneumonia in March 1617 and died soon after. Buried at Gravesend, England, at the age of 21, Pocahontas was never to return to her homeland.

FOR MORE INFORMATION:
Superintendent, Colonial National Historical Park, P.O. Box 210, Yorktown, VA 23690; 804-898-3400.

INDEX

Bold numerals indicate map reference.
Italic numerals indicate an illustration.
State abbreviations are in parentheses.
NF = National Forest
NHP = National Historical Park
NHS = National Historic Site
NM = National Monument
N MEM = National Memorial
NP = National Park
NP & PRES = National Park
and Preserve
NRA = National Recreation Area
NS = National Seashore
NWR = National Wildlife Refuge
SHP = State Historic Park
SF = State Forest
SP = State Park

PICTURE CREDITS

Cover photograph by Tim Thompson
2 Jean Higgins/Unicorn Stock Photos
5 Laurence Parent

PAUL REVERE'S JOURNEY
8, 9 David Muench
10 Stock Boston/Michael Dwyer
11 Corbis-Bettman
12 (upper) Stock Boston/Spencer Grant
12 (lower) James P. Rowan
13 (upper) Pauline Revere Thayer Collection Courtesy, Museum of Fine Arts, Boston
13 (lower) Jeff Gnass Photography
14 David Muench
15 (upper right) Courtesy of the Concord Museum, Concord, MA
15 (lower left) Craig Aurness/Woodfin Camp & Associates
16 (upper) Alan Briere
16 (lower) The Bettman Archive
17 James P. Rowan
18 Alan Briere
19 (both) Alan Briere

THE FARAWAY LAND
20, 21 Alan Briere
22 Jeffrey Allen Photography
23 Kendall Whaling Museum, Sharon, MA
24 (left) Alan Briere
24, 25 (lower) Alan Briere
25 (upper right) Kendall Whaling Museum, Sharon, MA
26 (upper) Terry Pommett
26 (lower) Kendall Whaling Museum, Sharon, MA
27 (upper) Kendall Whaling Museum, Sharon, MA
27 (lower) Alan Briere
28 (upper) Alan Briere
28 (lower) Jeffrey Allen Photography
29 Alan Briere
30 Bernard Boutrit/Woodfin Camp & Associates
31 (both) Alan Briere

JOHN BROWN'S RAID
32, 33 Tom Till/Photographer
34 Fred Hirschmann
36 (upper) Andre Jenny/Unicorn Stock Photos
36 (lower) Alan Briere
37 (upper right) Alan Briere
37 (lower left) Aneal F. Vohra/Unicorn Stock Photos
38 (upper) Eric Long Photography
38 (lower) Corbis-Bettman
39 Larry Ulrich Photography

40 Pat & Chuck Blackley
41 (upper left) Dave G. Houser
41 (lower right) Andre Jenny/Unicorn Stock Photos

THE LOST COLONY
42, 43 Jeff Gnass Photography
44 (upper) Jeff Gnass Photography
44 (lower) John Elk III
45 J. Faircloth/Transparencies, Inc.
46 (upper) John Elk III
46 (lower) Corbis-Bettman
47 John Elk III
48 The Indian Village of Secoton by John White, The Bridgeman Art Library, British Museum, London
49 (upper) John Elk III
49 (lower) Jonathan Wallen
50 J. Faircloth/Transparencies, Inc.
51 (both) Kelly Culpepper/Transparencies, Inc.

DANIEL BOONE'S KENTUCKY
52, 53 Terry Donnelly
54 (upper) Alan Briere
54 (lower) William Strode/Woodfin Camp & Associates, Inc.
56 (left) William Strode/Woodfin Camp & Associates, Inc.
56, 57 William Strode/Woodfin Camp & Associates, Inc.
57 (upper) Laurence Parent
58 Terry Donnelly
59 (upper) Tom Till/Photographer
59 (lower) William Strode/Woodfin Camp & Associates, Inc.
60 (both) William Strode/Woodfin Camp & Associates, Inc.
61 Washington University Gallery of Art, St. Louis, Gift of Nathaniel Phillips, Boston,1890
62 National Park Service, Andrew Johnson National Historic Site
63 (upper left) Jonathan Wallen
63 (lower right) Larry Ulrich

TEXAS REVOLUTION
64, 65 Laurence Parent
66 (upper right) Tim Thompson
66 (lower left) Laurence Parent
68 Laurence Parent
69 (upper right) John Elk III
69 (lower left) Corbis-Bettman
70, 71 (upper) The Bettman Archive
70 (lower left) Tim Thompson
71 (right) Laurence Parent
72 Laurence Parent
73 (both) Laurence Parent

THE WILD WEST
74, 75 Ric Ergenbright
76 (upper left) Buffalo Bill Historical Center, Cody, WY
76 (lower right) Frank S. Balthis
78 (upper) Buffalo Bill Historical Center, Cody, WY. Gift of Howell H. Howard
78 (lower) John Elk III
79 Courtesy of the Irma Hotel, Cody, WY
80 Buffalo Bill Historical Center, Cody, WY
81 (upper left) Lee Foster
81 (lower right) Laurence Parent
82 Buffalo Bill Historical Center, Cody, WY. Gift of Mr. I.H. "Larry" Larom and Irma D. Larom
83 Dewey Vanderhoff
84 (left) Dave G. Houser
84 (right) Jan Butchofsky/Dave G. Houser
85 Dave G. Houser

THE GOLDEN SPIKE
86, 87 John Elk III
88 Corbis-Bettman
89 George H.H. Huey
90 (both) George H.H. Huey
91 (both) George H.H. Huey
92 (upper) Lee Foster
92 (lower) Gerd Ludwig/Woodfin Camp & Associates
93 George H.H. Huey
94 Scott T. Smith
95 (upper left) Chuck Place
95 (lower right) Scott T. Smith

KLONDIKE GOLD RUSH
96, 97 Jeff Gnass Photography
98 (upper right) Jean Higgins/Unicorn Stock Photos
98 (lower left) Kim Heacox/Ken Graham Agency
100 (upper) Ken Graham /Ken Graham Agency
100 (lower) Corbis-Bettman
101 Fred Hirschmann
102 Fred Hirschmann
103 (upper) Fred Hirschmann
103 (lower) Tom Bean
104 Dave G. Houser
105 (upper right) Fred Hirschmann
105 (lower left) Mark Kelly

LAND OF FIRE
106, 107 Brad Lewis/Photo Resource Hawaii
108 Richard Alexander Cooke III
110 (upper) David Muench
110 (lower) George H.H. Huey
111 Richard Alexander Cooke III
112 (left) Rita Ariyoshi

112 (upper right) Rita Ariyoshi
112 (lower right) Laurence Parent
113 Jeff Gnass Photography
114 Jeff Gnass Photography
115 (upper left) Richard Alexander Cooke III
115 (lower right) Fred Hirschmann
116 Jack Jeffrey/Photo Resource Hawaii
117 (upper left) Rita Ariyoshi
117 (lower right) Jim Cazel/Photo Resource Hawaii

GAZETTEER
118 Terry Donnelly
119 (both) George H.H. Huey
120 (both) John Elk III
121 John Elk III
122 John Elk III
123 (upper right) Catherine Karnow/Woodfin Camp & Associates
123 (lower left) A.Gurmankin/Unicorn Stock Photos
124 Phyllis Kedl/Unicorn Stock Photos
125 (upper right) Wayne Levin/Photo Resource Hawaii
125 (lower) Al Harvey
126 (upper right) Martha McBride/Unicorn Stock Photos
126 (lower left) James P. Rowan
127 Ted Rose/Unicorn Stock Photos
128 Aneal F. Fohra/Unicorn Stock Photos
129 (upper) D. Donne Bryant
129 (lower) Clementine Hunter/Mildred Hart Bailey Cane Rive Collection
130 (both) James P. Rowan
131 Courtesy of Dorchester County Tourism Office, Cambridge, MD
132 (both) Martha McBride/Unicorn Stock Photos
133 Terry Donnelly
134 Alan Briere
135 (upper) Robert Perron/f/Stop Pictures, Inc.
135 (lower left) Mae Scanlan
136 Jan Butchofsky/Dave G. Houser
137 (upper right) Fred Hirschmann
137 (lower left) Tom Till/Photographer
138 F.B. Grunzweig/f/Stop Pictures, Inc.
139 (upper right) Jan Butchofsky/Dave G. Houser
139 (lower left) Larry Ulrich Photography
140 James P. Rowan
141 (upper right) Jeff Greenberg/Unicorn Stock Photos
141 (lower left) Jean Higgins/Unicorn Stock Photos

Back cover photograph by George H.H. Huey

ACKNOWLEDGMENTS

Cartography: DPR Inc.; map resource base courtesy of the USGS; shaded relief courtesy of the USGS, Michael Stockdale, and Mountain High Maps® Copyright © 1993 Digital Wisdom, Inc.

The editors would also like to thank the following: Lorraine Doré, Dominique Gagné, Pascale Hueber, and Valery Pigeon-Dumas.